Dateline: White House

To Suzanne Nutter —
with my admiration
for a woman who
has set great
goals for herself.
May all your
dreams come true.

Helen Thomas

February 9, 1976

Dateline: White House

Helen Thomas

Macmillan Publishing Co., Inc.
New York

Macmillan Publishing Co., Inc.
866 Third Avenue, New York, N.Y. 10022
Collier Macmillan Canada, Ltd.

Library of Congress Cataloging in Publication Data

Thomas, Helen, 1920–
    Dateline : White House.

    1. Presidents—United States—Biography. 2. Presidents—United States—Wives. 3. Washington, D.C. 4. United States—Politics and government—1945–   I. Title.

E176.1.T43   973'.0992 [B]   75-30625
ISBN 0-02-617620-3

First Printing 1975

Printed in the United States of America

Grateful acknowledgment is made to Holt, Rinehart and Winston, Inc. for permission to publish two lines from "Mending Wall" from *The Poetry of Robert Frost*, edited by Edward Connery Lathem. Copyright 1930, 1939, © 1969 by Holt, Rinehart and Winston, Inc. Copyright © 1958 by Robert Frost. Copyright © 1967 by Lesley Frost Ballantine. Reprinted by permission of Holt, Rinehart and Winston, Publishers.

To my beloved husband Doug and my family

Contents

Acknowledgments

Many reporters are asked whether they intend to write a book. I always used to say "maybe someday."

But one day, out of the blue, Grant Dillman, UPI vice president and my boss, asked, "How would you like to write a book?" I thought why not and I am now grateful to him for his kind encouragement. But it was far from a one-woman endeavor and I owe so much to many, starting with my husband, Douglas B. Cornell, a great newspaperman, and the Thomas family—they always encouraged me and understood my daily joy in covering the White House and my devotion to history in the making.

This book would not have been possible without the dedicated assistance of Diane Beury, who did so much to help me organize my chaotic newspaper clippings and writings of more than thirty years into some order, and her husband, Tom Beury, who also pitched in to help in so many ways.

I am indebted to Alvin Spivak who helped me recall some of those shared humorous and poignant moments during the Kennedy and Johnson eras, and to Assistant Secretary of Defense for Public Affairs Joseph Laitin for his witty memories of LBJ. Martha Mitchell's personal recollections were important to the book.

I am also indebted to Helen Smith for her kind assistance through the years and for being an extraordinarily able press secretary; to Jean and Robert Baldwin, my dear friends, who were always there during the Texas years; and to Larry Steinman of Austin for his friendship.

I also want to express my appreciation to Jeannette Hopkins, a great editor, who helped to put it all together.

I cannot overlook my friend Ayesha Abraham who read my Arabic coffee cup and said "everything is going to be fine" or the other women who inspired me, friends like Eleni Epstein, Dr. Pauline Stitt, Dr. Anne Caldwell, Betty Lersch, and Gloria and Dorothy Ohliger. My special gratitude to the Macmillan Publishing Co., which thought I could bridge the gap from reporter to author.

Introduction

I will never be blasé about covering the White House. I still experience a sense of awe when I walk through those black iron gates, waved through by the policemen, my press pass dangling around my neck.

It all has a special meaning for me because I know if my parents were alive they would have been very proud to share, albeit vicariously, some of these great moments in history with me. My parents had emigrated from Lebanon at the turn of the century to Winchester, Kentucky, where I was born August 4, 1920. When I was four years old we moved to Detroit, drawn, as were many other Lebanese and Syrian families, to the auto city with its promise of jobs. My father, George Thomas, owned a grocery store. He was a quiet, compassionate man who loved people. He was interested in the world around him. My mother, Mary Thomas, was strong-willed and had a burning sense of justice. Both gave their nine children security and love. During the Depression they distributed groceries to many families in our neighborhood. My parents were just and good. From them we learned compassion. We competed in that large family, but we also shared.

My father and mother could neither read nor write but they respected education and wanted us all to have a college education.

Growing up in the Thomas household meant long lively sessions at the dinner table, debating everything under the sun with my sisters Anne, Isabelle, Josephine, Barbara, and Genevieve, and my two brothers, Matry and Sabe (my other sister, Kate, was married and had her own home, also with a big, wonderful family), and my uncle Basily Rowady. We loved history and literature. Most of all, we had a deep and abiding commitment to learning. We absorbed both the American and Arab cultures and grew up with their proud traditions.

When I was a child a young woman friend of my parents came to our house and I asked her many questions. "You're so inquisitive," she said in annoyance. I didn't know what the word meant—but she was right. I was and always will be inquisitive, I guess.

I made up my mind at Eastern High School in Detroit when I worked on the school paper that journalism was the career for me. A teacher praised my work—and I liked the by-lines! After I was graduated from Wayne University (now Wayne State) in the midst of World War II, I headed for Washington, D.C. I worked as a hostess in a restaurant until I landed my big plum—a copy girl job on the now defunct *Washington Daily News* for $17 a week.

I was delighted to run for coffee for the reporters and editors and, even more, to hover over the UP ticker, hearing the bells when the bulletin stories were breaking. For years after I had moved to Washington my mother would ask, "When are you coming home?" I knew I couldn't, for Washington was the place for me, a journalist's paradise.

I had just been promoted to "cub reporter" on the *News* when I lost my job in a massive cutback, so I went knocking on doors at the National Press Building until I got another job with United Press, later to become UPI, for $24 a week. I shared an apartment with my good friend, Betty Lersch, who went to work for Transradio and our walk-up became a gathering place for midnight conversations. One friend who often dropped by was Allen Drury, who worked for UP before he became a successful author.

My job with UP was to file the Washington City News ticker and write local radio news. I had to be at work at 5:30 A.M. and for twelve years I went to work before the sun rose.

I had been hired primarily because young men were being drafted. After the war, women reporters were fired to make way for the men who would return. Only a few of the men came back to their old jobs, however, and my job, with its long hours, was hardly a lure to returning veterans, so I managed to hang on. But I was outraged then at the priority given to men in the news business.

I went to my first White House party when President Franklin D. Roosevelt and Mrs. Roosevelt invited the press corps to a Christmas gathering in 1944. During the late forties and early fifties I wrote a column, "Names in the News," for the national UP radio wire and interviewed many Washington celebrities, including Perle Mesta, the "hostess with the mostest," who invited me to many of her renowned and magnificent parties. Occasionally, I covered Bess Truman, diffident and somewhat shy in the limelight, but very much an individual.

In the late fifties I was promoted to cover the Justice Department and a string of other federal agencies. The big news was school integration. I helped out in 1954 when the Supreme Court handed down the historic *Brown* v. *Board of Education* decision, which ordered the end of school segregation.

It is hard to remember any tranquil years in Washington. There were three wars—World War II and the Korean and Vietnam wars. There were assassinations of leaders—John F. Kennedy, Robert F. Kennedy, and Martin Luther King. There were riots in the cities—Detroit, Newark, and Washington burned.

I have observed eight inaugurals on the Capitol steps and the oath-taking by Gerald R. Ford in the East Room. During the years I covered the White House, all three Presidents were cut off—John F. Kennedy was slain in office, Lyndon Baines Johnson was forced to renounce reelection, and Richard M. Nixon became the first President in history to resign.

My sense of awe at the responsibility I have assumed has grown with the years. Presidents are human beings, and I have always tried to be conscious of that fact, trying not only to be accurate but compassionate. For some of them it has been a "splendid misery," but I have seen Presidents in moments of glory bursting with their own sense of being, caught up in public adulation. I have also seen Presidents in despair, overburdened, brooding, emotional, seeking understanding.

The Presidency awed me, but Presidents do not. Perhaps I have always expected too much of them, but I believe that when they reach the highest office in the land, they should live up to the greatest honor that can come to a person in American political life. Some have stood the test better than others.

I have always thought that a President should know right from wrong.

"It's easy to do what is right if you only know what is right," LBJ used to say when faced with a crisis. FDR said the White House should be "a place of moral leadership."

When a President deals in less than the truth, the country is the victim. Too often in my years at the White House there has been a lack of candor and a misjudgment of the character of our people in this democratic society. Secrecy in matters of public interest can be destructive.

At the White House I see instant history and I watch the man who has push-button power of life and death over all our lives. For that reason I hope that only the most highly principled person will occupy the Oval Office. It has not always been so.

As a reporter, I do not sit in judgment (although it may sometimes seem otherwise), but I do believe that our democracy can endure only if the American people are informed. The people decide, and therein lies the transcending greatness of the land we love.

I remember Kennedy's quote from the Bible in the speech he had prepared for delivery in Austin, Texas, his next scheduled stop after Dallas: "Lest the Lord keep the city, the Watchman watches in vain."

I remember a dinner Nixon gave for retiring Chief Justice Earl Warren, whose Supreme Court decisions Nixon had castigated in public. The gentle white-haired Warren raised his champagne glass and said: "I leave with malice in my heart toward none."

I remember the peaceful march on Washington in 1963 to promote the cause of civil rights and the rabbi who said that the greatest sin of all in the Hitler era was "silence."

We all know now that an arrogance of power at the pinnacle tainted the country and diminished us all. How the mighty have fallen, the men who did not know where the line was drawn. "Watch what we *do,* not what we say," said John Mitchell. In the end we did.

Instant communications and round-the-clock journalism make possible a constant vigil on the Presidency. Anyone who goes into public life surely now understands that privacy has no priority. But the honor of service, of holding the public trust, must be more compelling.

It is a function of our democratic system that reporters go to the White House every day to watch the President at work. I have always felt especially privileged to be a United Press International reporter covering the White House beat. In more personal terms, it is exciting, demanding, inspiring—and sometimes depressing.

I have traveled thousands and thousands of miles with Presidents, but often I felt I have seen only airfields and hotel press rooms, the arrivals and departures. In many ways since the beginning of the Kennedy administration, I feel that I have lived the life of the President, on the sidelines at least. When the President moves in public, reporters move with him. When he travels officially or on vacation, we tag along.

In a wire service, a reporter gets inquiries from all over the country and from abroad. We cover all of the President's public events when he speaks to groups at the White House, and all photographic sessions—Presidents often drop hot news during a picture-taking. LBJ announced his defense budget that way, and when Nixon was angry with reporters and none were around he told the photographers, "There will be no gasoline rationing." We got the story from the cameramen and ran with it.

Presidents are often impulsive and impromptu. That is why reporters are never too sure when the day begins how it will end. I try to get to the White House before nine in the morning, get a cup of coffee as soon as I hit the press room and then read the *Washington Post, The New York Times*, and the news report on the UPI ticker. Usually, if an evening event is scheduled I rush back later to my apartment, grab a bite, take a quick shower, and dress. I was happy when the long skirts, blouses, and matching jacket ensembles came into style because I could change my blouse and be dressed for a new occasion. Sometimes I bring a gown to the White House and change that night in the ladies' room.

I often return to the White House press room late at night after a State Dinner or other event to write another story, an "overnighter" for the morning papers. Then, perhaps, I head for Nino's, our favorite Italian restaurant, which stays open to four in the morning. If it is earlier, I may go to the Calvert Street Cafe, an

Arab restaurant owned by Ayesha Abraham, an immigrant from Mount of Olives and my second mother. There the "clientele" is a mixture of VIPs from the Arab and other Washington embassies, Georgetown law students, an occasional Congressman, itinerants, and Palestinian refugees. Martha Mitchell has been there often, a favorite customer of Ayesha's. Liz Carpenter brought Ayesha an American flag from Lyndon Johnson's office in honor of Ayesha's becoming an American citizen. I relax and enjoy the food, the Turkish coffee, the music, singing and dancing by guests or belly dancers. Sometimes Ayesha plays the drumbaka. Sometimes she reads my coffee cup. She would look into the dregs of my coffee and find my future. She tells me only the good news, and I believe her. Her predictions often hit the bull's-eye.

Once when I told her I was traveling West with Lady Bird Johnson, she said I would not go. "My bag is packed," I insisted. "We're leaving tomorrow." The next day, the First Lady came down with laryngitis and cancelled her trip. Ayesha never let me forget it.

"Are you going to put me in the book?" she asked. "Yes," I replied. "But you are a whole book."

"Then why don't you write one," she said. "And put me on television."

I met my husband, Douglas Cornell, while he was covering the White House for the Associated Press and I for UPI. We were rivals and friends from the fall of 1960. We tried to beat each other on stories, as all reporters do.

In 1966, Doug's wife died. Five years later, Pat Nixon scooped me, to her delight, by announcing our engagement at a White House retirement party arranged for Doug by President Nixon. The Nixons sent us many photographs of that memorable occasion. One was inscribed, "To Helen and Doug—with happy memories of the surprise engagement announcement at the White House." It was signed "with affection, Pat Nixon."

We were married on October 16, 1971, in St. John's Church—known as the "Church of the Presidents"—within sight of the White House across Lafayette Park. The one Lebanese touch to the solemn ceremony came when a family friend, Freda Saloum, tossed up silver coins that clattered into the pews and aisles.

We had two receptions, a rather formal one at the American Newspaper Women's Club. There, Tricia and Ed Cox, Herbert Klein, White House Director of Communications, Ron Ziegler, Martha Mitchell, and many Washington friends from government, embassy, and press circles joined us. Liz Carpenter came from Texas bearing a silver cup inscribed: "To Helen and Doug—Happiness always from the LBJs." The other reception, very informal, was a stuffed lamb feast at Ayesha's restaurant, with champagne and belly dancing. After I was married, Mrs. Nixon gave me a post-wedding luncheon at the White House.

I was fifty-one at the time, and the notes I enjoyed most came from my single women friends who said that my getting married at that age had encouraged them.

I have been a women's libber all my life and discrimination against women at all work levels has always been distressing to me. Throughout my career I've tried to move forward in this male-oriented profession. My biggest ambition was to be a good reporter, knowing full well that in my career you are only as good as your last story.

My first big chance came in 1959 when I was elected president of the Women's National Press Club. During my year in office Soviet Premier Nikita S. Khrushchev came to visit Washington and the State Department had him scheduled to deliver his one address to the press at the National Press Club, from which women reporters were then excluded.

With other militant newswomen, I put up a battle to be present at that history-making event and we forced the United States Government on its honor not to schedule visiting heads of state for their one press appearance at places where women reporters were barred.

It was a tough battle and the Washington newspapers gave us full coverage. In the end we won a small victory. A number of women reporters were allowed to attend the luncheon and I, as president of the Women's National Press Club, sat at the head table when the shrewd Communist leader made his famous "We will bury you" speech. When I was introduced to Khrushchev, he took one look at my dark hair and eyes and said that I looked like the women from Soviet Georgia.

Women reporters have had to break down other doors of press strongholds, but once the doors have been opened, I have made it a policy to walk right in. When the National Press Club, after much debate, opened its membership to women, I joined. I also joined Sigma Delta Chi, the formerly all-male journalist society. And when the Gridiron Club, Washington's most exclusive press club, invited me in 1975 to become the first woman member in its ninety-year history, I did not hesitate. That year was a landmark for me because I also became president of the White House Correspondents Association, the first woman to serve in that position.

But professionally, I was even more honored to become the UPI bureau chief at the White House, the first woman to head a wire service operation at that flash point where news can break at any time.

I have often been asked if I ever get bored. "Never," is my answer. Every day is an education.

Reporters, I believe, should remain skeptical and untiring in their quest for answers to demanding questions, especially questions put to those who hold the public trust. I believe the greatest contribution a White House reporter can make is to keep an eye on the President, to help keep democracy alive.

After I was elected to the Gridiron Club I was teased a lot. At the Gridiron's annual dinner, President Gerald R. Ford said, "You've gone co-ed, which is great, but I don't want to overlook Helen Thomas. I learned that long before I ever became President. Through the years Helen has practiced a finely balanced blend of journalism and acupuncture. She has praised me when it was earned—and needled me when it was necessary and I have always been grateful for her fairness." I appreciated that.

To the journalistic credo: "Get it first, but first get it accurate," I would add, "and be fair."

Dateline: White House

Chapter 1

Kennedy: The End of the Beginning

On Thanksgiving Day, 1960, Jacqueline Bouvier Kennedy came to the door of her home on N Street in Washington's fashionable Georgetown to say good-bye to her husband, President-elect John F. Kennedy. With Caroline, in a smocked white dress, they tried to form a loving family tableau for photographers, but Jackie, eight months pregnant, barely managed a smile to hide her distress. Many would agree she had every right to be irritated. JFK was flying off in a jaunty mood to recuperate from the rigorous campaign in the warmth and elegance of his father's home in Palm Beach, Florida, and he was leaving her behind.

As a wire service reporter, I had stationed myself near the entrance of the Kennedy house and I could see this family vignette at close range. It told me a lot: Jackie Kennedy, the young, glamorous, cultured creature who would soon dazzle the world as First Lady, was human, vulnerable, shy, a woman who feared and dreaded her future life in the White House and didn't try too hard to cover up the afternoon's rift between husband and wife.

She had already given the press and public some insights into the type of apolitical, impish, many-faceted individual she was. Early in 1960, when someone asked where the Democratic National Nominating Convention should be held, she replied brightly, "Acapulco." At a press tea in her Georgetown home, she curled up comfortably in an upholstered chair and told reporters candidly, "I don't like crowds." And in the final heat of the Presidential campaign, when she was seated next to a Democratic Party bigwig at a fund-raising affair, she looked at him demurely and said, "You won't make me talk about November [and the general election], will you?"

Nothing in my background heretofore had prepared me for Jackie's elegant ambience and hauteur. I grew up in a family of Lebanese immigrants in Detroit. My father instilled in his children the love of learning but he had little entree to the social register. I had done odd jobs in the college library and in my brother's gas station to earn my tuition. Although as a reporter, I had covered politicians, diplomats, and government dignitaries for years in their lovely homes, they all seemed more down to earth. Jackie was to the manner born—a former debutante whose finishing school style was polished at Vassar and perfected at the Sorbonne. She made it clear in many ways that she represented the American aristocracy. Sometimes she was aloof even from the funloving inbred Kennedy clan.

Like other reporters who dogged Jackie, I was always the party-crasher, seldom the invited guest. I covered her from a cool distance. She introduced me and other reporters to the world of the international jet set, of the exclusive high society of Palm Beach, Newport, and other blue-blooded resort retreats, of the horse and hunt country, of yachts and high fashion and French antiques.

Jackie was already getting caught up in the vortex of worldwide adulation and curiosity during those days when I staked out the Kennedy federal-style house on N Street along with a crowd of other reporters. If she seemed confused and unhappy then, I could sympathize with her. After all, she was about to have a baby and the Kennedy house was bristling with activity. Energetic young men who had served in the campaign, new appointees, cabinet-members-to-be, Secret Service agents, servants, members of the expansive Kennedy family, and Jackie's hairdressers paraded through the front and back doors at all hours. JFK was making preinaugural announcements from the steps.

These were exhilarating times for most everyone else. The nation was stirring again after eight years of Eisenhower tranquility, after eight years of feeling older than we should have. Reporters who stood outside the house on N Street hour after hour, day after day, waiting for tidbits of news were caught up in the excitement. We were numb with cold but we knew we were recording a fascinating period in history and from a privileged vantage point. But when Kennedy left for Palm Beach on Thanksgiving Day, most of us breathed a sigh of relief and went home for some badly needed rest. I was a frazzled, weather-beaten wreck and for a rare change that night I took time to put my hair in curlers. I was about to crawl into bed when the office called and said, "Get to Georgetown Hospital!" Jackie had been rushed there for an emergency Caesarean operation. I dressed in three minutes and bolted out of my apartment into the street, motioning for a taxi while still buttoning my jacket and taking down my hair.

Kennedy got the news when he landed at the Palm Beach airport. He sped back to Washington in the press plane. In flight he learned he had become the father of a son. For the next ten days Georgetown Hospital was an even more tumultuous scene than N Street had been. Reporters badgered nuns, nurses, doctors, police, family, and friends for any morsel of news about Jackie and her three-weeks premature baby, John, Jr.—the first baby ever born to a President-elect. Kennedy, the proud, concerned, and dutiful father, made daily hospital visits and drew still more crowds. Once I buttonholed him in a hospital corridor and asked, "Do you want your son to grow up to be President?" JFK, who had known pain and illness much of his adult life, answered thoughtfully, "I just want him to be all right."

From Thanksgiving night until the day Jackie and John, Jr., went home, I was among those reporters who practically lived at Georgetown Hospital. Once I was shuttled back to N Street, however—on the day Kennedy was scheduled to hold his first formal meeting with President Eisenhower. My job was to check him out of his house as he departed for the White House and to call UPI. Kennedy recognized me immediately and, grinning broadly, complained: "You've deserted my child!" That quote hit every paper in the country. It was my first taste of Kennedy's dry wit.

Thereafter, I always felt completely at ease with him. I could be incredibly flip and he never made me feel that I was disrespectful. He loved to repartee with the press.

Jackie, on the other hand, played hide and seek with the press from the minute she came home from Georgetown Hospital. She went in through the front door at N Street and a few hours later slipped out the back door for her tour of the White House with Mamie Eisenhower. It was a one-hour tour and Jackie, who was recuperating, used a wheelchair part of the time. When she left she cried hysterically. An aide told me later that Jackie thought the White House looked like a hotel that had been decorated by a wholesale furniture store during a January clearance.

That same day she took her children—John, Jr., and three-year-old Caroline—to the Kennedy home in Palm Beach, determined to stay in seclusion until the January inauguration, and perhaps beyond. The name of the game for her was, "Avoid the press at all costs." For us, it was, "Cherchez la femme!"

My own route to the White House press room had been made possible probably in part by my election as president of the Women's National Press Club, spurred by Dorothy Williams, a former UPI reporter and club president. It gave me some stature with my bosses. During my administration I had annoyed many Club members by offering a luncheon platform to Nina Popova, one of Russia's leading women. I had felt it was important to hear dissenting views. After my term ended, I toured Russia and came home with a written interview with Mrs. Nikita Khrushchev.

The Kennedy-Nixon debates were on at the time and I watched one of them at the American Embassy in Moscow. It was clear that the Russians wanted Kennedy to win. They were still bitter over the Nixon-Khrushchev "kitchen debate" the year before and there was no love lost for Nixon. Later, ironically, when I came back twice to Moscow with Nixon, he was heralded as a friend, a promoter of "détente," at least by the Kremlin leaders.

When I returned in the late fall of 1960, the Presidential campaign was coming to a close and I got the Kennedy's front door as my beat. Merriman Smith, chief of the UPI White House bureau, and Alvin Spivak, who was on the staff, both great reporters, led me by the hand in the journalistic protocol of covering the White House.

I was sent to Palm Beach, Florida, in December 1960 to join Merriman Smith in covering the Kennedy family. The Kennedy forces took over several rooms on the ground floor of the ultra-modern Palm Beach Towers Hotel for press rooms, in an improbable setting of relaxed resort living. We sat at our type-writers in shorts and slacks, working hard, surrounded by vacation-ers at play.

Pierre Salinger was the Press Secretary and he managed to survive the ordeal better than most because of his keen sense of humor. His briefings were witty, warm, and headline-making with all the world hungry for any morsels about the Kennedy family. The atmosphere was casual. Salinger smoked cigars, often wore shorts, and was frequently photographed from the backside until Kennedy put his foot down and ordered the stocky secretary to dress less informally.

During those early days in Palm Beach, I got to know Jackie's personal secretary Mary Gallagher and she became a wonderful friend. When Jackie was going to fly back to Washington with her children for the inauguration, Mary arranged for me to travel with her. But if I thought I was going to get a big scoop, I was sadly mistaken. During the flight, Jackie walled herself off with her staff on one side of the plane so that I could not approach her. I got the message. On the other hand, I could observe her and saw that she was shy and faced the awesome prospect of becoming First Lady with some trepidation. I felt sorry for her.

When we landed at Washington National Airport, a crowd waved and beckoned to her, and she stepped forward, smiling, but then hesitated. She could not quite bring herself to go to the fence for some campaign-style handshaking.

From these fascinating, preinauguration days on I became an around-the-clock President watcher. I was assigned to cover Jackie, low man on the totem pole with United Press International's White House news team, and I jumped at the opportunity. The White House would be the news center of the world once the Kennedys moved in. I hadn't always been so savvy. In the early 1950s, a young unmarried Senator offered to take me home from a party at the Pakistan Embassy. My friend, Eleni Epstein, fashion editor of the *Washington Star*, telephoned me the next day and asked me what I thought of him. "He's kind of dull," I said. His name was John F. Kennedy.

Actually, I, in effect, assigned myself to cover the White House after the Kennedy inauguration. I was sent over to cover the President going to church on a Sunday, the day after the inauguration, and I just stayed on, reporting every day until my editors automatically assigned me there.

I have to confess that after I was assigned to cover John F. Kennedy and his family in the President-elect period, I was like the woman who came to dinner. I did not want to leave. I had a ringside seat to instant history and I didn't want to give it up.

Heavily bundled up against the cold that snowy Sunday morning, I got in a "pool" car in the motorcade with Kennedy when he decided to attend mass at his parish church, Holy Trinity, a couple of blocks from his N Street home. He hadn't broken with the routine of his past life. As we rode down N Street, Kennedy stopped his driver, got out of the car, and picked up the newspapers on the doorstep of the Georgetown home where he had lived for many years. Then he knocked on the door of a neighbor, Ben Bradlee, then with *Newsweek*.

Suddenly, on impulse, Kennedy decided to walk to church. I hopped out of the press car and trudged behind him in the snow. After mass, we went back to the White House. Later in the afternoon, Kennedy, looking over his new offices, popped into our messy press room, and we chatted about light things, the weather and the newspapers he regularly read, *The New York Times* and the *Washington Post*.

In the years to come I covered him many Sundays on his way to church. Kennedy was self-conscious about being followed by reporters to church. Once he asked me if I were Catholic and I told him no (I was Greek Orthodox). One day the thundering herd, as he called reporters and cameramen, rushed into the Oval Office for a brief picture-taking, and he asked me if I was going along on a forthcoming trip to New York. "No, Mr. President," I bemoaned, "I only go to church with you." When I was checking him out as he boarded a helicopter on the ellipse near the White House sometime later, he remembered my remark. "You get all the good trips," he said with a grin.

An excerpt from one of Kennedy's speeches reflected his religious faith: "With a good conscience our only sure reward, with history the final judge of our deeds, let us go forth to lead the land we love, asking His blessing and His help, but knowing that here on earth God's work must truly be our own." Kennedy, a devout Roman Catholic, used to get down on his knees at night and pray.

When Mrs. Kennedy went to mass, as she did only sporadically, we would hang around outside the church with the news photographers, then follow her in. Our perseverance was rewarded on Good Friday of 1961 in Palm Beach. She must have realized the press would be there on a holy day, but she appeared in a bandana, a short, sleeveless dress, sandals and no stockings, and, to make the story even better, Peter Lawford called for her in Bermuda shorts and bare feet. The photographers went wild. Pictures of the stockingless First Lady and her barefoot chauffeur were printed in newspapers across the country.

Jackie used her brittle wit, her Secret Service agents, and sometimes both, to retaliate. She pegged my good friend and relentless competitor, Fran Lewine of the Associated Press, and me from the start as the two who were always following her. She called us "the harpies." One Sunday she spotted us on the steps as she went to church and passed word to the Secret Service agents that "two strange-looking Spanish women" were after her. The word filtered back to us, as intended. It was a brilliant carom shot since Fran is Jewish and I'm of Arab descent.

Jackie made me and all reporters feel like intruders. She seldom spoke to me in the three years she was in the White House although we saw each other often. She had no sizzling hostility toward reporters in those days, she just ignored us, regally. But she was totally, completely aware that we were there. Once she returned from Hyannis Port, Massachusetts, with a German shepherd puppy her father-in-law had given her. The press knew she had named it Clipper and sent her a note on Air Force One asking what she would feed it. "Reporters," she scrawled.

She read practically everything we wrote with a hypersensitive eye and protested to Pierre Salinger, the President's Press Secretary, when she thought we had invaded her privacy too blatantly. In her own complex way, she appreciated Pierre's plight. One day she sent him a favorite photograph autographed, "To Pierre, from the greatest cross he has to bear." Salinger kept it in his home on Lake Barcroft, Virginia. When he showed me the photo, he said, "Not so . . . not so." But in fact he was constantly caught in the crossfire. It was decided Jackie was news and that, therefore, he rather than her own press secretary should make the "news" announcements about her. "News is news," he said. I couldn't agree more. The public's appetite for news about Jackie was voracious and her inability to comprehend it made for strained relations with us, to put it mildly. She once even expressed the forlorn hope that she could walk out of the White House unrecognized.

I was a regular on the White House reporting team by now and, when not covering Presidential news, I would often team up with Fran Lewine to zero in on Jackie. In all fairness to Mrs. Kennedy, I'll admit we were insatiable, and so were our editors. We interviewed customers and merchants in those elegant stores and salons along posh Worth Avenue where the Kennedys shopped in Palm Beach. (That's the first time I ever saw a hardware store with wall-to-wall carpeting.) We interviewed Jackie's hairdresser, her pianist, her caterer. I even interviewed the owner of the local diaper service. We were called the diaper detail; but, then, so were the agents who protected the Kennedy children.

Secret Service agents went overboard (sometimes literally) to do Jackie's bidding, in the name of security. They served as chauffeurs, servants, nannies, swimming and water skiing companions, and, at times, they seemed embarrassed at the lengths she would go to avoid the press. I always knew that when the agents shoved us around, orders had come from the top.

One such fracas occurred when a crowd of reporters was standing in the MATS terminal at Washington National Airport waiting for Jackie to return from her semiofficial, month-long tour of India and Pakistan. Security men on Jackie's plane, a DC-6, were tipped off and the pilot was ordered to pull into an American Airlines hangar. UPI photographer Roddy Mims and I were standing outside behind a chain link fence, and could see the plane land at the opposite end of the field from the waiting press. At that moment, a maintenance man came by on a motorcycle and Roddy jumped aboard. They reached the security area as Jackie was walking down the ramp and Roddy got some terrific pictures. But Clint Hill, the head of Jackie's Secret Service detail, who had been on the plane with Jackie, came charging after him yelling, "Give me that film! Jackie's giving me hell. She's giving me hell!" Clint, who was a very personable man, ranted and apologized simultaneously. Amid the furor, Federal Aviation Administration and airport police moved in, took Roddy into a security office and demanded to see his credentials. Clint demanded that he turn over the film. At that, Roddy called UPI's Merriman Smith, our boss and then the senior White House correspondent. Smitty marched into Salinger's office and Salinger, to his everlasting credit, told Clint to have Roddy released and to return his film. He knew the First Lady could not confiscate a news photographer's pictures.

Jackie's war of independence from the press never ceased. During her first year in the White House, she gave a luncheon for the press and arranged matters so that she would sit near friends and women writers who were not on the daily "Jackie" beat. And when she gave a press reception in Paris and was mobbed by the foreign press, she snubbed American newswomen. A *Women's Wear Daily* reporter inquired whether she read that paper. Jackie said coolly, "I try not to."

Jackie once impishly suggested that women reporters be held at bay by Presidential aides holding bayonets. She told Kennedy, jestingly I presume, that he should find a foreign assignment for me. She also wanted to relegate women reporters covering a White House State dinner to a post behind the potted palms.

Jackie did like UPI's Stan Tretick, however, and selected him to take photos of her son's christening. But then she hired her own photographer, Richard Avedon, and gave him carte blanche, to the consternation of other photographers who were competing fiercely for First Family pictures. At times, she even seemed to be posing for pictures or setting up some engaging family scene for the benefit of photographers. Once she found an old sleigh, brought it to the White House and hitched up Caroline's pony, Macaroni, to

it. Kids piled aboard as Jackie led Macaroni around the South
Lawn of the White House. Photographers captured the moment
and one of their pictures became the First Family's 1962 Christmas
card.

In an interview I had with Jackie, she said, "People must be as
sick of hearing about us and Macaroni [Caroline's pony] as I am."
They were and they were not.

Jackie often avoided White House and other official functions.
"The boss can't do a thing with her," Dave Powers, a favorite
Presidential aide, used to say. The record bore him out. She did
not, for example, attend the Distinguished Ladies Reception in her
honor at the time of her husband's inauguration. And when
Congressional wives gave a brunch for her, she was in New York at
a performance of the London Royal Ballet. The President, looking
somewhat embarrassed, showed up in her stead. Jackie also failed
to appear at a reception of several thousand exchange students on
the South Lawn. We asked social secretary Tish Baldrige why?
"Same old sinuses," Tish replied. A check showed that Mrs.
Kennedy never had a sinus problem. During the reception she was
upstairs in the family quarters, peeking through the windows
occasionally and laughing like a mischievous child.

In some respects Jackie's formidable sense of privacy was
understandable. She didn't want her two children to grow up in the
fierce white glare of worldwide publicity. When I asked her in an
interview what was her greatest joy in living in the White House,
she said, "Seeing my husband be a great President." She said she
had the "most affinity" for Mrs. Harry S. Truman among all the
first ladies because "she brought a daughter to the White House at
a most difficult age and managed to keep her from being spoiled."

Politics must take second place to her family, she told me. "The
official side of my life takes me away from my children a great deal.
If I were to add political duties, I would have practically no time
with my children and they are my first responsibility. My husband
agrees with me." She was devoted to her children, constantly
planning to try to give them a normal childhood.

What I couldn't understand was Jackie's desire to have it both
ways. When she was creating the image of a concerned First Lady,
she wanted press coverage. When she was flying off on her

Friday-to-Tuesday weekend trips, she wanted to pull the velvet curtain closed. She fought the reality that first ladies, like their husbands, belong to the public.

So we brought long-range binoculars, rented cabin cruisers, and made desperate attempts to become more athletic. Jackie's weekends were spent boating, swimming, water skiing, and riding to the hounds at Glen Ora, the Kennedy estate in Virginia near Middleburg; at Newport, Rhode Island, her own old summer home; at Hyannis Port, the site of the Kennedy compound on Cape Cod; at Camp David, the Presidential hideaway in the Catoctin Mountains (named for David Eisenhower; formerly FDR's "Shangri-la"); and, toward the last, at her new Atoka, Virginia, estate on Rattlesnake Mountain.

We were exhausted keeping up with Jackie's energetic forms of relaxation. As we trailed her, we tried to blend in with the local scenery, although I'm sure we didn't. I, for one, was strictly an indoor girl and preferred spectator sports. In Middleburg, we wore slacks and bulky sweaters and mingled with the horse set in the tavern at the Red Fox Inn, picking up local gossip about life-styles in Jackie country. (Never, before Middleburg, had I heard of a drug store that sold only horse medicine.)

Jackie never acquired a taste for politics. But as First Lady she captivated men who ran the world—de Gaulle, Nehru, Ayub Khan, Haile Selassie—even Khrushchev. In the White House she was called "the queen" and she was a regal, imperial First Lady if there ever was one, certainly with the press.

"She would be more at home in Buckingham Palace," we would mutter.

Toward the end Jacqueline began to enjoy her position on the pedestal and to comprehend more fully what she meant to the country. But she never came to terms with White House correspondents. Even though she had been an inquiring photographer herself for the old *Washington Times-Herald*, she deeply resented prying White House reporters, particularly prying female reporters. We were the thorn in her crown. Jackie was charmingly at ease with men, children, and animals. She was constantly on guard with women of the press.

The irony is that Jackie Kennedy unwittingly gave a tremendous lift to me and many other women reporters in Washington by escalating our beat, covering the First Lady, to instantaneous front-page news. Eleanor Roosevelt had made front-page news before her with her liberal activism, but Jackie, in her diametrically different fashion, was news twenty-four hours a day. She, her husband, and her children set a new and dizzying high in First Family newsmaking. One biting quip from Jackie or a spill from a horse could launch a thousand headlines. There was a mystique about her, in and out of the White House.

President and Mrs. Kennedy set a dazzling new style in White House entertaining. Elegance, informality, and culture arrived simultaneously. It was a long way from the time, as Perle Mesta told me, when Kennedy, then Senator, upset her by coming to one of her parties in tennis shoes. Dinner party lists sparkled with names like Stravinsky, Sandburg, Stokowski, Kazan, Stern, and

---

THE WHITE HOUSE
WASHINGTON

January 17, 1963

Dear Helen:

Thank you so much for your note.

I want you to know that I appreciated your thoughtful efforts on the interview as well as your helpful and informative articles on many of my projects in the last two years.

With my good wishes for a happy and less hectic New Year,

Sincerely,
Jacqueline Kennedy
(Signature)

Miss Helen Thomas
1711 Massachusetts Avenue
Washington 6, D.C.

Casals. In place of Guy Lombardo and Fred Waring, who were favorite entertainers during the Ike and Mamie Eisenhower era, guests now enjoyed Jerome Robbins' "Ballets: U.S.A.," the American Shakespeare Festival Theatre, the National Symphony Orchestra, and the Air Force Strolling Strings.

The red-coated Marine Band played lively music in the marble foyer of the first floor as the guests arrived, instead of sitting by in formal silence for the President to make his grand entrance. Small round tables supplemented the stiff U-shaped tables so long used at formal dinners, and fires glowed brightly in every fireplace. Mamie's mammoth floral arrangements were replaced with dainty centerpieces. White tie attire went out during the Kennedy administration—black tie was the most JFK would tolerate. When Jackie came to the White House, men and women were allowed to mingle at coffee after dinner for the first time. Earlier, as at other Washington parties, women had left the men to brandy, coffee, and cigars after dinner.

The Kennedys gave their first precedent-setting, or shattering, party—a Sunday reception for new Presidential appointees—nine days after JFK's inauguration. There were open bars in the State Dining Room during an official function, and butlers strolled among the guests with trays of champagne and mixed drinks.

We wrote about the "open bar" and there was the devil to pay. The Baptist Belt and the Women's Christian Temperance Union were outraged. At first the Kennedys knuckled under, but later the practice was quietly resumed and, during White House social functions, you could walk up to a strategically placed bar for a cocktail. The practice, as these innovations often do, became standard White House routine. Once when I was covering a Kennedy party from the sidelines, Jackie teasingly urged me to take a huge glass of champagne from the tray that a butler was holding temptingly close. I laughed and went along with her playful gambit.

In the Eisenhower days guests used to say they felt they had to be as proper as the military, but under the Kennedys they lit cigarettes, laughed, swapped stories and jokes, and reveled in being there. As for the open bar, guests were "higher" on the knowledge they were present at a special place than they could ever have gotten on alcohol. Artists and intellectuals especially relished these evenings, gratified that at last they were being recognized by the Republic.

The Kennedy cultural highpoint was the visit of Pablo Casals, the great cellist, who had vowed never to return to his native Spain while Franco ruled. After Kennedy introduced him, the room was hushed. Like Picasso, Casals was old but beyond age. The Kennedys were celebrating a great man.

The Casals dinner and other Kennedy extravaganzas haunted succeeding First Families; they seemed to feel compelled to meet and surpass the challenge. Early in the Nixon administration I asked Presidential Press Secretary Ronald Ziegler about an upcoming social event. In his line of questioning I knew he was trying to get my assessment of how the Nixons were doing in that department. I thought they were doing fine, but did recall some of the entertainment in the past. "Pablo Casals, Pablo Casals," he bristled. "That's all I hear." I had not even mentioned the famed cellist. The Nixon administration's sensitivity to the Kennedy social legacy was reflected further in a memo to H. R. Haldeman, Nixon's number-one assistant, from Lucy Winchester, Mrs. Nixon's social secretary, on February 14, 1973: "The second Nixon administration could reap a great harvest by a judicious program of press follow-through on the entertainment of the first four years," Mrs. Winchester told Haldeman. "The Kennedys had Pablo Casals perform once and by their follow-through have established President Kennedy firmly in the public's mind as the cultural President. This is not true! An effort should begin whereby performers are programmed for press interviews on a timely basis. For example, Isaac Stern and Leonard Bernstein should discuss the performance for Golda Meir at President Nixon's last dinner for Prime Minister Meir; Van Cliburn should discuss having performed at the White House and in Moscow, and he should comment on the President's commitment to excellence in the arts."

The irony is that not only President Kennedy, but Johnson, Nixon and Ford also encouraged the arts. Kennedy appointed a special counsel on the arts and urged the creation of a National Cultural Center; Johnson pushed through the legislation that created the National Endowment for the Arts and Humanities;

Nixon increased the Arts Endowment from a few million dollars to eighty million plus. President Ford, through his wife, Betty, a professionally trained dancer, has continued to support and spotlight the country's artists.

In the Kennedy administration, where art and culture seemed especially favored, I remember also the magnificent White House dinner on April 29, 1962, attended by 179 noted guests, including 49 Nobel Prize winners. Kennedy made a short but sparkling speech and opened by denying a report "that this is the President's Easter egg-head roll on the White House lawn."

Then he paid a famous and revealing tribute to his honored guests: "I think this is the most extraordinary collection of talent, of human knowledge, that has ever been gathered together at the White House, with the possible exception of when Thomas Jefferson dined alone."

Earlier on that bright spring day, Linus Pauling, the Nobel Prize-winning nuclear scientist, one of the invited guests, had marched in a ban-the-bomb demonstration in front of the White House. He completed his stint in the picket line, went to his hotel, changed into a tuxedo, and returned to the White House for dinner where President Kennedy greeted him with an appropriate sally: "I'm glad you decided to come inside."

At these parties, Jackie, basically shy, gravitated to those she knew. She was very much a guest at her own parties. Once the flowers and menus were planned she did not have to see that visitors were comfortable, but then no First Lady had such hostess chores. There are always aides to handle the amenities. But she did mastermind a number of the magnificent State Dinners. And she was a star; people, especially men, were intrigued by her and they basked in her attention. She was at ease in that milieu, amid the majesty of White House State Dinners, and she missed only one of these—when Haile Selassie came to Washington. The young First Lady liked the diminutive Ethiopian emperor and went with Kennedy to greet him at Union Station, but she flew on to New York, en route to a vacation with her sister in the Greek Isles aboard Aristotle Onassis' yacht.

There are many memories of Jackie at White House festivities. Jackie, beautiful in her Parisian gowns that she had "smuggled" into the White House through her sister, Lee Radziwill, or her secretary, Mary Gallagher, while pretending that most of her formals were purchased from American designers. Or carrying her elegant gold cigaret case and her small gold cigaret lighter, which she would hand to the nearest man when she wanted to smoke. Sidney Poitier had a difficult time getting her lighter to work but when he finally succeeded she looked at him as though he had invented fire.

President Kennedy became displeased with the family image that began to emerge after reporters wrote about the dunking parties at "Hickory Hill," the seven-acre McLean, Virginia, estate of Attorney General and Mrs. Robert F. Kennedy. Their parties made headlines when guests, including Ethel Kennedy, took impromptu leaps into the outdoor pool, dressed in their glamorous gowns and tuxedos.

Even the lively private parties at the White House made news. Their guests couldn't resist talking about the marvelous times they had, and when Jackie danced the twist at a private party with Defense Secretary Robert McNamara, the news hit papers across the country. JFK was incensed. He felt the image of Jackie gyrating in the Presidential mansion would distress Middle America. Several years later, Christina Ford was able to perform her sensuous twist in the East Room without creating any public stir whatsoever, which shows how rapidly precedents are set.

I remember one formal White House function where women of the press had questioned Jackie's guests too eagerly. She complained that we were ill-mannered. She also thought we were dowdy. I thought we looked fine. We couldn't afford expensive wardrobes on a reporter's salary, though we conformed to Jackie's style with bouffant hairdos and the bare-arm look of the day, even though not all of us were built for it, I'll admit. My selection of long gowns at the time was limited to two. One was an off-the-shoulder black sheath. When I wore it to one State Dinner, Jackie appeared that night in a black velvet off-the-shoulder sheath of her own. She reacted with startled surprise to my off-the-rack imitation. *Washington Post* columnist Maxine Cheshire wrote about the coincidence the next day.

Foreign audiences were always captivated by Jackie, particularly when she spoke their language. She was fluent in French and learned enough Spanish to get by. In Mexico City, when the President and Mrs. Kennedy were on a speaking platform with Mexican President Lopez Mateos, Kennedy admired the watch Lopez Mateos was wearing. In keeping with a gallant Mexican custom, Lopez Mateos took off the watch and gave it to him. Then Jackie spoke to the assembled crowd and Mateos spontaneously broke into torrents of praise for her beauty, her style, and her perfect Spanish. Kennedy took off the watch and pretended to give it back. The two presidents broke up in laughter.

Jackie's White House restoration program was without precedent. She restored the President's home to its illustrious past to almost universal bipartisan acclaim. She renewed our pride in our heritage. She brought the Mona Lisa to the United States. She made the White House a showcase for the best in music, poetry, and art. She upgraded entertainment in the White House so that guests could actually enjoy themselves. Only during the Kennedy era (at a private White House party) was "Hail to the Chief" played with a twist beat. "That's Jack's favorite song," she used to kid.

The tempo at the White House, under the influence of both Jackie and JFK, was definitely upbeat. Chiefs of state landed in helicopters on the South Lawn where Caroline Kennedy and nursery school friends played on trampolines and swings in the tree houses. The movie theatre ran cartoons. I broke the story that Jackie was setting up a nursery school in the solarium on the third floor for Caroline, and had integrated it with one black student, the young son of Deputy Press Secretary Andrew Hatcher.

The youngsters would often watch from the third floor balcony during a ceremonial arrival of a head of state on the South Lawn. When Algerian President Ahmed Ben Bella arrived, the children mimicked and echoed every order given during a troop review. "Present Arms" and "Attention" they called out to amused and some embarrassed smiles. After that incident Caroline's class was banished behind the glassed-in solarium, where they could see the pageantry but not be heard.

I had a field day with Caroline stories and so did other reporters. She captured national attention during the President-elect days when she wandered out onto the patio of Kennedy's Palm Beach villa during a news conference, wearing her pajamas, a robe, and her mother's high heels. "Where's my Daddy," she asked a television technician. "He's over there, honey," the technician told her, pointing at Kennedy, who joined in the laughter.

Caroline and her brother John, Jr., were the joy of Kennedy's life. He would come out of the Oval Office, clap his hands, and they would come running, along with all their little friends. Kennedy liked to show them off, and even had photographs taken when Jackie was not around.

Caroline's most quoted remark was made when she was three years old and wandering around the White House. "Where's your Daddy?" she was asked.

"He's upstairs with his shoes and socks off, doing nothing," she said.

Once when Eleanor Roosevelt came to the White House, the President's daughter tagged along as the former First Lady and other guests went on a tour of the family quarters. "Isn't it sad Mommy isn't here," she told Mrs. Roosevelt. Jackie was in Palm Beach at the time. Then when Kennedy turned to two men in the party to ask whether they wanted a drink, Caroline piped up, "They've already had a drink, Daddy, there's their glasses."

Caroline used to accompany her father to work in the morning. She and John-John would romp with him in the evening, frequently going to his office to pick him up.

"Daddy," she once reproached him, when she saw him combing his hair, "you're not going to make a speech."

Her relationship with her father was warm and close. She adored her mother also and learned from Jackie to say imperiously: "No photographers."

The Kennedy youngsters brought life to the White House. The PT-Boat tie clasp (which LBJ later barred aides from wearing), the expressions "vig-uh" and "terrific" were symbolic. So were the White House parties that focused on the intellectual and fun-loving side of American life. The country rejoiced in the Kennedy exploits, although some Republicans, perhaps in jest, who considered Caroline a political threat. Mrs. Clare B. Williams, assistant to the Republican National Chairman, told a GOP audience that there "ought to be a law against lady politicians under four years old. There is one in Washington who is giving us fits." Once when Senate Majority Leader Mike Mansfield was asked why the Democrats in Congress were trailing Kennedy in the polls, he quipped: "He's got Caroline."

Unlike the First Lady, the President maintained an easy camaraderie with the press. He liked the press—well sometimes. He realized that our constant probing was a direct reflection of the prevailing public mood, one he could never get from his aides. He considered us a necessary, abrasive force, although there were times when he undoubtedly wanted to banish us to Siberia.

When Jackie Kennedy ordered the planting of tall rhododendron bushes on the South Grounds to shield Caroline's playground from public view, Pierre Salinger produced a twenty-six-year-old landscaping plan and made the astounding claim that this was all part of a National Park Service beautification program. JFK perceived the gaping holes in this bit of subterfuge and the plans for the rhododendron plantings were scaled down.

We had other skirmishes with Kennedy. It was never one big love affair between Kennedy and the press as many people seemed to think. But we were never considered "the enemy." There was never the insidious campaign of hatred against the press that developed in the Nixon era.

Kennedy had no Chief of Staff, no Sherman Adams and no H. R. Haldeman, Nixon's top lieutenant. Shortly after his election, Kennedy let it be known that he would run his own show. He was not going to be tied down to a formal staff system with a chain of command like Eisenhower's. Kennedy's aides had no trouble getting into the Oval Office. Kennedy ran a loose ship; he was an ad hoc operator. When the *Washington Post* told a Presidential assistant it was preparing a chart of the White House staff, the assistant said it could not be done.

"Draw a circle instead," he advised, "and put the President in the center with the lines running out to the assistants on the rim of the circle."

President Kennedy knew that effrontery and aggressiveness are the marks of the conscientious newsperson. A speed-reader, he used to devour the wire service reports and some ten daily newspapers. Nothing escaped him—he even read the "women's pages" and the society columns. He would observe mournfully, "I'm reading more and enjoying it less." He relished the daily banter with the press. Kennedy had a burning curiosity; he wanted to know all the major news and all the trivial gossip about the people around him.

Shortly after Tom Elliston, a reporter for the U.S. Information Agency, became the father of twins, Kennedy spotted him sitting in the lobby outside the President's Oval Office. Kennedy was en route to an important conference but he stopped and asked the new father, "What did you do, sneeze?"

In my work with UPI in those days, when I wasn't Jackie-watching, I was constantly trailing or questioning Kennedy. Sometimes I guess I was rather brazen in my questions. But he was relaxed about it all. He was an inveterate tease and quipster himself.

"Helen would be a nice girl if she'd ever get rid of that pad and pencil," Kennedy told Salinger early in the game. From Palm Beach on I had followed him with pad and pencil, openly writing down everything he said. He had apparently tired of the scrutiny.

On one occasion, Salinger decided to call reporters and photographers into the Oval Office for a picture-taking session. I was the only member of the writing press in the lobby at the time and I marched into the President's office—the lone "pad and pencil" reporter amid the covey of cameramen.

Kennedy looked up, surmised the situation at once and said, "Well, if it isn't Miss Thomas of the Universal Press."

Both "Lucky" Pierre and I have total recall of the telephone call I made to him at three o'clock in the morning to find out whether one of Caroline Kennedy's hamsters was dead. An AP story had just come through saying so and my editor had ordered me to match the story. Pierre could not have been more tolerant, but I had to wait for my answer (yes, the hamster was dead) until later in the day.

The lobby of the West Wing—before Nixon built the big, new, corporate-like White House press headquarters—was the gathering place for White House "regulars." The press center was a small, oblong, and usually jampacked room just off the West Wing entranceway. But the lobby itself was commodious and from that vantage point we could see and sometimes interview the President's visitors—at least those who came in through the front door.

I was constantly amazed by Kennedy's grasp. In the midst of a hectic schedule he would notice some minute detail and find the humor in it. Just before Jackie received her $7,000 Somali leopard coat from Emperor Haile Selassie, I had purchased a fake leopard number of my own, for a sale price of $40. One chilly autumn day, I wore my bargain coat to cover Kennedy's arrival by helicopter on the ellipse. I was standing in a jumble of reporters, aides, tourists, and cameramen when he stepped off the chopper, spotted me and yelled over the crowd, "Everyone's wearing leopard these days!"

When I turned the tables and teased him, he was never offended, and he usually had a comeback. On St. Patrick's Day, 1962, there was, appropriately, a large party at the White House attended by a number of "Irish Mafia" types. I walked up to the President, who turned the conversation to Caroline. He wanted to boast that she had thought up the name Leprechaun for the pony given to her by Ireland's President Eamon de Valera. "It's a great day for the Irish," I observed. "What are you doing here?" he shot back with a big smile, knowing full well my Mediterranean origins.

That spring I covered, from the sidelines, the President's working luncheon with German Chancellor Konrad Adenauer. Such occasions, in contrast to formal State Dinners where no business is done, are predominantly stag. They always make me realize how little political power women have in the world. In a toast the Chancellor said his state visit had been beneficial "although we know these communiqués are written in advance."

After lunch, Kennedy escorted Adenauer to a waiting limousine as I asked him about the meeting. "You'll be getting a communiqué from me," he said.

"Is that the one you wrote before he came?" I asked. Kennedy threw back his head and laughed, and everyone joined in.

AP's Douglas Cornell and I once saw Kennedy in a dramatic moment at a reception in the Blue Room after he had had a bitter confrontation with Roger Blough, chairman of United States Steel

Corporation. Blough informed Kennedy that his firm was raising steel prices. Kennedy thought he had a commitment from steel's "Big Five" to hold the line. "Six o'clock, six o'clock, they came in and told me," Kennedy raved to Doug and me. We had a good story because we knew that Kennedy was not going to take that lying down. Within a day or so, the steel companies rolled back their prices under government pressure.

Kennedy admitted at a news conference later that he had said, "My father always told me businessmen were SOBs."

Kennedy's essential intellect and wit allowed him to look both at life and people with detachment and compassion. He let the world in on his jokes and he lampooned everything and everyone, including himself. Of his job as President he said: "The pay is good and I can walk to work." Of his wife he said, when Jackie dressed in a large flamboyant hat to greet a visiting head of state, "What are you trying to do, ruin my political career? Take it off!" Of his Vice President, composing a birthday telegram to Johnson, who was known for his super-sensitivity, he admitted, "This is worse than drafting a state document." And of Nikita Khrushchev, with whom he had had an unnerving cold-bath meeting in Vienna, he said thoughtfully, "He has his good days and bad days, too."

Kennedy was chummier with the press than any other President I have covered because, in a sense, he was one of us; that is, one of our generation—the first President born in the twentieth century. He knew about our deadlines, problems, policies—and about our shenanigans. For one thing, he knew full well that reporters satirized members of the handsome Kennedy clan at every opportunity. The President provided a convenient target with his youthful looks, that unruly shock of hair, his Boston accent, the awkward jab of the forefinger when he answered questions. So was Jackie, sometimes the ultra-sophisticate and sometimes the wide-eyed little girl with the Marilyn Monroe voice.

In 1961, I played Jackie with some—but not much—trepidation in the Women's National Press Club's annual show spoofing politicians. I sang a song that poked fun at the way Jackie constantly flew off to exotic lands or to the New York theatre.

Vice President Johnson was the ranking guest in the audience of some four hundred—Jackie had declined our invitation to attend—

and local papers gave our dialogue and lyrics full coverage. The next day I had a friendly confrontation with President Kennedy in the Rose Garden. He was standing with a group of reporters and visitors, but when he saw me, he folded his arms in a characteristic stance, and said teasingly, "I've been reading all about you." "It's all true," I admitted, while the others standing around guffawed. I sang that same song ten years later at another dinner of the Women's National Press Club with Pat Nixon, Tricia, Julie, and David Eisenhower in the audience. They were amused.

Kennedy demonstrated his intimate knowledge of a more serious press corps matter during the visit of Venezuelan President Romulo Betancourt to the United States. At that time, in 1961, women reporters in Washington were waging their uphill fight for the right to cover major speeches made by local and visiting dignitaries at the then all-male National Press Club. Women were allowed to listen to these newsmaking noon speeches at the NPC, but they were not permitted to eat there, and they had to sit in a tiny balcony as male reporters dined at round tables in comfort and style in the ballroom below. We may as well have been in purdah.

As president of the Women's National Press Club, I had sent cables to a number of foreign leaders, including Nikita Khrushchev, urging them to speak at our club instead of the National Press Club, on the grounds that we would provide a balanced and integrated audience. Betancourt was apprised of this matter but he addressed a segregated National Press Club luncheon, anyway. Then he went to the White House for a lengthy meeting with JFK. When their meeting ended, Kennedy, as was his custom, escorted his guest through the lobby of the West Wing. A number of reporters, mostly women, stopped the two presidents in a corridor and asked for a comment. "I just told the National Press Club that I felt it might be a good idea to permit women correspondents to join their club activities," Betancourt said somewhat sheepishly.

"There's one of your revolutionaries right over there," Kennedy interjected, pointing at me. "Here she is trying to bring her own revolt into the White House."

Over the laughter, I told Betancourt loudly, "We forgive you, officially."

"But not personally," Kennedy said. He expressed my feelings precisely.

During the Kennedy era, I became the first woman to close a Presidential press conference, but I didn't do so with any great aplomb. Merriman Smith, the senior White House correspondent who traditionally brought these conferences to a close with his loud "Thank you, Mr. President," was out of town. It was my national television debut and I regretted I only had time to comb my hair and freshen my lipstick, especially since I knew my family would be watching. I studied the clock, and at what I thought was the appropriate time, I stood up and said my line, straight—"Thank you, Mr. President"—but I was drowned out by a chorus of newsmen still seeking recognition. It was a terrifying moment for me; I was about to lose my place in history—and still more important, with Smitty. I waited a few minutes until Kennedy was struggling to answer a complicated question, then I shouted, "Mr. President!" as though seeking recognition myself. When he looked my way, I said emphatically, "Thank you."

"Thank *you*, Helen," he said. He was grateful to me for getting him off the hook. The conference broke up in laughter.

A few hours after one of these televised matches with reporters, I saw President Kennedy standing at a side entrance of the White House, puffing on a cigar and looking very self-satisfied. I was waiting to travel with him and I teased: "Boy, you really handled that one." I was particularly impressed by the way he had reeled off some esoteric statistics about how many gallons of molasses went into the daily Cuban sugar production process. He laughed and confessed, "Someone came in and gave me the figures a few hours before the conference."

Salinger used to say that in the preparation for a news conference, Kennedy's aides could predict what questions newsmen would ask ninety percent of the time but they were always floored by the questions from women reporters. Kennedy once called a press aide at seven o'clock in the morning to forewarn him that a newswoman "has chewed your tail off." When the tart-tongued May Craig, famed for her pink hats and dark blue suits, asked Kennedy at a news conference what he had done for women lately, he grinned and said: "Obviously not enough."

If Kennedy's wit was a dominant feature of his administration, it was aided and abetted by Pierre Salinger. Once, confronted with the fact that he had strayed from the prepared text of a statement, Salinger replied, "I'm a textual deviate." Pierre had good rapport with the press. It was a joy to go to his briefings. He mixed with reporters and with the Kennedy family and he was a good pipeline to JFK. He had been through the campaign and he was a friend of the President. And when pushed by reporters, he would tell us the truth.

Salinger was the kind of public official you could reach with a human problem. He pulled me through a painful situation once after I had a lively interview with Anthony F. Matarrese, the pianist for the Marine Band Combo which played at Kennedy parties. Tony told me that the actor, Peter Lawford, then married to Pat Kennedy, came down the grand staircase snapping his fingers, and a few other tidbits about a private party. The story outraged President Kennedy and Tony was threatened with the loss of his job. When I went to Salinger and made an emotional appeal for reconsideration, Salinger sympathized, smoothed over the problem and Tony was back at the piano at the next party.

Covering the Kennedys was a three-ring circus. On weekends we could count on not being in Washington. In the fall and spring off we went to Middleburg, Virginia, to cover Kennedy and Jackie, a horsewoman, in the hunt country. In the summer it was up to Hyannis Port, Massachusetts, where the entire Kennedy clan would be gathered. Over the Christmas holidays the destination was Palm Beach, where the Kennedys had a Spanish-style ocean-side villa.

Kennedy tried many times to duck the press. And there were times when many of his friends—from the jet, Georgetown, Hollywood, and yachting sets—were arrogant and disdainful of reporters. They made it clear they could barely tolerate us. He himself never wanted us around when he was at the helm of his sailboat, the *Victura*, or when he was cruising in the *Honey Fitz*, the Presidential yacht; or in the *Marlin*, the family yacht, off Hyannis Port, Newport, or Palm Beach. Then he demanded privacy, and, like all other Presidents, he got angry with reporters who ignored his wishes.

But we had to follow him. When the President is on the high seas anything can happen and it's essential that the press be there to provide an objective report to the people. We covered these Presidential yachting parties—as best we could—in rented cabin cruisers, with reporters perched perilously on the bow, peering through binoculars, trying to take notes in the ocean spray, with photographers snapping pictures through telescopic lenses. I'm sure our presence, in our casual yachting attire, zigzagging across the open seas in our rented boats with their hired crews, did little to enhance the dignity of these Presidential armadas.

The President's yacht was always escorted by Coast Guard boats and other vessels carrying Secret Service agents. The agents expended much of their time and energy trying to thwart the press, to drive a wedge between us and the President's boat—while tourists in private boats often came close enough to the Presidential party to wave and take pictures with standard cameras. The logic in this always escaped me. The Secret Service men seldom knew who the tourists were, but they knew every reporter in the press boat well; while they knew we were often annoying we were not a security threat.

The orders to hold us back went out, and this time they came from the President, not Jackie.

Once a Secret Service boat kicked up a wake in the path of the press boat that sent reporters scurrying for life jackets. Kennedy so resented our intrusions that he deliberately turned away when the press boat was in sight. Photographers called him "Jack the Back" on such occasions.

One day Al Spivak, my friend and former colleague on the UPI White House staff, was peering at the Presidential yacht from the bow of the press boat—the *Honey Chile*, in this instance. Al was startled to see JFK staring back through binoculars. Kennedy kept this up, off and on, throughout his excursion that day, and Al mentioned the incident to Pierre Salinger.

"He's tired of being stared at," said Pierre. "He was retaliating."

Al had another theory. The shapely wife of a Secret Service agent was aboard the press boat that day, sunbathing in a skimpy bathing suit, and Kennedy was known to appreciate beautiful women.

The best part-time reporter the UPI had at Hyannis Port was Larry Newman, a local writer who lived with his wife in an elegant home just across the road from the Kennedy family enclave. When Kennedy's boat, the *Victura*, went aground with the President at the helm, Larry was the only reporter to see the mishap. The UPI story appeared on the front page of the *Washington Post* the following day. Kennedy was furious. Flying back to Washington from the Cape on Air Force One, he sent Salinger back to remonstrate with Al Spivak, the UPI pool man that trip.

"The President says that UPI story in the *Post* is absolutely false," Salinger told Al. "We can't have the captain of the Ship of State, a former naval lieutenant, going aground. We want a retraction."

Al: "I can't do that."

Salinger: "Why not?"

Al: "Because I've got these pictures right here of the *Victura* going aground."

Newman had taken pictures of the *Victura* and her skipper at the moment of truth. Salinger threw up his hands and walked away. Newman got a personal call from Kennedy, who wondered just how the story had leaked out. Kennedy admitted that a lot of people had been on the dock. Then he got to the point, according to Newman.

"Have you thought," asked Kennedy, "just what the Republicans will say about the commander-in-chief of all the armed services running a little sailboat aground?"

Jackie many years before had painted a watercolor of Kennedy standing at the helm of the *Victura* in a Napoleonic pose. Kennedy liked the painting but wondered, Newman wrote in *Parade* in November 1964, where she got the idea that "I have a commander-in-chief complex."

Despite the trauma and turmoil and the Presidential chill, those trips to Kennedy's oceanfront retreats were in part fun and games for reporters. Merriman Smith, particularly, was in his element when he hired a cabin cruiser and sailed the seas in pursuit of the President. Smitty, the author of several books about Presidents and Presidential politics, was a tough, compassionate, brilliant, complicated, at times irascible man—and a Pulitzer-prize winning reporter. He gave me the best basic training a wire service reporter could ever have. Write everything, was his advice.

Smitty and Cornell, who covered the White House regularly for the Associated Press, were the most professional newsmen I ever had the privilege of emulating. They were cool, competent, and able to write beautifully under tough, pressure-cooker conditions. The two major wire services—UPI and AP—have thousands of client newspapers, radio, and television stations all over the world and a wire service reporter must transmit the news the minute it breaks. Smitty impressed me early in the game with the fact that a wire service reporter covering the President is on a deadline twenty-four hours a day. Doug, who became my husband, was a formidable rival and a great writer under deadline pressure.

When Smitty was around, there was never any question about who was in charge of the UPI White House coverage. But one breezy October day, when we were covering the Kennedys at Newport, he found it necessary to give me a little lesson in protocol. Smitty was in command of the press boat that was chasing the Presidential yachting party around Narragansett Bay. He was equipped with all the paraphernalia a sailing reporter could need, including a walkie-talkie. But as an added protection, he gave me another walkie-talkie and stationed me on high, dry land, at the site of an old Revolutionary War cannon, where I had a sweeping view of the Bay. I was to wait for Smitty to call on his walkie-talkie and dictate a story. Then I was to rush to the nearest phone and call the story in to the Washington UPI. I sat on the cannon in my pink stretch slacks and manned my post for a couple of hours without hearing the first beep from Smitty. Finally, I began to shout frantically into my radio, "UPI one to UPI two, UPI one to UPI two."

Smitty came on the air, clearing his throat. There was a painful silence and then he said, with the utmost patience: "*This* is UPI one. You may come in now, UPI two."

Jackie Kennedy sometimes used a government helicopter to go fox-hunting, and when we could see the chopper arriving from our outpost at the Inn, we would race across winding country roads and peer through fences and foliage to see her land—running the very real risk that we would get picked off by a hunter's stray rifle shot. Despite her protestations to the contrary, Jackie took chances. She tumbled off her water skis a number of times on Nantucket Sound off Hyannis Port.

Several times when at Palm Beach, JFK and Jackie and some of their jet-set friends swam off the *Honey Fitz*, the 96-foot Presidential yacht, several miles out in the Gulf Stream where the water was calm, but where merchant ships dumped garbage and sharks were often sighted. We incurred the displeasure of both the President and the First Lady when we wrote that they swam in "shark-infested waters."

Some days later Jackie told reporters invited to a party at the Kennedy Palm Beach home that the stories were inaccurate. "There was no danger at all," she said softly. Maybe. But as the Kennedys swam, Secret Service agents hovered nearby in water-jet speedboats with rifles at the ready.

We called such pursuit "protective coverage." Most Presidents chafe under such vigilant reporting. I've always understood the desire for privacy Presidents and their families express. On the other hand, I have felt even more the need to have an independent observer, i.e., the objective reporter, when a President is in public, and is possibly in harm's way. Four Presidents have been assassinated and several, including FDR and President Ford, have been directly threatened—and that gives any reporter pause.

The New Frontiersmen who came into the White House at the start of the Kennedy era were pretty cocky, almost inviting the fall that inevitably came. Within a few months they were bragging "The boss has mastered the job." Then came the Bay of Pigs. In April 1961, Kennedy sanctioned the invasion of Fidel Castro's Cuba by 1,400 Cuban exiles, a plan inherited from Eisenhower. The invasion was quickly crushed by Castro. Told that the rebel cause was hopeless unless he committed United States forces, Kennedy refused to do so. I thought it the better part of valor. Pacing up and down in the Rose Garden at 3:00 A.M., Kennedy decided to accept full responsibility for the catastrophe rather than risk an invasion of Cuba. He paid a heavy price but it taught him never to use his Presidential authority until he was aware of the facts and had estimated the consequences. His family was very defensive as he came under critical fire from many quarters. "One mistake, one mistake," said Eunice Kennedy Shriver, in exasperation. But his popularity polls rose again after he admitted it was his fault. The American people, I find, can take a lot if a President levels with them. If he lies too often on important issues, he is finished in their eyes.

The second time around in an eyeball-to-eyeball confrontation with Soviet leader Nikita S. Khrushchev, Kennedy used his power effectively. On October 14, 1962, American U-2s brought back photographic evidence that the Russians were delivering missiles into Cuba capable of destroying every major city on our Eastern seaboard. He went on the air to tell the American people about the crisis and of the blockade of Cuba which he ordered.

The day he sent an ultimatum to the Kremlin to remove the missiles, Kennedy walked through the West Wing lobby. Smitty buttonholed him. "It's been a very interesting day," Kennedy told him.

Khrushchev capitulated on October 27 and had the courage to retreat. Kennedy, respecting his pride, made no big claims of victory.

Later in 1964, Lyndon Johnson, speaking on the campaign trail of those frightening hours, said that, "Kennedy was the coolest man in the room, and he had his thumb on the nuclear button." All the Presidents I have covered have seemed acutely conscious of the presence of the man with a "little black bag" with the nuclear codes who follows the President wherever he goes.

Salinger's own big test came during the 1962 Cuban Missile Crisis when he kept inquisitive reporters at bay while an anxious administration debated its next move in the nuclear chess game. Kennedy's credibility was far from 100 percent. He had been slated to make a speech in Chicago when suddenly a "cold" brought him back to Washington, or so reporters at the time were led to believe. But when several high-level Kennedy assistants, with a startling lack of originality, also developed "colds" in different parts of the country and headed back to Washington, the press began to put clues together. Lights began to burn late at the State Department and black limousines, arriving and departing, were a giveaway that a diplomatic crisis was underway.

In the aftermath of the missile crisis, Arthur Sylvester, Assistant Secretary of Defense for Public Affairs, said to the New York Deadline Club, December 6, 1962, "It would seem to be basic, all through history that a government's right—by government I mean people—that it's inherent in that government's right—if necessary to lie to save itself when it's going up into a nuclear war. This seems to me basic." Sylvester's candor touched off a furor in journalistic circles. The debate was the forerunner of "the credibility gap" that caused the downfall of two of Kennedy's successors.

Kennedy lived with the realization that he held life and death nuclear power over the world. He was proud of the test ban treaty he negotiated with the Russians because, as he stressed in a speech I covered, "three hundred million people could be killed in one hour in an atomic war." He saw it as a "nuclear Sword of Damocles, hanging by the slenderest of threads, capable of being cut at any moment by accident or miscalculation or by madness."

Kennedy, it always seemed to me, wanted to set the world on a course that would ultimately make all-out war unthinkable.

In talking of the quest for peace, Kennedy would often quote a Chinese proverb: "A journey of a thousand miles must begin with the first step." He took a giant first step in a speech before the United Nations in September of 1963 when he challenged the Soviet Union to embark on an era of "peaceful cooperation" and consider a joint expedition to the moon. "I believe the problems of human destiny are not beyond the reach of human beings," he said. He also produced a test ban treaty barring nuclear tests in the atmosphere, outer space, and under water; a disarmament program; the Peace Corps; and an assault on poverty and on mental illness. Although his civil rights bill was botched, Martin Luther King, Jr., said of him: "I think historians will have to record that he vacillated like Lincoln, but he uplifted the cause far above the political level."

Kennedy and King visited many times at the White House. Their most emotional meeting was August 28, 1963—on the day 200,000 people marched on Washington in a beautiful, peaceful demand for immediate equality for blacks, gathering along the Mall between the Washington Monument and the Lincoln Memorial. That evening, after King's moving and impassioned speech, "I have a dream . . . ," King went to a reception at the White House.

When Kennedy saw him, he extended his hand and said, "*I* have a dream."

Tragedy haunted the Kennedy family, in and out of the White House. On August 5, 1963, Press Secretary Pierre Salinger came rushing into the West Lobby, hastily summoned reporters and announced: "The President is leaving in five minutes to go to Hyannis Port." Jackie had been rushed to Otis Air Force Base Hospital from her Squaw Island summer home to have her third child.

I staked out the hospital during those sorrowful days. Two days after his birth, Patrick Bouvier Kennedy was dead from a hyaline membrane disease, a lung ailment. Kennedy, grief-stricken, was there when the tiny infant died, at 4:04 A.M., in a giant pressure chamber at Children's Hospital Medical Center. In the days that followed, Kennedy came to see his wife daily at the Air Base Hospital.

Kennedy and his wife left the hospital hand in hand. She had suffered a lot and her doctor relayed the word that she had made a "satisfactory recovery" but should curtail her activities.

The vibrancy of the Kennedy era reflected the ebullient spirit of the man himself. I always sensed that he felt he had a short time to live. So live it he would. One could tell by what he said that he had an overwhelming sense of fate after two close brushes with death. The first came in 1943 when his PT-109 torpedo boat was rammed by a Japanese destroyer in the South Pacific, and he swam for hours, towing an injured crew member, until they reached land. The second was in 1954 when he underwent a major operation in New York's Hospital for Special Surgery. Kennedy had first injured his back playing football; the injury was aggravated when his PT boat was rammed. Twice Kennedy was placed on the critical list and given last rites.

Kennedy always tried to conceal the pain of his ailing back. Once, forced to use crutches for a few days after he had injured his back planting a tree in Canada, he stayed out of public view until he could put the crutches away. He also suffered from adrenal insufficiency, a mild form of Addison's disease, and often his face looked puffy and dark, apparently from the cortisone treatment. This illness too was kept secret.

He used to joke to his Secret Service agents when discussing security details: "If they're going to get me, they're going to get me even in church."

But no matter the shadows he may have felt around him, Kennedy joked about what he would do when his White House days were over.

"It has recently been suggested that, whether I serve one or two terms in the Presidency, I will find myself at the end of that period at what might be called the awkward age—too old to begin a new career and too young to write my memoirs."

On a brisk, sunny day in March 1963, Kennedy made an unscheduled visit to Arlington National Cemetery with his friend, Charles Bartlett, a Washington newspaperman, and as he stood in front of the Custis-Lee Mansion, looking at the lovely sweeping view of the Potomac, the Lincoln Memorial, and the Washington Monument, he said quietly, "I could stay up here forever."

I was with Kennedy when he went to Arlington National Cemetery again on Veterans' Day, November 11, 1963, to pay his respects to the American war dead. He took his son, John-John, with him. Kennedy's military aide, Gen. Chester V. (Ted) Clifton, had been teaching the youngster to salute and to march like a soldier. Kennedy appeared pensive and alone on that sad anniversary. After a while, Kennedy realized that his son was not in the amphitheater where the ceremonies were being held and I heard him tell a Secret Service agent, "Go get John-John. I think he'll be lonely out there."

Two weeks later Kennedy was buried on a gentle hill at Arlington, surrounded by thousands of other slain veterans, near the Custis-Lee Mansion.

Not until the trip to Dallas, Texas, in November 1963, had Jackie Kennedy traveled with her husband on any political trips. They were not her cup of tea. But after the death of their son, the Kennedys had, from my observation, grown closer together. They

appeared genuinely affectionate toward each other, although the
night before they departed Jackie showed up late, and apparently
reluctantly, at a reception in honor of the Judiciary. She looked as
if she had been crying.

She had returned only a short time before from a two-week
vacation in Greece and a cruise on the Aegean and East
Mediterranean seas on the luxurious 303-foot yacht *Christina*
owned by Aristotle Onassis, a friend of her sister, "Princess" Lee
Radziwill. She was still recovering from Patrick's Caesarean birth
and death. Reporters had followed the Onassis yacht from island to
island as Jackie water-skiied, swam, dined, and danced until dawn
each day. She did not give the impression of being a lady in
mourning. As the newspapers began chronicling the hijinks,
Kennedy had blown up and cabled her to come home.

I always felt that when Jackie agreed to go to Texas she was
trying to make amends to JFK for the sensation she created with
Onassis in Greece. She had traveled around the world with her
husband, but the trip to Dallas in November 1963 was her first
purely political trip as First Lady in the United States. Two days
before she left she called her former social secretary, Tish
Baldridge, and said: "You're going to be very proud of me; I'm
going to start campaigning."

I watched President and Mrs. Kennedy leave the White House
by helicopter from the South Grounds that day as they departed on
the first leg of their trip to Texas. It was raining but, as usual,
Kennedy was hatless. He had John-John by the hand. He took his
son on the chopper ride from the White House to Andrews Air
Force Base where he and Jackie boarded Air Force One for Texas
and John-John came back home to the White House with a Secret
Service agent.

I was preparing to depart on a vacation to Detroit to see my
family the following day. I had my bags packed and was having
lunch in a Washington restaurant with Fran Lewine and Pierette
Spiegler, a member of Mrs. Kennedy's press staff, when we heard
the news on a transistor radio. Kennedy had been shot. Fran and I
bolted out of the restaurant, hailed cabs and rushed to our offices.

"You're on vacation," my boss, Julius Frandsen, said.

"No, I'm not," I told him. The wire reports said Kennedy was still alive and I was sent home to pick up my suitcase and then get to Andrews Air Force Base where a press plane was standing by to fly to Dallas. En route, I heard the news on the cab radio. Kennedy was dead. I was stunned and did not want to believe it.

The Kennedy era ended Friday, November 22, 1963, as the President's open car, leading a motorcade through Dallas, passed by the Texas School Book Depository. Kennedy was shot from the rear. Smitty was riding in the press pool car about 200 feet behind the Presidential limousine. From a Secret Service agent he learned that Kennedy died—his head cradled in Jackie's arms—as the car sped to Parkland Hospital in Dallas, although Kennedy was not pronounced dead until twenty-two minutes after the blood-spattered limousine pulled up to the hospital's emergency entrance.

Smitty was aboard Air Force One when it took off from Love Field in Dallas for Andrews Air Force Base, carrying the body of the dead President, and he witnessed the swearing in of Lyndon Johnson as the new President.

I was in that mad scramble of stunned and distraught reporters who watched the Presidential jet return. Smitty saw me and yelled at me to dictate his copy to the office from our phone at the airfield, while he went on to the White House. He had written a beautiful, simple story, but it broke my heart to dictate it. In the material Smitty thrust into my hands was the text of a speech that Kennedy had intended to deliver the night of November 22, 1963 before the Texas Democratic State Committee. Kennedy was to have warned that "hate, suspicion, and fear could divide and weaken the country . . . and end the dream."

I went back to the White House press room, which was jampacked with reporters and cameramen, all of us waiting for word on the plans for the state funeral. We also had to keep in mind that we had a new President to watch—Lyndon Baines Johnson.

A policeman tipped me off that the Kennedy casket would be brought into the White House a few hours past midnight. I was told that when Jackie had got off Air Force One and when Angier Biddle Duke, the U.S. Chief of Protocol, rushed up to her and asked: "Is there anything I can do for you?"

"Yes," she said, "find out how Lincoln was buried."

Sargent Shriver, Kennedy's brother-in-law and at that time head of the Peace Corps, took command of arrangements, even to the black crepe hung on the windows, which Jackie later ordered rearranged. The White House policemen paid their respects to the fallen President on Saturday morning. Kennedy's office was already being stripped of all his belongings and a distraught Jackie came into the Oval Office and directed the moving.

Robert "Bobby" Kennedy, whose grief was so profound, stayed at the White House all night after the casket was brought in. He and Jack had been so close for so many years. Jack had defied the charges of nepotism to name his brother Attorney General and, indeed, Bobby was the lightning rod for Kennedy's opposition. They liked Jack but they could not stand Bobby, so they said. In an unbelievable stroke of fate Bobby was to be slain himself, also on a campaign trip, five years later.

Bobby was the only member of the family in the East Room when a Gawler's Funeral Home representative opened the casket. When he saw his brother's body, he collapsed. He was taken to the Green Room and a White House doctor was summoned. It was the only time the casket was opened.

I remember Jackie's Spartan courage and control that weekend. Kennedy's funeral had unparalleled grandeur and Mrs. Kennedy had masterminded it. She had always seemed to think of herself as a queen and in November 1963 she carried herself with majesty. To the family she said, "We must just get through this."

She was the pro. When her moment came, she was ready.

Many wanted her to continue to live the legend of the grieving widow forever. But Jackie was more realistic. I was not surprised when she married Onassis. Before that big event, a friend cautioned her: "But, Jackie, you're going to fall off your pedestal."

Her response was searing, logical, and pure Jacquelinian. "That's better than freezing there," she said.

I have seen Kennedy, Johnson, Nixon, and Ford savor the Presidency. I have also seen them in their troubled moments. But it is people who turn them on; that is, the worshipful crowds, the shining eyes, and the smiles on the faces of men, women, and children when a President comes up to a fence to shake their hands, always accompanied by tense Secret Service agents.

Kennedy liked crowds, especially the young with whom he felt a special rapport, as they did with him. Whenever he spoke to young groups on the South Lawn or in the Rose Garden, he would point out the magnolia tree planted by Andrew Jackson. He would give his definition of happiness, taken from the Greeks. "Happiness," he said, "is the fullest use of one's powers along lines of excellence."

Striving for excellence was one of Kennedy's primary goals. In the decade that followed his death there have been inevitable reassessments. Revisionists have questioned his accomplishments and his place in history. If spirit can be assessed, as I think it can, Kennedy was an outstanding President. He led the people with a sense of hope and direction, a feeling that there was more to fulfill in their own lives and for future generations. No President since then has inspired such ideals of life and pride in ourselves and our history. He also brought glamor and humor to the White House, and a spontaneous wit that touched the mansion even on dark days.

"If we cannot end our differences, we can at least make the world safe for diversity," he would say. He had known war and it made a difference. He knew sadness and great joy. I don't think anything in my years at the White House can compare to the death of Kennedy. I still feel the pain of his death and think it's natural when people ask "where were you when Kennedy died?" It was somehow like a death in the family, a personal loss.

Chapter 2

LBJ: The Texas Brand

I made the mistake of most reporters and chief executives—we ignore or pay inadequate attention to Vice Presidents. Yet I have witnessed three successions of Vice Presidents to the Presidency since coming to Washington in the middle of World War II— Harry S. Truman on the death of FDR, Lyndon B. Johnson when Kennedy was assassinated, and later Gerald R. Ford when Richard M. Nixon resigned—and I should realize by now that Vice Presidents are to be taken seriously.

The Presidency was what Johnson actually wanted, but during the 1960 Democratic convention Kennedy offered him the number 2 spot. Johnson told us later, "I wanted to be Vice President about as much as I wanted to be the Pope of Rome."

In the Johnson suite at the Hilton Hotel in Los Angeles, in the summer of 1960, Johnson's Texas friends were divided over whether he should join the Kennedy ticket. In chats with us later, Johnson recalled that, "Senators came in begging, 'Please don't run.' One said, 'If you run I'm going to shoot you between the eyes,' then he came around again and said, 'If you *don't* run I'm going to shoot you between the eyes.' I asked him what happened and he explained, 'I'm running for election.' He thought my name could help him."

Speaker of the House Sam Rayburn finally argued Johnson into going on the ticket. "How can you say that when at 2:00 A.M. you told me not to?" Johnson asked.

"Because I'm a much smarter and wiser man today," Rayburn

answered. Rayburn had another motive also. He told Johnson he did not want Richard Nixon to win the Presidency. Nixon had called him and President Truman traitors.

Mrs. Johnson had sided with those who opposed his lining up with Kennedy. A reporter friend of mine who was in the Johnson suite on that night told me that, when Kennedy left his quarters en route to the Johnson suite, word spread quickly. Mrs. Johnson urged her husband to decline JFK's offer. There was a last-minute confrontation between them in the bedroom. Mrs. Johnson was wearing a beautiful dressing gown with a low-cut neckline. LBJ tapped his wife's breast with his forefinger as he said emphatically, "Don't you know that the Number Two spot is just a heartbeat away from the Presidency?"

After he made the decision to accept, Johnson told us, "All my delegation cried. A good many wouldn't speak to me. Friends came in tears and said, 'Don't do this. How can you?' "

Many men had chafed under the impotency of the Vice Presidency, and Johnson, a commanding, zestful six-foot-three man with the rangy physique of a ranch hand, full of energy and ambition, had to feel especially frustrated in that role. After he became President he told us, "If I had my druthers I would have been happy to be elected Senate Democratic Leader for a lifetime." Capitol Hill had been a more compatible milieu, because there he could best utilize his talents to "get things done." He needed to be with people, to press against them, to be where he could literally count the heads of those who sided with him.

Several days after John F. Kennedy's funeral I saw his successor seated in the chalk-white Oval Office. The occasion was the first official picture-taking session of the new thirty-sixth President at work. The late November sun filtered through the glass curtains and the room seemed ghostly. Kennedy's new bright red rug just then being installed had already been replaced by a pale green one and Johnson's old Senate desk with the inlaid leather top had already been moved into the President's office. President Johnson was seated near a sofa in a rocker similar to the one President Kennedy had used. I was stunned. At first I thought that it was insensitive of Johnson. But then I realized he was trying to impart a sense of continuity, and that the gesture was not fraudulent. And, in fact, Dr. Janet Travell, the White House physician during the Kennedy years and the early part of the Johnson administration, recommended the use of specially-designed rockers for LBJ as well as for JFK. Still, Johnson was not a rocking chair man and we all knew it. He was trying to put his own stamp on the White House and establish a link with President Kennedy at the same time. From the outset he wanted to be all things to all people.

The morning after his initial sitting with White House photographers, he took a 6:00 A.M. walk outside the White House grounds, the way President Truman used to do. Later, at the Burning Tree Country Club, he played golf, just as Eisenhower did. LBJ wanted to be a big, strong, individualist President—omnipotent, omniscient, and omnipresent. He also wanted to be identified with Kennedy, with Truman, with Roosevelt, and with his mentor, Sam Rayburn, the great former Speaker of the House. Especially with Roosevelt. If anyone was his hero, it was FDR. "He was like a Daddy to me," Johnson often said. From Roosevelt, Johnson learned how to manipulate for desired political results. FDR was the all-time pro on that score and LBJ learned at his master's feet. Political scientist Richard Neustadt, author of *Presidential Power*, felt that LBJ wanted to be a Roosevelt-Eisenhower—that he wanted to be loved like Ike, as the great stabilizer, while achieving revolutionary, Rooseveltian-like results in the field of social reform. Johnson himself once told us that he wanted to be "progressive without being radical" and "prudent without being reactionary"— a philosophy that I felt straddled the middle and tried to have it all.

As LBJ groped to establish his own Presidential image, I kept wanting to shout, "Just be yourself, Mr. Johnson, just be yourself!" This was a larger order than I realized at first. LBJ, like the partly-parched, partly-verdant Texas hill country he came from, was marked by many contradictions. He was coarse and courtly, rude and considerate, tyrannical and thoughtful, cruel and compassionate. He had a giant ego and a giant inferiority complex. He was true to the image of Texas, a big man with a big appetite and big ambitions and big loves—for his family, for women, for the people, for the country, for the world. He was larger than life. He was also self-conscious about his Texas origins—more so than any other Texan I've ever known. He had worked his way through Southwest

Texas State Teachers College doing janitor's work part of the time and I felt he should have been proud of this background. He was, in a way. But he was also extremely defensive in the presence of the Eastern Establishment intellectuals he had inherited from the Kennedy administration. The fact that the tall Texas President could sit on the john and brief the patrician C. Douglas Dillon, the Secretary of the Treasury, explains to a large degree why he never established complete rapport with his urbane and erudite Eastern aides—the men from Harvard, the Phi Beta Kappans, the Rhodes Scholars—Kennedy had appointed. "With my background, I don't think I will ever get credit for anything I do in foreign policy, no matter how successful, because I didn't go to Harvard," LBJ once said.

He had a complex nature. In his speeches he could preach economy and spending in the same breath; he could use Lincolnesque and cornpone language alternately. In his private conversations he could both invoke the Bible and revel in salacious language in relating one of his earthy barnyard stories. But then so did Lincoln. Late in his administration we saw him as a man who could, in the same week, praise our fliers in Vietnam for their accurate bombing and then fly to Rome for peace talks with the Pope; we saw him as a man who could preach openness and honesty and practice secretiveness and deception.

But in the beginning he was majestic. In that black hour after President Kennedy's assassination he immediately assumed the responsibilities of national and free world leadership. He might have fallen apart. Kennedy had flown to Texas in November 1963 at Johnson's own invitation. The young President was murdered in full view of the Vice President, who rode in the third car behind the death limousine—a tragedy unparalleled in our history. Johnson was afraid for his own life in that hour, and on many occasions later. Of that I am certain. But he took command firmly and swiftly and he held the country together. "He's a good man in a crisis," Mrs. Johnson always said, and in this case she was absolutely right.

Johnson stood outside Emergency Room One in Dallas' Parkland Memorial Hospital, offering comfort to Jackie Kennedy, until an Assistant White House Press Secretary announced that JFK was dead. Then he sped to Love Field, boarded the Presidential jet and

took the oath of office from a Texas woman judge who was an old
family friend. An hour after the announcement of Kennedy's
death—with members of his party and Kennedy's party and Mrs.
Kennedy and President Kennedy's body aboard Air Force One—
LBJ gave his first Presidential order: "Let's get this plane back to
Washington!"

En route he began to summon members of Congress and the
Cabinet to immediate meetings in Washington. From the moment
he became President, he was conscious of destiny and going down
in the pages of history. Even on the plane headed back to
Washington from Dallas, his face grave, surrounded by the
grief-stricken Jackie and other Kennedy and Johnson followers,
LBJ turned to his wife and said: "Lady Bird, why don't you make
some notes. . . ."

Merriman Smith of UPI and Charles Roberts of *Newsweek*
magazine were the only reporters aboard Air Force One on this
epic flight from Love Field in Dallas to Andrews Air Force Base
outside Washington, and I quote from an article that Smitty wrote
some time later:

Johnson in this terribly trying hour was everything a leader should be
under great emotional stress—calm, deliberate, considerate and perhaps
above all, as realistic as an ice pick.

He was a picture of well-coordinated activity—talking by radio-
telephone to Kennedy's mother, Rose, and remembering to inquire about
her paralyzed husband, Joseph P. Kennedy; dictating to a secretary what
amounted to the minutes of this dreadful hour, and stopping to tell a
member of his small staff to set up a Cabinet meeting for that night. LBJ
was walking down the aisle of the main passenger compartment, running
an errand of his own, a sheaf of papers in his big hands, when he stopped
to talk to me briefly:

"I'm trying to keep you posted on everything I'm doing because it is
extremely important for the people at an awful time like this."

I thanked him and explained that my partner in the press pool, Charles
Roberts, and I were writing as rapidly and in as much detail as time
allowed.

"I know, I know," he said almost impatiently. "God knows, the last
thing I wanted was to become President in this way. But I'll tell you one
thing—"

He paused to punch a big right forefinger into my chest forcefully as if
to make his point in boldface italics:

"Now that I am President and with God's help, you're going to live long enough to write that I was the best President this country ever had.

"And you know why you're going to write that? Because I'm going to try like hell—I'm going to try so hard that you'll be forced to write something like that."

What amazed me at the time was that Johnson, speaking in a low voice, almost a whisper, did not seem at all to be bragging. He was taking a fiercely determined oath and that was what he set out to do.

I was standing on the tarmac at Andrews Air Force Base in Maryland waiting to call in Smitty's story. I saw Lyndon Johnson's face as he stepped off that plane at the base and walked down the ramp behind Mrs. Kennedy, and it was ashen. He was stricken, grieved, frightened, but he worked around-the-clock in the next weeks to show the world that there would be no lapse in American leadership. For two days during the Kennedy funeral, he worked quietly in the Executive Office Building, across West Executive Avenue from the White House. Johnson did not want to enter the White House as President until after the funeral was over. He didn't think it fitting. He met with a continuous parade of national and world leaders. When Eisenhower came in, I saw Lyndon Johnson take out a big yellow legal pad and take copious notes. So did Ike. LBJ conferred with Ike often after that.

But Johnson was a man who loved power and adulation, and while the tragedy of Kennedy's death was still with him I could observe a growing mood of euphoria.

Two weeks after Johnson became President, Pierre Salinger arranged a reception in the family quarters so that Johnson could get acquainted with members of the foreign press. I covered the event and could sense the new feeling of well-being and determination. He stepped out onto the Truman balcony with a glass in his hand, looked toward the Washington Monument and said proudly, "There have only been thirty-six of us." The visiting writers were impressed with the personal generosity of LBJ's hospitality, but a few looked startled when he undid his belt, pulled his pants out from the waist and said, "See how much weight I've lost in these two weeks." It was not a dignified gesture but it was pure Johnson. He wanted sympathy.

Some days later Johnson told a group in the Rose Garden, "The most stimulating thing in my kind of work is the feeling that people care about me." As the weeks rolled by he became more intoxicated with the majesty of the Presidency, but he didn't want to lose touch. "I don't want to be king," he said. "I just want to see people. All day long they call me Mr. President. I wish they'd just call me Lyndon."

Lady Bird Johnson moved into the White House while the nation was still traumatized over the Kennedy death. The psychological burdens were heavy. "Somehow we must find the strength to go on," she said. She had been riding with Johnson in the motorcade in Dallas when Kennedy was slain. "We didn't want to be President," she used to say in the first months.

The First Lady issued a statement when the Johnsons moved into the mansion.

Dear Friends:

The President and I know and understand the anguish each of you has been through these last weeks, and we are also very much aware of how you labored hard and long to help us in many ways. We are looking forward to meeting all the members of the White House staff.

Once installed at 1600 Pennsylvania Avenue, she said to us she "walked on tiptoe and spoke in a whisper." To her, it was awesome and never quite home. The Johnsons were really at home only on their Texas ranch along the banks of the Pedernales.

A restless man who had to keep moving, LBJ complained about "lonely acres" and "that big black fence" that kept him pent in. He did not always take too kindly to some of the protocol of the Presidency, particularly to entertaining the stream of foreign visitors. Of some heads of state, he would say, "I would be as delighted to see them now as you would be to see your mother-in-law coming when you're headed for a ball game." He would often escape to his Texas ranch to get away from all the Congressmen, also, and "all those poster kids" he had to pose with in Oval Office ceremonies.

His 400-acre spread along the peaceful Pedernales River renewed his spirits and brought him serenity. He insisted he could accomplish more among his Hereford cattle herds and whitetail deer than in Washington, D.C. There he could walk to inspect a fence or take a dip in the heated pool, or play dominos with cronies who still called him "Lyndon." He told us often of his father, Samuel Ealy Johnson, Jr., who refused to stay in a hospital in Austin when he knew he was dying. Johnson said his father "put on his pants" and told him, "I'm going home where the folks take care of you when you're sick and they care when you die." In the end, LBJ did the same thing.

Johnson often invited reporters to barbecues at the LBJ ranch where mariachi bands would play and Mexican cocktails—margaritas, made of tequila and lime juice—would be served. I had been there once when Johnson was Vice President and had entertained a group of touring United Nations delegates with a barbecue fiesta of ribs, brisket of beef, deer meat sausage, pinto beans, cole slaw, and apple turnovers. I remember small executive planes landing like birds, debarking ambassadors who warmed quickly to his open, friendly manner. As host, LBJ reigned. He'd circulate among the guests, mount his horse for picture-taking, and introduce notables from a microphone. His barbecues were always gracious, and I once made a faux pas by wearing slacks to one when patio skirt and blouse would have been more appropriate.

I was introduced to what became Johnson rituals—a ride at sundown in the white Lincoln Continental to look into the eyes of the deer, an afternoon aboard his cruiser on the Granite Shoals (later renamed Lake LBJ) the next day, then a fried catfish dinner topped by pecan pie at the white-framed native stone ranchhouse, which we tagged "the Texas White House."

There was no place to hide on the ranch. LBJ's intercom and other communications gadgetry created a "Big Brother Is Watching You" atmosphere. Johnson used the intercom to conduct ranch business. He barked orders to his foreman and the Secret Service alike. One weekend when reporters Garnett "Jack" Horner and Jack Sutherland were staying with their wives at the guest house, they discovered Johnson's line was open. They heard Johnson tell aides he wanted the newsmen to come to dinner and before the invitations arrived, they accepted. Johnson realized later that they were tuned into his conversations and one of the ranch hands came by the next day to pick up their radio "to be repaired."

One "must" in our ranch schedule was a nighttime stroll led by Johnson over to Cousin Oriole Bailey's for a chat. She was an elder Johnson relative, a lively woman who had once obviously been voluptuous. She looked at us through thick-lensed spectacles, and sassed LBJ, to his great delight. She became famous for Johnson's affection for her and for her own folksy assessment of life.

When I first called on her during Johnson's Vice Presidency, with Perle Mesta and two other reporters, all weekend house guests at the ranch, we woke her up and she came padding out in bare feet. Her home was weather-beaten and needed painting and she obviously lived frugally. I wrote a story about her, describing her "ramshackle house." She was furious and asked Johnson, "Does Helen Thomas sleep with her shoes on?" Johnson never let me forget it. When I wrote to thank him for the exciting weekend at the ranch, he wrote back:

Dear Helen,

I was down at Cousin Oriole's recently and you have no idea how much your story is in circulation along the Pedernales. Visitors just pass the ranch by now to stop at the most famous landmark of all, Oriole's house. You girls have an elevating influence, however. She sleeps with her shoes on, so no one will catch her otherwise. And after you referred to her house as "ramshackle," she's hit me up for a paint job.

                                        Affectionately,
                                        Lyndon B. Johnson

On Sundays, when he was President, the wire service reporters would drive the seventy miles to the Texas hill country from Austin, and later the eighty-five miles from the press headquarters in San Antonio, to find the President at church. He wanted coverage of worship services only on special occasions, like Christmas Eve or Easter, but we felt that we should go wherever he went whenever he was out in public. Besides, such coverage gave us important background. We could see that his spirit was renewed by the local preachers like Father Wunibald Schneider, and we could recognize the origin of a phrase or gesture in his speeches later. Johnson received solace also from Evangelist Billy Graham and

Dr. George Davis, pastor of the National Christian Church in Washington, where Johnson was an elder. Davis officiated at the religious service before Johnson drove to the Capitol Hill on Inaugural Day, January 20, 1965.

I was invited as a guest to those services by LBJ, along with a thousand dignitaries, friends of the Johnsons, and other members of the press. Yet when LBJ came out of the church and descended the steps, he stared at the mob of photographers and asked petulantly, "What are you doing here?"

Johnson was the most ecumenical President I covered. One Sunday, he attended a Roman Catholic mass at St. Francis Xavier with Luci, about a mile away from the ranch. Then with the whole family in tow he attended services at Trinity Lutheran Church, which adjoined the ranch. Rev. Norman C. Truesdell, the young church pastor, had become Johnson's good friend. "It's not right to gripe and bitch and say I don't want to be involved," said Truesdell from the pulpit as we did a double take. "That is your responsibility."

Only once did Johnson suffer a severe rebuke from the pulpit in churches he attended. At services at Bruton Parish in Colonial Williamsburg, Virginia, Rev. Cotesworth Pinkney Lewis preached a sermon against the Vietnam War. Johnson, sitting in a front pew, was furious, but said nothing after the service. Mrs. Johnson complimented the pastor on the "wonderful choir."

Lyndon Baines Johnson had to have it all, and whenever I heard him tell the story of old Mrs. Lurana Fidelia Stribling who, in the early 1900s amassed one of the largest ranch empires around Johnson City, I felt he was talking about himself. Once one of her lawyers, exasperated by the way she was buying up one ranch after another, said to her, "Mrs. Stribling, how much land do you want? Do you want all there is in the country?"

And Mrs. Stribling replied, "No, I don't want it all. All I want is my own and all that joins it."

You simply had no choice but to relax and relish his all-embracing presence. There was no alternative.

During his first two years in office, Johnson proved that he was, as he claimed to be, "a can-do President." He had a reputation as a wheeler-dealer and arm-twister, but he thought the treatment he applied to get bills through Congress was simply old-fashioned American politics at its best, including the ingredients of cajolery, flattery, patronage, and sometimes knowing where the bodies were buried. He had vast intellect, a knowledge of people and their motives, and the style of a riverboat gambler. While deriding opponents mercilessly he also could compromise, quoting his favorite expression from Isaiah, "Come, let us reason together." And he made no permanent enemies because he knew he might need them as friends some day. He had a mammoth ego and an inferiority complex to balance it.

Though he reveled in glory, Johnson was wounded in the early days by the resentment and bitterness of the Kennedy cult. My opinion on this score was shared by many others—C. Douglas Dillon, for one. In an oral history he donated to the Lyndon Johnson Library in Austin, Dillon said that the Kennedy clansmen would walk into LBJ's office often and tell him, "This is the way we used to do it."

"It was an inevitable problem, given the situation," said Dillon. "Larry O'Brien was the only one who was able to make the complete transition." Kennedy New Frontiersmen became, in the Johnsonian lexicon, "those touch footballers" or "Harvard boys."

When Johnson thought he was being unfavorably compared to Kennedy, he would retort quite accurately, "I don't have charisma but I get things done." His achievements on the domestic front were monumental. He picked up John Kennedy's Grand Design and tried to build a Great Society. Johnson was haunted by the Great Depression and I felt he truly wanted to improve the lot of the underprivileged everywhere, that—with the help of God and the Congress—he would create a modern Utopia where jobs, food, health care, homes, and education would be available to all.

Within months after he took office, Johnson, with more Congressional experience than any other American President, had won Congressional approval of the controversial, Kennedy-sponsored $11.5 billion tax cut bill, a move that spurred the economy to a new high rate of expansion. He soft-soaped, cajoled, finagled, influenced, and bargained with his old colleagues on the Hill until they went on to approve the Kennedy-initiated Civil Rights program, which did more to protect the rights of blacks than any measure since Reconstruction days. He told me and other reporters that his concern about civil rights was very personal. When his black cook, Zephyr Wright, accompanied the Johnson family on their drive to Texas, she couldn't go to the bathroom at gas stations where they stopped. Johnson was outraged. He pushed his own pet Medicare program through Congress. Under his prodding, Congress responded generously to administration requests for federal aid to education and voted out the long-bottled-up immigration reform bill, wiping out the prejudicial quota system based on national origins.

It was Johnson's personal intervention in 1964 that averted a nationwide rail strike and it was his personal touch as "mediator" that helped to forestall a steel strike which could have seriously crippled the economy.

Johnson put the LBJ brand on the nation in those first two years and the effect was sometimes searing. He told George Reedy, the second of his four press secretaries, that he wanted to see his name on the front page of the nation's newspapers "every day." He could be derisive against real or imagined enemies.

But when in difficulty, Johnson never hesitated to look to the group of elder statesmen who had served past administrations. Among them was Dean Acheson, Secretary of State in the Truman era, much respected in the field of diplomacy. But Johnson was not always respectful, to put it mildly. During one agonizing session Johnson went into a tirade and vilified a public official. Acheson spoke up, saying, "Mr. President, there is no job in the world that would make me take that from you." LBJ could be a tyrant with the lashing tongue of a Texas bullwhip. I ceased to be shocked by his swings from praise to anger, from high exhilaration to deep despair.

The triumphant 1964 Presidential campaign helped ease his inferiority complex and reinforce his ego. Johnson was now a President elected by the people, not merely a successor to a dead President. The convention, held in Atlantic City, New Jersey, in late August to coincide with LBJ's August 27 birthday, was a week-long political extravaganza, and Lyndon Johnson was the undisputed star from start to finish. On the night of his nomination, the some 3,500 delegates and contributors gave him a tumultuous ovation while outside the convention hall his brand and portrait exploded in fireworks in the sky.

I had also been assigned to cover the divisive Republican convention, when, after much internecine fighting, the Republicans chose Senator Barry Goldwater as their standard-bearer. On the first day back on my regular White House beat, President Johnson reproached me with, "You're a member of the White House press. What were you doing in San Francisco?" I tried to explain that I had no control over the assignments from my Washington and New York editors, but to Johnson my side trip to the GOP convention was a personal affront.

In the following weeks I covered enough of his campaign to "redeem" myself in his eyes. During this gruelling, two-month coast-to-coast marathon, with his wife and daughters now 100 percent behind him, President Johnson made up to twenty-five speeches a day, pouring out the same litany of jokes and promises over and over and over. He was an incomparable combination of medicine man, evangelist, and statesman. He promised voters not just a great, but the greatest, happiest society in all history. He was exhausting. Sometimes he orated fourteen hours, his voice getting more and more hoarse from impromptu speeches on street corners. When he capriciously stopped his motorcade, we had to run the length of as many as ten cars to hear what he had to say. While we knew his standard speech by heart, he could flay his opponent extemporaneously, so we had to listen closely. The campaign was an emotional orgy for him. He smothered the country with his cracker barrel campaign style, unchanged since the days when he first ran for Congress from the tenth Texas district. He made grandiose, overblown, stemwinder speeches. One observer said he campaigned for reelection "with all the fervor of an evangelist smoking out pockets of heathens." When the crowds roared their approval of his speeches he walked on clouds. "They have a baby-like faith in me," he said once. On one occasion Johnson was so buoyed by the enthusiastic reception he received from a crowd of blacks that he boasted, "Those Negroes go off the ground when they see me. They cling to my hands like I was Jesus Christ walking in their midst."

He said he had heard about a great preacher in Senator Barry Goldwater's native Phoenix and one Sunday morning there at the height of the campaign, Johnson decided to attend his service. Johnson's motorcade stopped at several street corners so he could commandeer the bullhorn himself, shouting "Come to the speakin'." He arrived late at church. For LBJ, the Sabbath was no let-up day. Thus, after invading Goldwater's home territory, he flew, on Sunday, to Long Beach, California, Las Vegas, Nevada, and then to San Francisco. Johnson plowed through days and nights on a natural reserve of adrenalin and said he took an occasional Seconal to get some sleep during those protracted days and nights.

Running with LBJ, of course, was the effervescent Hubert H. Humphrey. President Johnson had gone to great lengths before the 1964 Democratic nominating convention in Atlantic City to eliminate Bobby Kennedy as a potential running mate. He took the Mack truck approach.

Sometimes, as I bucked crowds and dove into a moving telephone car, I wondered whether I would survive. I felt like a stunt woman, but the only thing worse than covering a campaign is not covering a campaign.

Johnson's advance men did their job superbly, arranging for throngs of people to turn out for the President. Inspired, Johnson got folksier and folksier, especially in his native South. He also demonstrated his political courage and candor when he arrived in New Orleans as if it were a Hollywood finale, and he touched on civil rights. "All I ever hear is nigger, nigger, nigger," he chided fellow Southerners.

He was riding high in the saddle and in the polls. He carried the latter inside his jacket where he could whip them out and read them to reporters. He also just happened to have with him a copy of the Senate vote on the Tonkin Gulf Resolution. It became smudged and soiled as he repeatedly pulled it out to underscore the Senate vote of 88 to 2 giving him carte blanche to take all necessary measures against aggression in Southeast Asia. The House backed him unanimously, 416 to 0.

Johnson was a tremendous campaigner, especially when he got wound up and milked the crowd with such questions as, "Whose finger do you want on the nuclear button?" implying that his opponent would be trigger-happy in the White House.

The momentum was with him and against his Republican opponent. Goldwater was a self-proclaimed hawk and LBJ became the candidate who was not going to send "American boys to do the work Asian boys ought to do for themselves"—a promise he later did not keep and which haunted him in the turbulent years that followed. Often he invoked the popular name of John F. Kennedy and contended that his opposition wanted to "lob one into the men's room of the Kremlin."

Campaign days lasted deep into the night, but reporters aboard Air Force One were particularly spellbound. Once after a few drinks he began to swagger with self-confidence that the great leaders were all dead. "I am the king!" he shouted. Press Secretary George Reedy, shuddering to think how the comment would look in the next day's headlines, ruled the remark off the record. Mrs. Johnson tried to halt such long-winded speeches sending notes to her husband on the platform: "Speech excellent. Time to stop!"

The "Lady Bird Whistle Stop" campaign in pursuit of Southern votes for her husband was unprecedented, at times miraculous, at other times incongruous. No other First Lady had taken on such a taxing political assignment for her husband, but she was a pro and had often stumped by his side.

We set out from Alexandria, Virginia, with flags flying and bands blaring. Johnson came to the railroad station to send us off with a fanfare and Democratic hoopla. Crowds shouted, "You're prettier than your pictures." Lady Bird was not photogenic and she was well aware the photographs did not do her justice. Close up she was very attractive, with magnolia-blossom skin and sparkling brown eyes.

Mrs. Johnson was happy and proud to let everyone know that she was a "Southern Lady" with her heart in Dixie. We teased her staff about the more noticeable drawl she acquired as the train chugged deeper into Alabama and Mississippi. Never did she falter or lose her cool on the four-day, 1,672-mile trip aboard the

Pennsylvania Railroad's "Queen Mary" with a red, white, and blue observation car.

I could keep track of the number of her speeches by the number of bruises I acquired, along with my colleagues, as we chased to the caboose along the rocking train on the rickety rails to watch her talk to the throngs. Forty-seven speeches later she wound up at the railroad station in New Orleans where her husband was waiting. Lights, cameras—it was an exciting and affectionate reunion and we all felt part of it.

At first the crowds at the crossings were friendly. "Hi Lady Bird" and "All the Way with LBJ" placards were held high as Lady Bird summoned votes for the President because "he's a forward-going man and a looking-ahead man." Then at the rural Chipley, Florida, railroad crossing, she laid it on the line after one man in an overwhelmingly enthusiastic crowd hollered, "Lady Bird, go back to your black bird."

"There are some who would have us ignore the South . . . who say we can win the election without it," she said, in a firm assertive voice, "but we have too much respect for it to take it for granted and too much love for it to ignore it."

Real trouble appeared when her bandwagon rolled into South Carolina, "Goldwater country." Mrs. Johnson obeyed the politician's cardinal rule and did not mention the name of her husband's opponent. But she was not afraid to take on his supporters. We were entranced with the charm of old Charleston, where we got off the train for a tour but we saw we were not exactly welcome when the signs on the front lawns of the quaint antebellum homes read: "Sold on Goldwater." The ladies of the houses were having no truck with intruders and kept their shutters closed, but we did see one or two women peering through their lace curtains.

At a rally in Columbus, South Carolina, the atmosphere was hostile. Teenage hecklers, holding up signs "We want Barry," tried to drown out the First Lady as she spoke. Holding up her hand, and mustering all her Southern gentility, Mrs. Johnson drawled to the emotional, racially mixed audience quietly: "In this country, we have many viewpoints. You are entitled to yours. Right now," she added firmly, "I am entitled to mine."

Her daughters, Luci and Lynda Bird, who were also not about to let the hecklers get away without a rebuttal, lectured youths in the crowd. "It's all right to disagree but not to be disagreeable," Luci remonstrated from the back of the train.

"Y'all are just in a state of confusion," Lynda Bird chided when she encountered loud disruptive protesters as the train rolled through Dixie.

We silently cheered them. Unbiased reporters we were, but we saw their courage and felt they deserved the respect to be heard.

The President, reading the news stories, called his wife later and told her: "I couldn't have been more proud of you." Johnson told us after the campaign that he had argued with his wife against taking the Southern tour, but she was adamant. "You just go to bed early," she told him.

There was no way of telling how many votes she was winning, but she ignited a fighting spirit and won the Democrats' admiration. Many found it wise to ride her hemlines. Representative Hale Boggs of Louisiana, then the House Democratic Leader, extolled the virtues of grits and red-eye gravy and in a suspender-snapping, tie-stripping performance along the route urged Southerners to rally to the First Lady's banquet. Alabama's George Wallace sent a large bouquet of red roses, and other Senators, Congressmen, and Governors along the tracks became more and more effusive in their introductions, calling Mrs. Johnson: "The First Lady of the World," the "Greatest First Lady in history," and "Mrs. First Lady of our nation." Editorials suggested "Lady Bird for Vice President."

After a grimy day on the road the 150-member press corps headed for the nearest shower. We carried away with us Lady Bird's "certificate of journalistic perspicuity," which read:

Having partaken generously of eight states of southern hospitality from Alexandria to New Orleans, day on day, daze on daze, eyeball to eyeball, elbow to elbow, weaved and wiggled the crowded aisle of the Lady Bird special in pursuit of the better story; having kept attentive to the primary mission on 1,682 miles—an objective crowd estimate and correct analysis of those events that alter and illuminate the political world; and having lost composure only when necessary to file and beat the deadline by phone or telegraph or ESP—

Now therefore, the above individual is awarded this certificate of journalistic perspicuity.

On election day, smiling but subdued, the President arrived with his wife at the Pedernales Electrical Co-op headquarters to vote. Asked if he had consulted any of his advisors, he said, "The only political advisor I consulted with is the one I slept with." It was a typical earthy remark.

That night his joy was boundless. Johnson ran in and out of reception rooms at the Driskill Hotel in Austin euphoric and glowing. After the results were announced, he stepped before TV cameras at the Municipal Auditorium at 1:40 A.M., parading his family across the stage. He spoke with the air of a man who had just been anointed. Now he was no longer an accidental President. Lyndon Baines Johnson, the self-styled man of peace, had won 61 percent of the popular vote, the largest percentage of the popular vote polled by any Presidential candidate. "Tonight," he said, "we face the world as one. Our purpose must be to bind our wounds, to heal our history. . . ."

I ask all of those who supported me and all those who opposed me to forget our differences, because there are many more things in America that unite us than divide us. . . . We will be better able to achieve peace in our time and try to keep our people prosperous. I would like to leave you tonight with the words of Abraham Lincoln: "Without the assistance of that Divine Being who ever attended us, I cannot succeed. With that assistance, I cannot fail."

By the time he left the auditorium around three o'clock that morning, Johnson had wound himself up into ecstasy. He invited us all to a massive, Texas-style victory celebration the next day back at the LBJ ranch. It started with a barbecue for 200, featured jazz and cowboy combos, and several truckloads of beef, beans, and corn. Hubert Humphrey, newly-elected Vice President, flew in from Minneapolis, and he and LBJ showed up at the party wearing identical cowboy regalia of shooting jackets, slacks, and ranch hats. They looked more like a vaudeville team than the newly-elected leaders of the free world.

At the height of the party, LBJ ordered up two horses for himself and his veep and Humphrey tried gamely to ride along beside his boss. But he looked ludicrously ill at ease and a groom finally led him and his horse back to the corral. Dismounting, he stepped in a cowpile and turned even that into a campaign speech. "I just stepped on the Republican platform," he said.

Later Johnson held up his own private poll, which showed he would lose only six states, right on target. Daughter Luci, who had stumped in selected areas and took the election drive personally, was unsatisfied. "I lost Georgia. I can't understand it," she said.

That was one of Johnson's happiest days in the Presidency. He was now rightfully entitled to be called "Landslide Lyndon," a title bestowed on him years before when he first won his Senate seat by only eighty-seven votes. Those were his glory days, and before they tarnished, we had copy galore. He began to build monuments to himself. He carefully restored his "birthplace," a small frame house near the ranch—we called it, irreverently, "the manger"—then his boyhood home in Johnson City. We traipsed through the white frame house with the yellowed mementos many times, with LBJ leading the pack. We attended news conferences in his plushly refurbished airplane hangar at the ranch. Later, LBJ State Park, across from the ranch, was completed after he left office. It was lovingly redeveloped and equipped with a visitors' center, museum, theatre, and more. The old ranch house that belonged to LBJ's grandfather, Sam Ealy Johnson, Sr., was restored, as was the country schoolhouse LBJ attended as a boy. Ultimately, the LBJ brand was to go overseas when a hill in Korea south of Seoul was named the Lyndon B. Johnson Hill. Visitors on the LBJ trail from Austin to Stonewall, Texas, could travel to a long man-made Lake LBJ, a refreshing oasis in a harsh ranch country, where LBJ used to cruise along the waves at a sixty-mile-an-hour clip, leaving a big wake. "Here comes Lyndon!" Secret Service agents would tremble, trying to steer their small speedboats out of his course. Once one went aground.

I enjoyed going to Austin because of dear friends I had made there. Bob and Jean Baldwin opened their home and provided the best in Texas hospitality to me and my press colleagues. We became habitués of the Headliners Club, a club of journalists and Austin businessmen in the Driskill Hotel. We could all gather there and all keep an eye on each other. Johnson also always wanted to know what we were up to and would call Joseph Laitin, the Deputy Press Secretary, now Assistant Secretary of Defense for Public Affairs, and ask about gossip or stories on reporters' social lives, sprinkling in ribald obscenities about us. And his Texas friends were not above providing us occasionally with some juicy tidbits about LBJ.

His four years in office after the mandate were difficult and painful. Besides the heat of the civil rights movement, he found that everything he did and said triggered protests. On his first trip to Vietnam he told troops at Camranh Bay, "Bring back that coonskin cap, and we'll nail it to the wall." Also, "We're going to take care of these little brown men," he said. Many people were offended.

The crisis in Vietnam had grown more ominous in August 1964, even before the Democratic convention. After North Vietnamese torpedo boats attacked U.S. destroyers in the Gulf of Tonkin off the coast of North Vietnam in that month, Johnson ordered the retaliatory bombing of North Vietnamese torpedo boats and bases. Still, he had convinced voters in November, and, I think, himself, as well, that he was the candidate most likely to bring about a quick and simple solution to the Vietnam conflict. He had told some of us on his campaign plane during one of his candid, off-the-record sessions, that peace was the overriding issue in his mind. "Everything else is chickenshit," he said. "Education is chickenshit. Crime is chickenshit. Inflation is chickenshit. Remember this—everything but peace is chickenshit."

Even with his mandate, however, Johnson had trouble getting a fix on his administration. Once after attending church, he told AP's Karl Bauman and myself he was firing the whole Cabinet, meaning undersecretaries and assistant secretaries who had failed to hand over their pro forma resignations at the start of his term of office. He wanted us to put out a story saying that they were all leaving, but we couldn't quote him because Johnson didn't want the wives "calling up and crying" about it.

With Johnson you were either for him or against him. There was no middle ground. When dovish Senator Frank Church of Idaho became more vocal on the Vietnam War, Johnson confronted him at a White House party:

"Where do you get your ideas?" LBJ asked Church.

"From Walter Lippmann," Church replied.

"Wa'al, the next time you need a dam in Idaho, you just ask Walter Lippmann," drawled Johnson.

When foreign ambassadors would suggest that the United States was being defeated in Southeast Asia, Johnson would demand belligerently: "How many troops have yo'all got in Vietnam?"

Johnson was determined to be a statesman during his last year in office and to concentrate on being President, disdaining politics. But Senator Robert F. Kennedy was not disdaining politics. He was preparing to announce his candidacy for the Presidency and he knew he would never be LBJ's choice.

The day Kennedy did announce for the Democratic nomination Johnson invited me and another reporter to ride with him in his limousine to the Shoreham Hotel where he was to speak before departing for Texas. As we sat back on the plush seat with Johnson next to the window and his telephone, I asked him what he thought of Kennedy's announcement. Johnson looked down at his cufflinks and asked me: "Do you like these?" He had answered my question. Some time later, during one of those many off-the-record press briefings, which now belong to the public domain, he told us: "I always felt Bobby wanted very much to run against me."

But Johnson was the complete political realist. From his years before the mast, he knew when it was time to pull into harbor—and he wanted to do it with dignity and pride.

Chapter 3

LBJ at Credibility Gap

It was natural for an old-line Texas politician like Lyndon B. Johnson, once he became President, to try to rope the press into his corral. Sometimes we in the press were docile, at other times we bucked. Johnson never seemed to be able to understand the need of reporters for independence.

President Johnson was, at first, so anxious to communicate, to be "a man of the people," that frequently, when he walked on the White House grounds, he would suddenly stride across the yard to the iron fence that encircles the mansion and extend his hands through the bars to the tourists outside. He called this "pressing the flesh." He wanted to touch the people and let them touch him. On two occasions I saw him open the big black steel gates on the South Grounds to let the people pour in as White House police and Secret Service agents snapped to, anticipating all kinds of trouble. Fortunately there was none: President Johnson was still enjoying great personal popularity.

His desire to communicate with the world outside the White House was surpassed only by his compulsion to hear, see, and know everything that was going on inside the White House—particularly with the press. LBJ maintained a closer, rockier, love-hate relationship with White House reporters than any President I've ever known. He had three news tickers in his office, along with a three-screen color television console that would beam in all the major network news shows simultaneously. AP's Karl Bauman used to call Johnson "Constant Reader," like the pseudonym for someone who writes frequent letters to the editor. He planned to keep on top of our reports, expected them to be favorable, and he let us know it if they weren't.

Initially, President Johnson seemed to think he could overwhelm reporters with his power as he did his aides; at the least he hoped to strike some kind of bargain with us. "You hep me and I'll hep you," he once told UPI's Merriman Smith in that slow Southwestern twang of his. "I'll make you a big man in your profession." It was incredible that a man like LBJ, who had been around Washington twenty-six years before he entered the White House, could make such a statement to a man like Smitty, who always wrote the truth as he saw it.

Soon after he moved into the White House, Johnson confided, in a chat with a small group of reporters, that he didn't expect them to count and report on how many drinks he took or "when I go into a strange bedroom." You heard a lot about bedrooms in those good old days, and the liquor flowed, but in public LBJ was a very circumspect and temperate man. He realized that reporters conveyed his image to the world, and we saw that he wanted the image to be a good one. Johnson's perspective of us as his personal public relations staff was opposed to our own image of ourselves as a pipeline to the people, reporting on public servants to make them accountable.

From the day he entered the White House until the day he left, LBJ tried to come to terms with the press. He didn't succeed. He had thrived on secrecy during his Congressional days and it was impossible for him to change his style. Johnson instructed a secretary in the office of the White House Press Secretary to jot down the name of each reporter alongside his or her question at press conferences. He wanted to know who was asking what and why. It was not a very subtle form of intimidation, I thought.

President Johnson knew so much about us reporters—what we said, what we did, where we went, what we joked about, when we were angry or restless—that we often suspected that the White House press room was wired for sound. Although we could never prove this, we knew for certain that LBJ had extensive intelligence reports compiled on everyone around him—including members of the press. We always felt Big Brother was watching.

"I go to bed at night and read my FBI reports," he would say, and we knew from the tone of his voice that there was plenty of personal gossipy detail in them. President Johnson had FBI and other security checks conducted not once but every year on his White House aides. It was not unusual for a trusted LBJ assistant to go home from the White House and find that, out of the blue, FBI agents had been around questioning the neighbors.

The contest with the press preoccupied, frustrated, and eluded Johnson throughout his Presidency. "Y'all have the First Amendment," he'd complain, as if the Founding Fathers had specially endowed the press to harass the President. Johnson hit the ceiling over some of the stories we wrote and never let us forget what he saw as our transgressions. After a press conference or news briefing he would go back to his office and stand over the tickers reading our stories as they came over the wire. A number of times a Presidental press aide interrupted me while I was dictating a story to my office to complain about my lead paragraph or my interpretation of a certain White House statement. I knew the criticism came directly from LBJ, but I certainly never changed a story because a President asked me to. The President thought nothing of calling a reporter after his story cleared the wire to tell him, "You got it all wrong," or to chide, "If I call a Congressman to wish him Happy Birthday, y'all say it's arm-twisting!" He let offenders know when he was displeased by looking right through a reporter at a gathering as journalists crowded around with questions.

Douglas Cornell of the AP was in Johnson's doghouse for some time after he wrote a captivating story about the President pulling his beagle's ears. The White House was bombarded with critical mail from dog lovers and the Humane Society went after the President. After that, Johnson pantomimed pulling his dog's ears every time he saw Doug. He said of the incident sardonically, "I enjoy seeing the press. I learn much from reporters. In the White House press corps alone there are at least half a dozen experts already on animal husbandry." LBJ had a long memory and he was not about to let a reporter forget.

I was his enfant terrible because I broke a number of stories about his daughters and their romances before the President himself knew what was going on—and that was the unforgiveable sin. Johnson once told me—in good humor—"You announced Luci's engagement, you announced Luci's marriage, you announced when she was going to have a baby and I resented it." When he was mad at me, he would walk right past me and chat with my opposition. When he was angry with the AP he would consort with the UPI. We always knew exactly where we stood with him. When Johnson was feeling kindly toward the press, we would fly with him as the "pool." When he was irritated, and that was often, the pool would be barred from Air Force One.

But if Johnson was quick to pick up the phone and admonish someone he thought had written an offensive story, he was just as quick to call up someone who had written a story that pleased him. In the beginning President Johnson treated reporters to a tumultuous, whirlwind courtship and he reacted like a jilted lover when we didn't respond to his wooing. He would shower us with gifts when we were in his good graces and call us every name in the book when we weren't. When he scored his sensational legislative record with the Congress during his first years in office he would pass out the pens he used to sign the bills to the press. I got many myself. I gave them to my nieces and nephews as a symbol of American history to pass on to their own children. Reporters received autographed photographs and other mementos of happy encounters. One Christmas we got a charm of an airplane, a memento of the 1964 campaign. Another Christmas he gave us deer meat sausages,* peach preserves, and pickled okra (for hors d'oeuvres), all put up at the ranch. Reporters are only human, and a Presidential gift is a souvenir to treasure. Cleve Ryan, a lighting technician and a favorite in the White House press room, got an LBJ photo inscribed, "To Cleve, who brings a little light into my life every day." I value the photos inscribed to me.

---

* The recipe for deer meat sausage, recommended for late Sunday breakfast with hominy grits, coffee, eggs, and biscuits, came from a "Fact Sheet on the LBJ Ranch":

½ deer	20 ounces black pepper
½ hog	8 ounces red pepper
25 ounces salt	2 ounces sage

Mix together for 200 pounds of sausage.

Soon after he became President, Johnson told AP's Douglas Cornell and myself one day when we were covering a story involving the Cabinet that he was going to have "an open administration." "I want you to know that anyone who comes to see me is going to see you," he said expansively. He meant that Presidential visitors would pass through the West Lobby, where reporters were staked out and could buttonhole them. But of course he had no intention of permitting a free exchange. We saw the officials he wanted us to see, and they were primed with the party line. More discreet callers came and went through the back door and the side doors when Johnson wanted to keep their visits off the record, which was often.

You can tell a lot about what is going on if you have the President's full agenda, but reporters are only given a highly sanitized schedule of Presidential appointments. The off-the-record visitors who would be a tip-off to a President's current preoccupation are often the most interesting.

Like his predecessors and successors, Johnson loved the element of surprise. He was a master of secrecy. He certainly had no intention of being predictable, and therefore vulnerable. "When I have something to announce, I'll announce it," he used to say. His secretiveness, in the end, led to the "credibility gap" that mortally wounded his second administration.

LBJ was obsessed by the conviction that if he did not publicly announce he was going anywhere, he could change his mind. He could not bear for anyone to know his travel schedule, not even his wife, who sometimes had to call the Signal Corps (which was in charge of White House communications) to find out when he would be heading for Texas. Once he decided, however, he seldom changed his plans.

Sometimes we would get a day's notice; at other times Johnson's Press Secretary would announce that he would be leaving for Texas "in an hour." Johnson thought that the President of the United States should not have to stop to consider any inconvenience he might cause. I traveled to Austin without any luggage, not even a toothbrush, at least once because Johnson did not feel it necessary to reveal his plans. Every weekend at the White House we had the excruciating go-round of trying to find out whether Johnson was going to travel or stay put. Successive press secretaries tried in little ways to hint at the possibility.

"A prudent man would pack a bag," Reedy would say. Succeeding press secretaries mentioned their "gut feelings" that Johnson was going home to Texas. Around holiday time, Johnson might announce he was going to Texas and tell reporters, "Y'all can tell your wives, your mistresses, and lovers." I remember LBJ's contorted maneuvers when he decided to visit the Vatican in 1967 at Christmas time. He thought he could just plop down on the Pope. Fortunately then, as at other times, Deputy Press Secretary Laitin stayed two jumps ahead of Johnson and arranged telephones for reporters. Laitin and other aides had learned to read LBJ's mind.

As a young boy, Johnson had been disappointed when he traveled twice to hear a famous Texas politician on the hustings. Each time the man did not show up. He learned a lesson on the impermanence of human plans at that time and never forgot it.

The complaints of the press only made him more recalcitrant. But we were each dependent on the other. If we were totally fascinated with Johnson's every move, he, in turn, had to be engrossed in us because we were inescapable.

"There's not a single reporter I'm afraid of," he once said, and he meant it.

Johnson's incompatibility with the press extended to press conferences, particularly on television. He preferred to hold them in the Oval Office and often on the spur of the moment so that the "experts" could not be rushing over to the White House to put him on the spot. He would call us into the Oval Office where he could sit at his desk, lean back in his swivel chair nonchalantly, and command the situation. Johnson never mastered the electronic media as Kennedy had, and in the end, TV mastered him. He once confided that he felt the televised news that brought daily reports and films of the horrors of the Vietnam War into American living rooms increased public hostility to his war policies.

Or, instead of Oval Office sessions, he would engage us in marathon "walkie-talkie" press conferences as he strode around the

South Lawn of the White House. He would first summon his dogs and then the press. There would be a call out in the West Lobby from a press aide, "The President is going for a walk," and with loud groans we would scramble out of the press room to join him. We called those press conferences the "Bataan death marches." Sometimes Johnson would go fifteen laps followed by a mob of dog-trotting reporters stumbling over each other to hear his conversation. Often he spoke in a whisper to bedevil us for questioning him.

In such situations we were completely at his mercy. We feared he would drop bombshell news and we would be unable to hear it unless we were striding at his side. A reporter who fell five or ten feet behind was apt to miss an important quote.

Some casualties resulted. Peter Lisagor of the *Chicago Daily News* bumped into a cast iron lamp pole and LBJ gave him a campaign button as a purple heart. Women reporters suffered most because in those days we wore tight skirts and stockings and those shoes with high narrow spiked heels. Johnson, I thought, thoroughly enjoyed our misery. I stashed a pair of flats in my desk in self defense for I found it necessary to push and shove like everyone else as we jockeyed for a position close to him in the melee. We loved it when Lady Bird would come along to break it up.

To be with Johnson in those early years was an endurance contest. He was a whirling dervish on those walks, romping with the dogs, flailing at his political enemies, berating the press. "Perpetual motion," we dubbed him. When he was not on a manic merry-go-round, he would retreat for days, morose, depressed, and just plain feeling sorry for himself. But no one mood lasted long.

I think we got our greatest insights about Johnson when he was on a talking jag and put everything off the record. We were never quite sure whether Johnson wanted us to write his observations without attribution or to keep the lid on. We suspected he wanted his views out, but he also wanted the element of deniability, a shield many presidents before and since have used.

Johnson finally abandoned his "walkie-talkie" press conferences in early 1965 on grounds that there were too many "leaks" and too many complaints from reporters about being unable to hear him.

LBJ held many off-the-record sessions, either in the family quarters or while flying somewhere on Air Force One. He would plant stories or court favor with reporters, but in unburdening himself he also gave us a few clues into his complex thinking processes, and he dropped some petty and some major news items. For instance:

He did not see how Franco-American relations could ever get back to normal, happy terms until after the death of France's General Charles de Gaulle.

Talking about the heady effects of power, he said, "Power is like a bottle of bourbon. If you take it a glass at a time, it's fine. But if you drink the whole bottle, you have troubles. I plan to take it a sip at a time and enjoy myself."

In one such session, he told us he had to make decisions on Vietnam every night, often in a minute. Johnson inveighed, "The generals only know two words—bomb and spend. The generals say the only thing better than one is two. Sure it's good to have two of everything, if you can afford it." Johnson told the press one day about a time when Kennedy had invited him to swim in the White House pool. They talked about the military and Kennedy said: "Don't you think the Founding Fathers were wise to provide for civilian control?"

Another time he offered a few scathing asides about the "Eastern establishment press." "The only people more bigoted are in Jackson, Mississippi," he once said.

It was in one of his off-the-record sessions, this time when we were flying to Texas on Air Force One after his gall bladder surgery, that he mentioned the startling news that he had been on tranquilizers for ten years—since his 1955 heart attack. In another such session he read us some handwritten notes he had taken during a lengthy meeting with General Eisenhower about the Vietnam War. Ike told him, he said, that the United States would have to stick to its guns in Vietnam and eventually might have to use tactical nuclear weapons if the Red Chinese came in.

Johnson scolded the press for basing stories on leaks but often he was the source of the leaks himself. Early in the game, for example, he used to refer to Jack Valenti, Special Assistant to the President, as "my Italian in the White House—he only raises my shades in the morning." Yet later, he complained that "there were stories calling Valenti a valet and there isn't a harder worker anywhere."

In his off-the-record news conferences, LBJ often resorted to barnyard analogies but we never reported them. When he was contemptuous of an official's mental capacity, he would be derisive. "He doesn't know enough to pour the piss out of his boot." Such talk was startling at first but we got used to his scatological approach. His free-flowing obscenities became routine. Once when a pilot was shot down over enemy territory, Johnson kept calling to find out if he had been rescued. He told a pool of reporters on Air Force One that when he learned that the pilot had reached safe lines, he said, "I felt so good it was just like having a good bowel movement."

LBJ could never stay away from the White House press room where reporters were constantly grinding out stories about him. He was the only President I've ever known who would drop by the press room unexpectedly and invite a couple of newsmen to the family quarters for lunch. Merriman Smith and Douglas Cornell, as top White House correspondents, were probably summoned to lunch by Johnson more than any other reporters in town. It was a command performance. They had to eat the same diet meals LBJ did and they ate them whether they had already had lunch or not. Doug said these meals invariably included diet tapioca pudding. Once Doug didn't finish his pudding and the President reached over and ate his leftover portion.

During these lunches LBJ would give reporters extensive, off-the-record briefings. Sometimes he wanted these confidential tidbits to leak out; other times he would deliberately plant a story, on the record, then, after it ran, if public reaction was not all he desired, he would deny it—the old trial balloon trick.

When Doug and Smitty were there, LBJ would talk throughout lunch, then would motion for them to come into his bedroom and he would dress, or undress for his daily after-lunch nap, talking all the while. Doug and Smitty would leave only after the President fell asleep, and return to the press room, often to hit a telephone and dictate: "A high administration source said today. . . ."

I was invited to lunch in the family quarters with the President on the day that Detroit was burning, when blacks were rioting in the streets. The President was enraged because the situation had gotten out of hand and he blamed Governor George Romney of Michigan. I had been standing in the West Lobby when I saw Johnson come out of the press office and hover over three news tickers in the corridor just outside. He was pointing to the smudged glass and finger marks on the tickers and was telling a secretary: "Now if you use a little Bon Ami. . . ." The President of the United States telling a secretary what kind of cleanser she should use to clean glass! But that was our President.

Johnson spotted me and greeted me with a drawling: "Have you had your lunch?" and invited me to join him in the family quarters.

"No, sir," I said happily. I was glad there were no opposition reporters around and I thought I might get an exclusive. "Can you wait a minute, Mr. President?" I asked, sprinting to the press room to put on some lipstick and run a comb through my hair.

As we walked over to the family side of the mansion, I struggled to keep up with his giant steps. I probably smiled loftily at the Secret Service agents as we went up the elevator and down the West Hall to the dining room, which was still papered with scenes of the American Revolution that Jackie Kennedy had discovered during her restoration project. (I learned later that Pat Nixon could not stand the battle scenes and would have preferred a more peaceful decor. Betty Ford had the wallpaper removed because she found it depressing and had the walls painted a bright yellow.)

Mrs. Johnson was away at the time, and Johnson summoned Tom Johnson (no relation), his Deputy Press Secretary, to join us and Mrs. Johnson's secretary, Ashton Gonella.

Johnson sat at the head of the mahogany table with a telephone near his knee. Near him was a bottle of hot green peppers and an electric pepper grinder. We ate Johnson's diet lunch, a thin slice of liver, lima beans, and pudding for dessert. When the cream pitcher was passed around, Johnson dumped the entire contents in his dish, leaving none for anyone else.

While he ate, he read with relish the stenotypes of his Press Secretary George Christian's latest news briefing. Some of the questions plainly irritated him. When he came to a question about his travel plans, Johnson mockingly said, "He just wants to go on a trip." I had to laugh, sharing that intimate moment and knowing how many times I had asked the question myself in frustration. There was a lot of salacious talk and LBJ kept twisting his electric pepper grinder as he complained that Governor Romney was reluctant to appeal to the White House for help because it would be humiliating. "I know how he feels. It's just like when you can't take care of your wife and you have to send out for a friend."

Afterward when we dropped in on little Lyn, Luci Johnson Nugent's baby, Johnson told aides: "If Lady Bird calls, tell her I'm in the bedroom with you know who."

Johnson reminded me with a smile as I left, that it was "all off-the-record."

When he was in a good mood and we were in Texas, Johnson would invite reporters and photographers to go for a ride around the ranch with him. Often it was hilarious, with our caravan kicking up the dust and Johnson honking his horn at the grazing cattle.

Once Johnson began to tease one of his prize bulls. "Mr. President, I wouldn't get too close to that bull," shouted a Secret Service agent. The other agents became so worried that they ran and got a submachine gun as Johnson jauntily strode around the bull. "Good God," an agent whispered to a photographer, "do you know that we're going to see the President killed by his own bulls?" On one drive around the ranch Johnson threatened to shoot up the tires of the Secret Service backup car unless they stayed 200 yards behind. Another time, as several women reporters piled into Johnson's white Lincoln Continental for the ritualistic drive at sundown around his hill country spread, Johnson poured Scotch into plastic cups. He handed me a hefty slug on the rocks, gave me a meaningful look and said, "This is off the record, isn't it?"

"Yes, sir," I said, as I took a gulp.

One day Johnson took a press entourage to view his new outdoor toilet. He summoned Garnett Horner of the *Washington Star* into the "Chic Sale" with him and passed on a scoop about a new appointment he was planning to announce.

When Johnson and Horner emerged, a photographer wise-cracked, "Oh, there is where the leaks come from."

"No," grinned Johnson, "that is a shithouse scoop."

On a Texas trip with LBJ, Tom Craven, a crack TV cameraman, driving at a forty-mile-an-hour clip in Austin, drove through a radar trap. An officer ordered him to pull up and began to question him. Craven said he had not seen any speed limit sign.

"Where are you from?" he was asked.

"I'm here following President Johnson," he replied.

"Get along, buddy," said the policeman. "You've got enough trouble."

We were closer to LBJ than to the other Presidents. We couldn't help it, he was everywhere. When Johnson was President it was a one-man country. He was so human you couldn't bear it. He took everything so personally that we reporters could never kid or kibitz with him as freely as we had with President Kennedy. He had an unlimited repertoire of homespun, politically-oriented stories, but there was no scintillating, spontaneous repartee. And he was offended if someone else made the cracks. I found this out the hard way. Once I walked into the Oval Office late, after the President had finished giving a little spiel to reporters, and he reprimanded me. "You just missed the speech I gave," he said. "That's all right, Mr. President. I'll pull out one of your old ones," I answered. It seemed to me like a harmless jest at his reputation for being so repetitious. The other reporters laughed, but LBJ glared at me and I knew he was thinking, "I hate smart-alecky women." Another time I was in his office when he said, "Helen, I'm looking for a woman ambassador." "I accept," I told him. Once again he stared at me as though I had overstepped my bounds.

President Johnson liked a good laugh, all right—when he was making the jokes or when the laugh was on someone else. I was in his office during his second term when he had a surprise visit from his grandson, Lyn Nugent, then about sixteen months old. President Johnson, who adored that baby, began to show him the wondrous gadgets on his desk and the buttons on his telephone (into which he could speak without lifting the receiver). "Isn't he smart? Isn't he cute?" the President asked, and I answered, "Yes, Mr. President. Yes, Mr. President." The White House photographer snapped numerous pictures of the fetching scene and LBJ sent me an autographed copy of one of the prints a few days later. I'm sure he did so with great relish because the picture showed the President and his grandson with their heads together, absorbed in each other—and I was at their side, craning my neck in an obvious and brazen attempt to read the mail on the President's desk.

Johnson had four press secretaries, possibly an all-time record for a President. "I never fired a press officer," LBJ said, in a typical Johnsonian rationalization. When, for example, it was arranged for Reedy to leave, LBJ never referred to his performance of duty but simply would tell us, we thought disingenuously, "Poor George Reedy, we had to get rid of him because he has hammer toes."

LBJ's first Press Secretary for a few months was Salinger, a Kennedy holdover. Johnson expected Salinger to give him a Kennedy-like image in the press. It didn't work. Then he went on to George Reedy, one of his long-time staffers and a former UPI reporter. Reedy was followed by Bill Moyers, whom we knew as Johnson's protégé, and he by George Christian, whom he borrowed from John Connally of Texas. When Johnson announced Reedy's appointment, he told us, "My desk will be his beat." But Reedy would puff on his pipe and tell reporters very little indeed. We felt that LBJ kept him under tight wraps most of the time. I remember that Reedy sometimes seemed petrified by Johnson's wrath, although he knew the boss very well. His hand would shake as he talked to us.

Johnson could hardly bear the daily press briefings his press secretaries gave in his name. The gatherings were held in Reedy's office and sometimes, in the middle of a sentence, Reedy would pick up the telephone which had been ringing insistently. He said nothing, he simply listened. Reedy would try to act nonchalant but we knew it was LBJ telling him how to handle a question since all telephone calls but the President's were blocked by the switchboard during the briefings. We often wondered whether the briefing was being piped to the Oval Office.

Johnson was very protective of his press secretaries when he thought reporters were being too hard on them. "You're always pick-pick-pickin' on George Reedy," he told us. "You're always badgering him." Those were the days when Reedy was standing before us twice a day at news briefings, fending off our questions.

In April 1964, LBJ sat with the poolers on a flight from Huntington, West Virginia, back to Washington and complained that the press was needling Reedy at his briefings, "picking at him, acting like he was a gladiator in the arena." Johnson said the briefings were a waste of time anyway and ought to be cut down to one a day (under Ziegler in the Nixon era they eventually were). "George knows a lot more than Pierre [he pronounced it Pear]. George knows what he's talking about. Pierre just bulled it through. He announced a lot of things I never heard of. Jack Valenti's the only man who knows everything. He reads every Cabinet paper and looks over everybody's shoulder and he tells George what is happening."

Johnson chided a *Washington Post* reporter who was not present for having asked him at his news conference if Defense Secretary Robert McNamara was a Republican. "I said I didn't believe in guilt by association," Johnson said. "And he went back and wrote his story and never said anything about guilt by association. I did it just to stick it up the *Washington Post*'s ass until they choked—they are always talking about guilt by association." Johnson grabbed partly eaten sweet rolls on the table and swallowed them fast. "Lady Bird would kill me if she knew I did that," he said.

Johnson realized, he said, that the magazines "will be colorful and stick it to me, but I always thought the wire services were pure and holy writ. But I never saw such confusion. They got everything screwed up. They said the hecklers at the World's Fair drowned me out. They never did. I was watching the demonstrators. I was smelling them, I had one ear on Lyndon and one ear on them, and they never drowned me out."

He told reporters, "I want to have you in my office [for press conferences for the regulars who come daily] and make experts of you. I want you to be the experts. When your editors ask about Johnson I want them to ask you. That's how I want it."

In early 1965, Johnson was again in high dudgeon over the "sniping" at Reedy and the complaints from the press about bad ventilation and overcrowding in the White House theatre where he had held his last news conference. He denounced the complainers as "a bunch of cry babies who weren't comfortable enough in the

President's own movie studio, where the President watches movies."

Still fuming, he recalled to us the time a televised news conference was arranged for him. He had expected merely to tape three statements, one of them about voting rights for Selma, Alabama. As he remembered, "Someone ran in, all out of breath, and said, 'Mr. President, Mr. President, you're late.' And I said, 'Late for what, I'm not on any time schedule.' And he said, 'But it's on live TV and they're having a fit.' And I said, 'Well, let them. Goddam it, I'm the President of the United States, and who the hell told them to put it on live television anyway.' So I finished what I was doing, and I went over there and I guess I was a half hour late but I walked a little fast and I was even a little out of breath when I got there."

During one get-together with a small group of reporters, Johnson was asked if he was upset about a spate of press complaints. No, he insisted for about twenty impassioned minutes, he expected this sort of thing. He said he had checked back and found that James C. Hagerty was attacked when he was Eisenhower's Press Secretary, "but then after he left everybody said he was the greatest in history." He said that Charlie Ross, Press Secretary to Truman, was abused "and they accused Kennedy of managing the news."

"Reedy is a great Press Secretary," he continued. "He calls me four or five times a day to get answers to your questions and he goes from office to office and stands and looks over people's shoulders to find out what's going on. And then he makes himself available to you two times a day—if it was me, I'd just do it once—and he has to listen to insulting questions. If I were Press Secretary and people insulted me the way they do him at those briefings, I'd say 'Fuck you!' And I wouldn't answer their questions. I'm not going to kiss the ass of any reporter."

He particularly complained about Douglas Kiker, then with the *New York Herald Tribune*, now with NBC, saying "I guess he's a nice young boy who will be all right when he grows up." He said other things about him that don't bear repeating. "He's trying to run his own war, but he won't be where the shooting is."

Once when Charles Mohr of *The New York Times* was trying to find out the salaries of the White House top echelon, a focal point of abrasion, Johnson decided to give him the "treatment." Laitin summoned Mohr one day to go walking with Johnson, and in their chat Mohr told LBJ of his problems in getting queries answered. "You didn't call me," said LBJ. "Ask me anything." Mohr put the same question to him, inquiring about staff salaries.

Johnson stalled, saying: "Here you are the reporter for *The New York Times* walking with the leader of the Western world and all you can think of is that chickenshit question. Here you have the most powerful man and he says he'll tell you anything. . . ." Johnson, of course, never answered the question.

When Bill Moyers became the President's Press Secretary, he was extremely glib and articulate, and seemed to be much more daring then Reedy had been. Once when I confronted Moyers with an answer he had given, he admitted, "I may shade the truth a bit." Moyers, nevertheless, was popular with reporters. Moyers was more than a Press Secretary. Johnson relied on him as an advisor, but Johnson grew to feel that his own image was not being enhanced by Moyers' activities in his behalf, and it did not sit well with Johnson when Moyers consorted with the Bobby Kennedy crowd. Moyers had begun with the high expectations of a beloved son, but lost favor when Johnson thought he was becoming too independent. Johnson even grumped that Moyers was starting to think *he* was the President.

My favorite story about Moyers' relationship with LBJ came from Johnson himself. Moyers had had religious training and the President used to refer to him as "mah Baptist preacher." As Johnson told the story, Moyers was saying grace before a White House dinner one evening in such a low voice that he could hardly be heard. "Speak up, Bill," bellowed Johnson. "Speak up."

"I wasn't addressing you, Mr. President," Moyers replied softly.

LBJ said that George Christian, his last Press Secretary, was the ideal Press Secretary. Christian stonewalled as much as his predecessors, perhaps more deftly. He was loyal to Johnson. He once came running into the press room white-faced to tell me I had gotten the facts of a story garbled. Johnson had been watching the ticker and had chewed him out. "You go tell that girl!" But when Christian came into the post, he seemed to be only marking time.

He seemed to be leaving the day he took the job. Ironically, after he left Washington and went back to Texas, he became active in Democrats for Nixon.

Johnson's Deputy Press Secretary, Tom Johnson, like Moyers before him, was a young Johnson protégé. He kept good relations with the press. He had been a White House intern and stayed on. Young Johnson was clued in and served as Johnson's Boswell in the last years. He would sit in with the President on his Tuesday luncheons with Secretary of State Dean Rusk, McNamara, and later with Secretary of Defense Clark Clifford and National Security Affairs Advisor Walt Rostow, and take notes. He stayed on at the ranch after Johnson went home and became his press officer, and is now publisher of the Dallas *Times-Herald.* Like Moyers, he was like a son to LBJ, the son he never had. But unlike Moyers, he never broke with him.

Johnson obviously had trouble keeping press secretaries. After all, LBJ was his own best spokesman.

He did not like to delegate power and had to know every detail of everything that was going on in his name.

When he underwent gall bladder surgery in October 1965, he made the announcement himself, giving as many details as he could. He understood well the impact on the country of Presidential incapacity and wanted the public to get a candid, reassuring report on his operation. When LBJ opened his eyes in the recovery room, Moyers, who knew his concern, was standing over him and said, so the story went, "Mr. President, the stock market opened steady." Moyers then provided us with a clinical description of the surgery that may have upset squeamish TV viewers hearing it, but such coverage is necessary when the man who is ill is President.

Shortly after the operation Johnson invited a pool of reporters to Bethesda Naval Medical Center to see him. A press room had been set up in a ward that had housed mental patients and when Johnson asked Moyers what had happened to the patients, Moyers told him, "We gave them press badges." That must have amused LBJ no end, considering what he thought of some of us. As cameramen were leaving, he summoned them back, pulled up his blue knit shirt and showed off the ugly twelve-inch scar slashed across his right rib cage. He wanted startled reporters to see that he got "two operations for the price of one"—removal not only of his gall bladder, but of kidney stones as well. The photo made every newspaper in the country and made him the butt of many jokes. But in a chat with UPI's Merriman Smith some time later, Johnson explained, "Hell, I know the touch footballers [meaning the Georgetown crowd whom he regarded as haughty] were shocked. But let me tell you something. Thousands, maybe millions of Americans were beginning to gossip that their President has cancer. That scar was right where it should have been for a gall bladder. And don't forget this, people with cancer don't go around bragging about it."

Johnson's acute understanding of the importance of his health to the nation was underscored by Cousin Oriole's response when I asked her how she thought he looked. "He looks tired," she said, "but he told me not to say that because I could start a depression."

When Johnson suffered, he wanted everyone to suffer. Proper announcements were made before he entered a hospital. And we became instant medical experts with every Johnson illness, as did correspondents who covered Eisenhower's heart attack and ileitis. Johnson used to write his own medical bulletins. He was furious when Deputy Press Secretary Laitin disclosed his weight—210 pounds. He wanted the country to feel sorry for him. But sometimes it wasn't serious—after he had a polyp removed from his throat, Johnson's doctors ordered him to stop talking, and when we asked Lady Bird how she felt about her husband being "speechless," she smiled and said, "We're going to make the most of it."

Neither Johnson nor any other President I have covered ever referred to a "crisis," even when there was one. It is abhorrent for a President to read or hear that there is a tense atmosphere in the White House. They seem to feel it will spread insecurity throughout the nation, or at least lead the populace to expect momentous decisions. The whole idea is that Big Daddy can take care of any problem that comes along.

Johnson had a particular phobia against the word "crisis." In one off-the-record marathon with reporters, Johnson denounced "What's that boy's name, with NBC, Nelson or Nessen, or something for standing up there Sunday like a carnival barker,

barkin' 'there's a crisis here at the White House, a real crisis, the
big black limousines are arriving' and hell, I'd been up all night and
I had just been asleep for three hours and I woke up and there was
Nessen saying what a crisis it was—such a crisis that I was just
finishing my nap."

The next day, Johnson said he was pleased to note that NBC's
John Chancellor redeemed the day with a "calm, factual account."
(Nessen, of course, was Ron Nessen, who later became President
Ford's Press Secretary.)

At times LBJ misled us; at other times he simply withheld all the
facts. It got so we began to mistrust everything Johnson said. He
could not tell us the time of day without arousing suspicion.

His first Christmas in the White House Johnson had aides put
out the word that he drank bourbon, a liquor that originated in
America, and water. Everyone knew, however, that he favored
Scotch. He did not think his credibility hung on that little fib and
thought it would please the bourbon industry. Once he grew
weight-conscious, he eschewed liquor for long periods and kept a
refrigerator full of Fresca.

We sometimes felt Johnson played with facts just to keep us off
guard. But, as with the boy who cried wolf too many times, we
eventually grew wary of believing what he told us. Like him, we
began to keep our options open after he misled us a few times.
Kennedy had had his "news management" critics, but reporters
covering Johnson now were writing about a White House "credibility gap." The label haunted Johnson's last years in office, and
added to his suspicion that he could do no right in the eyes of the
press. I never felt that was true. He had many things to be proud of,
and we reported them. But he was constantly seeking understanding and not quite sure he had it.

One afternoon, for example, I was in the West Lobby where
reporters sometimes relaxed in the traditional men's club atmosphere when I read a dispatch from Saigon that indicated that
Johnson had ordered the use of gas warfare in Vietnam. I do not
believe that I ever saw him more perturbed than that day.
Vehement denials were made on his behalf but that was not
enough; Johnson kept coming through the lobby, looking more
and more disturbed. He had seen victims of the horror of gas

warfare in World War I and he seemed to be seeking reassurance
that we did not believe he would resort to that verboten weapon.

He may often have found news stories about himself irritating,
but photographs he loved, cherishing even the old family album.
Shortly after becoming President he drafted Yoichi Okamoto away
from the United States Information Agency to become his personal
photographer. Okamoto took a pictorial history of Johnson's White
House years and LBJ used to pass personally on every picture
released from the White House. He could not stand photographers
who tried to shoot the right side of his face. "Okie, do I look like
this? Do I look like this?" he would ask angrily. Johnson had
feuded with photographers when he was Number One on Capitol
Hill. He used to order them out of his office and flip if a
cameraman tried to get a shot of his right profile. The joke around
town was that Johnson's right profile was as remote "as the
backside of the moon." When Johnson left the Presidency he took
with him to the LBJ Library in Austin truckloads of photographs,
about 250,000 in all.

Early in the game, I had found out that presidents might change
but that the enduring motto at the White House is One Picture Is
Worth a Thousand Words. Photographers are called many times a
day to the White House, reporters rarely, though we tag along
anyway.

Occasionally, LBJ was jealous even of the attention Lady Bird
got from the cameramen. On the Pacific tour in 1966, Lady Bird
was getting big play in the Asian capitals, and once when
newspapers with Lady Bird heavily featured on the front pages
were spread out in the Johnson's hotel room, Johnson inquired of
Liz Carpenter: "And where's *my* picture?"

Covering Lady Bird Johnson was strenuous also, but less
frustrating than covering LBJ. I will never again be as rugged as I
had to be covering Mrs. Johnson. It was adapt or die. Sheer
survival impelled me. Climbing mountains pursued by gnats, riding
Snake River rapids in Wyoming, watching from the beaches as
she—not I—snorkeled in the barracuda-filled Caribbean, bobbing
in a flotilla of rubber rafts down the Rio Grande.

My athletic prowess had peaked in high school gym class, but no newswoman wanted to be left behind when Lady Bird set out on her adventures. Lady Bird watchers had trouble keeping up with this woman who had the stamina of steel. We datelined copy from Moose, Wyoming, and Panther Junction, held our breath as the antelopes were shooed off a dirt airstrip at Presidio, Texas, as we landed, sent out typewritten copy by Pony Express from the Big Bend, in Texas, which seemed as remote to us as the planet Mars. My friends laughed at my grim expressions in news photos taken on these adventures.

Sometimes we returned to "civilization" to honor the birthplace of John Quincy Adams in Quincy, Massachusetts, the Hermitage, Andrew Jackson's home, in Tennessee, Thomas Wolfe's birthplace in Asheville, North Carolina, and Robert Frost's Vermont. The theme—to preserve our historical heritage. I remember on one trip to New England, Mrs. Johnson paused at a marker in the village of Ripton, Vermont, home of the poet Robert Frost. She read aloud his "Mending Wall" engraved on a rustic plaque:

> Something there is that doesn't love a wall,
> That sends the frozen ground swell under it.

A bit weary of our road show I piped up: "And we have miles to go before we sleep." Mrs. Johnson, recognizing the other lines by Frost, looked at the tired member of her loyal troop and laughed.

Our tour leader and wagonmaster Liz had an answer for everything, and helped us find telephones, which were prized beyond baths or comfortable shoes. Our offices probably imagined they were sponsoring vacations. But they could see that we were working by the reams of copy we filed.

Because of my dark hair, I was often taken for Lady Bird, particularly at a distance, by crowds along the fences at airports. As we rode in the motorcade "wire car"—the telephone-equipped vehicle for reporters—people would shout, "There's Lady Bird" as I drove by. I would wave back, automatically but graciously, I hope.

Mrs. Johnson knew us by our first names, as all First Ladies had come to know the female reporters who track them. She accepted us but her aides sometimes found us an irritant. "Get out of the picture," was a frequent top-sergeant command to us by one of her aides as Mrs. Johnson would be positioned for a photograph looking toward the horizon. Cameramen had less gentle imperatives for the blue-jeaned women reporters who jockeyed for position to get a better view. We had a few choice words for them, too, but mostly there was a camaraderie in the "We're all in this together" tradition.

LBJ was always observant of one's appearance. I was running for the press chopper one day for the flight back from New York when he beckoned me, and his aides grabbed me and hoisted me aboard. "You can sit in Lady Bird's seat," he said. He looked at me, took a comb out of his pocket, brushed it off, handed it to me and said, "Here. Comb your hair. You're a mess." I dutifully primped. I was not embarrassed. Johnson was always doing the unusual, and he was the most fastidious man I have ever met, impeccable in his own appearance. He didn't tolerate sloppy appearance among the White House staff.

LBJ was the only President who invited me, as he invited many other reporters, to ride with him in his bullet-proof bubbletop limousine. I was not immune to the thrill of riding with the President of the United States. I was standing with Peggy Stanton, then of the American Broadcasting System and later the wife of an Ohio Congressman, outside Blair House waiting for the President to arrive and to deliver a foreign visitor to the guest house, when Johnson, who was heading back to the White House, a two-block ride, waved us over to his black limousine and told us to jump in; "Wave to crowds," he said, "as if you are Luci and Lynda." And we did.

Johnson always felt that newspaperwomen gave him a better shake than our male colleagues, and he said so often. At one of his last sessions with a gathering of newswomen, he said to some of us, "Y'all are more accurate." Besides, he had Liz Carpenter around and she was more than just the Press Secretary for "the ladies' " side of the White House. When Johnson needed new ideas, or sharp, timely jokes, he would call on Liz, one of the wittiest and warmest human beings ever to hit Washington.

I sometimes thought Liz Carpenter understood LBJ better than he understood himself. But she was also protective of him, and neither LBJ nor his associates understood, until it was too late, how much the escalation of the Vietnam War hurt him, increased domestic strife, and ruined his popularity standing. In early 1968, Johnson had set the wheels in motion to run again, or at least he gave that strong impression. He brought former aides back on board at the White House to rev up the machinery, and Liz began holding sessions on campaign strategy at her home, even attended by Lady Bird Johnson. I ran into Liz once in that period and she said to me: "How can we win the next election?"

"Easy, Liz," I replied. "End the Vietnam War." She looked stunned. The White House did not understand how deeply the country felt about Vietnam until it was too late.

Chapter 4

The Johnson White House

Loving a good party, especially one in his honor, LBJ had fox-trotted through his inaugural night, going to several lively balls at downtown hotels. He wound up in the hospital a few hours later stricken with what his doctors described as a cold. "What I have," the world leader told his medics with lofty anger, "is F-L-U."

Shortly after Johnson became President he announced he did not want to see his staff or officials on the Georgetown cocktail circuit. Work was to be the watchword of his administration. Another Johnsonian edict was that no staff members' names were to show up in the social columns. One aide used to groan when her name appeared in the party prints. Johnson read the columns avidly and never failed to mention an item involving his staff. But he obviously was not referring to his own social gatherings. Johnson was the "host with the most" during his White House years. The Johnsons rarely, if ever, dined alone. During his years on Capitol Hill, Johnson would often call Lady Bird up at 8:00 P.M. to inform her he was bringing ten friends to dinner. Zephyr Wright, the family cook, learned to be ready for anything. Fried chicken, country ham, home-baked pies—there was always plenty to go around prepared in advance and stored in the freezer.

As President, LBJ wooed members of Congress with Texas hospitality. He never forgot his old friends down Pennsylvania Avenue at the Capitol where he had spent his happiest years in Washington. Over long drinks, he would brief the lawmakers and dance with their wives.

He never stood on ceremony. On December 23, 1963, he woke up at 7:00 A.M. and decided it was a fine day to give a party for members of Congress and their wives. Never mind that a heavy snowstorm had hit the town. His wife, Lady Bird, who long ago had learned to adapt to his impromptu hospitality, summoned the staff, and they reached members of Congress. Most of them accepted the invitation.

Lyndon Johnson was known among women reporters as the dancing President, at least until Vietnam engulfed the White House in gloom. He loved to glide around the dance floor with a beautiful woman in his arms, enjoying the music provided by the Marine Dance Band or by combos. In 1964, when he was seeking reelection he would try to dance with every woman in the room, the beautiful and the plain ones, so they could go back home and tell their friends, "I danced with the President."

"I think I danced with a woman from every continent," he told me after a party for the Diplomatic Corps.

When teenage Luci Johnson, the hottest dancer I've ever seen in the White House, performed the "Monkey," the "Watusi," and all those other wild and impassioned dances of her day, everyone thought it was great. And I agreed. She even did the "frug" with her Dad.

Johnson always tried to dance with every woman reporter at his parties. He waltzed me around the White House dance floor and once while we were dancing, he looked at me through bloodshot eyes and lamented, "Oh, Helen, if you only knew how hard it is being President." I went to the press room as soon as possible and filed a feature story. I didn't feel there was anything private about our dance floor conversation.

Sometimes President Johnson was an overly enthusiastic dancer. At one private party, early in his administration, he danced until 3:00 A.M., twirling one pretty girl after another around the floor. Mrs. Johnson's patience finally wore thin and she asked Tony Matarrese, then pianist and leader of the Marine Dance Band, to play, "Goodnight, Sweetheart." When Tony complied, President Johnson stopped in the middle of the dance floor, glared at Tony fiercely, and stuck out his tongue in a childish display of temper.

Tony just kept smiling and playing the First Lady's request until the guests departed.

Once during the Johnson era, White House social aides wanted Tony and his piano inside the huge fireplace in the Blue Room to make more room for dancing guests, but Tony balked at this, in the interest of self-preservation.

Mrs. Johnson was assisted by her social secretary, Bess Abell, and by her press secretary, Liz Carpenter who I always thought of as the White House's female P. T. Barnum. On a summer night in 1964, the Johnsons broke a precedent by giving a State Dinner in honor of German Chancellor Ludwig Erhard in the Rose Garden, just outside the President's office. Metropolitan star Robert Merrill was one of the performers. The next summer they scored another first by staging a marathon Festival of the Arts in the White House. Festivities began at ten in the morning, and continued until midnight. A collection of contemporary American sculpture was exhibited in the East Garden; paintings and photographic exhibits were hung in the corridors of the East Wing. Poetry and prose, drama and ballet, symphony and jazz programs were staged in the East Room during the day and on the half-shell bandstand on the South Lawn that night. The highlight was a buffet supper for 400 guests served at tables with lighted candles, artfully arranged in the President's back yard, with the floodlit Washington Monument as a backdrop. But overshadowing the magnificent day was the Vietnam War, with many elite guests vocally protesting U.S. involvement. Johnson vowed never to hold another similar gathering.

As a hostess, Mrs. Johnson was consistently chic, charming, and considerate; as a host LBJ was consistently unpredictable. He took reporters completely by surprise on the night of March 30, 1965, when the Johnsons gave a State Dinner for President and Mrs. Maurice Yameogo of Upper Volta. Several Cabinet members, including Defense Secretary McNamara, and some 150 other very, very important guests were present. Early in the evening the President and his guests learned that the American Embassy in Saigon had been bombed. (I got the news from my UPI desk. I stay in constant touch with the office when covering a White House party, because if a story breaks you've got a roomful of top policy-makers right there. And, in a time of crisis, they are often more willing than usual to talk to you.)

President Johnson was visibly stunned by reports of the bombing incident. He presided at the dinner for Yameogo but afterwards, when guests had filed into the East Room for dancing, he abruptly left the party with President and Mrs. Yameogo for a midnight visit to the Lincoln Memorial. Lloyd Hand, then Johnson's Chief of Protocol, told me what happened. The young black West African leader was a devotee of Abraham Lincoln and his visit to the memorial had been planned by protocol officers weeks earlier.

Johnson was standing nearby when Hand told Yameogo it was time to leave for this appointment. "I want to go, too," said the President. Johnson rode in a limousine with President and Mrs. Yameogo during the short motorcade to the memorial. I was in the "pool" that went along with them. With Johnson in the middle, the three of them walked arm in arm up the rain-dampened steps to the floodlit base of the imposing Lincoln statue. As they stood there, Hand asked Yameogo what he thought of the memorial and he replied in his native French, "Fantastic!" The young African president had tears in his eyes, Hand told me later.

Johnson escorted the Yameogos back to the President's guest house and then went to his Oval Office. His other guests were still dancing in the East Room, but Johnson did not rejoin the party this night.

President Johnson remained an unnervingly erratic White House host until the last. In 1968, when his days as President were coming to a close, he and Mrs. Johnson gave a 6-to-8 P.M. reception for friends and aides. As the party was breaking up, he invited a group of women reporters to the family quarters where he launched into a stream-of-consciousness discourse about his dreams and aspirations; his view of the Presidency and what he had hoped to accomplish as Chief Executive; his impressions of General Charles de Gaulle, and more, which I will get to later. I was carrying a small inconspicuous notebook, as Liz always urged us women reporters to do, and within minutes I had used up every sheet of paper in it and was grabbing for anything and everything I could find to write on. I scribbled notes on the back of White House matchbook covers, on paper napkins, and on the margins of one of Mrs. Johnson's magazines.

As the President held his impromptu session in the second floor Oval Room, Lady Bird kept wafting in and out in various stages of attire, as she changed from her cocktail dress into dressing gown. "Now Lyndon . . . now Lyndon," the First Lady would say, but her husband continued to talk for a good hour. When he finished, he handed each of us a gold charm bracelet with the Presidential Seal on it and said, "Now you know this is all off-the-record." We moaned in unison. We were frustrated, but also a bit relieved. It would have been exceedingly difficult to run to a phone and dictate a fast, comprehensive story out of this rambling, discursive Presidential dissertation. When LBJ put everything off-the-record it meant we could go home, type up our notes leisurely, and file them away for the time they could be used. Whenever a President or other news source puts something off-the-record, you respect his wishes or you lose the source and your friends in the business. It's a matter of honor. However, almost all off-the-record confidences eventually come to light after the source has left office or after so much time has passed that the ban becomes meaningless. With LBJ, I used off-the-record conversations only after he died.

I have many memories of White House parties. I remember in particular singer Sarah Vaughn crying at the end of a memorable evening at the White House during the Johnson era. The popular black singer, described by the First Lady as a "musician's musician," was the star performer at the State Dinner honoring Japanese Prime Minister Eisaku Sato. President Johnson had danced with her twice and Vice President Hubert H. Humphrey had twirled her around the White House foyer where the Marine Dance Band played for the dinner guests. When the evening was over, she broke into tears and told White House social secretary Bess Abell: "Twenty-five years ago I couldn't get a room in this town. But tonight I sang at the White House and danced with the President."

During the anti-Vietnam demonstrations the Secret Service intensified its investigations of entertainers scheduled to appear at the White House. A number of artists saved the Service the trouble by declining to appear before the President because of their opposition to growing U.S. involvement in Vietnam's civil war.

Mrs. Johnson was aware that the war was dividing the country and punishing her husband physically. LBJ was being awakened with battle reports from the frontlines. She considered the telephone calls from the twenty-four-hour situation room at four o'clock in the morning "horrendous."

Toward the latter part of her White House years, Mrs. Johnson initiated "women doer" luncheons spotlighting women who made contributions to their communities. Celebrities were invited and frequently Johnson would drop by to say hello. But the luncheons came to a swift halt after black singer Eartha Kitt lashed out at the lack of compassion on the part of the Johnson administration and delivered a stunning diatribe in the Blue Room against the Vietnam War. It upset Mrs. Johnson and shocked the other guests.

"You send the best of this country off to be shot and maimed," Miss Kitt cried out. "They rebel in the streets. They will take pot . . . and they will get high. They don't want to go to school because they're going to be snatched off from their mothers to be shot in Vietnam."

It was one of the most dramatic moments I have ever observed in the White House. As I took notes, I was stunned, but I thought she had a right to speak her mind. Pale, the First Lady rose with tears in her eyes and looked directly at the singer. With a trembling voice but with dignity she said: "Because there is a war on—and I pray there will be a just and honest peace—that still doesn't give us a free ticket to not try to work for better things such as against crime in the streets, better education, and better health for our people."

Johnson had dropped in but had left before Miss Kitt began. He had, however, been taken aback during his brief stay when she asked him: "What do you think about delinquent parents?" He had brushed her aside.

Afterwards, one guest after another got up to speak in defense of Mrs. Johnson and the war. With two Secret Service agents watching intently from a doorway, Mrs. Johnson, clasping her hands nervously, commented that "Violence will not solve all the problems."

When reporters made a dash for the telephones in the press

room, Liz Carpenter exhorted them to heed the pleasant news in the luncheon. She did not think Miss Kitt should be the focus of our stories. But we had to cover the news and this was news.

In the White House, where movements were orchestrated from the first to the last step, where aides gave the President and the First Lady briefing papers on visitors and places they were to stand were marked with tape, the impromptu and the unexpected could throw the machinery out of kilter. But it was the unprogrammed occurrence that made headlines for us.

At least one other White House performer—Canadian-born singer Carol Feraci—followed in the "tradition" set by Ms. Kitt. Ms. Feraci had passed her Secret Service test and was performing at the White House with the Ray Conniff singers on January 28, 1972, when she stopped the show by pulling a long blue chiffon scarf out of her bosom reading, "Stop The War!" The guests booed Ms. Feraci and applauded their host, President Nixon. Ms. Feraci was whisked away by the Secret Service for questioning, and later released. Once again I wrote a straight story, but I couldn't help thinking that the young singer's actions had helped to penetrate that protective velvet curtain that shielded President Nixon from dissident voices in the land.

During President Johnson's last two years in office, it became more important than ever for reporters to cover White House parties for Johnson often pronounced some major new Vietnam policy in his toasts to guests.

The massive antiwar demonstrations and marches were upsetting to Johnson and to his entire family. During one candlelight vigil, Johnson could not stay in the Oval Office. He came through the lobby, and I asked half-seriously if he was going to the fence and talk to the protesters. He glared at me and said testily: "I'm going to call you Sarah McClendon." That was all right with me. Sarah is a reporter who has a mind of her own and knows how to put a President on the spot. I once heard Johnson say with bravado, "I'm not afraid to have Sarah ask me a question."

I was pained for the Johnson family whenever the demonstrators we met all across the country would chant: "Hey, hey LBJ, how many kids did you kill today?" For a sensitive man like Johnson

such catcalls were torture, but I also understood the tensions which
provoked the cruelty.

———————————

The first time I saw the Johnsons was in 1960 when I was a guest
at their home. Then Senate Majority Leader, Johnson was seeking
the Democratic Presidential nomination, and as part of the
buildup, Lady Bird's aide, Liz Carpenter, suggested that she should
have newswomen to dinner. After a sumptuous Southern-style
meal, we formed a semicircle around Mrs. Johnson, who sat with
hands properly folded and replied to our questions. Suddenly a tall
man crashed the party. It was LBJ himself just back from a party at
the National Press Club. He sat right down on the floor and began
to speak nonstop. He acknowledged with pride that Lady Bird had
been his tireless helpmate, personally speaking to voters on his
behalf during his Senate race and traveling for him even after she
had been badly bruised in an automobile accident.

Vain, insecure, needing an excess of adulation and love, Johnson
was at times impossible, but his wife was always confident that
reason would prevail. She knew that when he hurt people he would
be remorseful later. He needed her, and that is what mattered.

On their thirty-first wedding anniversary, Mrs. Johnson said:

All these years have been spent in public life. Watching Lyndon in the
Presidency, there is something a wife feels which is quite apart from
devotion. It is deep compassion for the man who must cope with problems
from Vietnam to Appalachia. They seek him out even to the shade of the
oak tree.

I was once called upon to introduce my husband at a dinner. I said he
was an exciting man to live with; an exhausting man to keep up with; a
man who has worn well in thirty years we've been together and most
importantly a man from whom I've learned that putting all the brains and
heart and skill you have into trying to make your government work a little
bit better can make a wonderful life for a man and his wife.

Often, I heard her say with a light in her eye, "Lyndon is a man
of many surprises" and "Lyndon has courage."

Accent the positive was always the First Lady's philosophy. She
did not want to see or hear the unhappy realities. When she viewed

the documentary film *USA* shown at the Hemisfair in San Antonio, Texas, in 1968, she complained that it lacked the "element of hope" in stressing racial discrimination. When her daughter Lynda Bird, then an expectant mother, told her of the horror of the Vietnam War as described by Lynda's husband, Marine Capt. Charles S. Robb, Mrs. Johnson said: "He shouldn't write you such things." She was pained when she ran into antiwar demonstrations and catcalls, which grew noisier during her last two years in the White

---

MRS. LYNDON BAINES JOHNSON

March 19, 1963

Dear Helen:

Friends from all over the country have been sending me copies of your story, and I can't tell you how proud I am of it! I was particularly pleased to get a copy from a friend in my home town—she had clipped it from a near-by Louisiana paper usually markedly unfriendly to everything that relates to this Administration.

No one knows better than I how far I fall short of measuring up to the colorful, capable woman you picture, but I love having you think of me in those terms. Thank you, Helen, so very much.

It was fun to have you along on the trip—and to have you here for the reception last night.

Sincerely,
Lady Bird
(Signature)

Miss Helen Thomas
The Boston House
1711 Massachusetts Avenue
Washington, D.C.

House. As the tempo of protest increased, we found ourselves slipping into side doors with her.

Lyndon Johnson understood the worth of his wife and was not too shy to say so. Many times I heard him say "I don't know how I deserved a lady like Lady Bird."

"She's the only one who can control him," remarked a friend.

When the day was done, and it could be at any hour, Johnson would step off the elevator leading to the family quarters and ask: "Where's Bird?"

"Here I am darlin'," she would reply.

In fact, no one in the Johnson family was afraid to show true affection for each other. Johnson and his wife used to walk around the South Grounds hand in hand. The more reserved Kennedys and Nixons never did in public, or at least the reporters never saw them, if they did.

When Johnson was sworn in as the thirty-sixth President of the United States, Mrs. Johnson said her feeling for him was one of "infinite compassion." She immediately looked upon her role "to be the calm sustainer and sometimes a critic for my husband."

"Deeds not words" would be her style, and "if I leave any footprints in the sands of time," she said, "it will be because he has been able to achieve something."

Johnson always pushed her to do more. He had complete confidence in her ability to move a mountain, if need be. "He lived," she said, "as if there was no tomorrow and those around him had to adopt the same philosophy to survive." She grew as a person and as a personality because she made up her mind to be a "doer" herself, and to make her own interests a cause. She left the White House more poised, confident, and happy.

Mrs. Johnson's image-makers in her press department at first decided that in the tradition of her populist husband she would properly fit into the mould of Eleanor Roosevelt whose social conscience activism was both praised and pilloried and whose humanitarian style became a cause célèbre.

I love the oft-told story of FDR asking an aide: "Where's Eleanor?"

"She's in prison, Sir," was the reply. (She had gone to study conditions in the nation's prisons.)

"I know, but what's she done now?" quipped Roosevelt.

Mrs. Johnson wanted only to be herself. She stumped for Johnson's antipoverty and "Great Society" programs in the hollows of Kentucky and visited "Head Start" programs for deprived children around the country.

In an interview I had with Mrs. Johnson in the sitting room of the rose-patterned Queen's Suite at the White House on May 27, 1964, she said to me, "I can serve some use to my husband in telling him what I saw, my feeling about it in learning from the people rather than statistics." She was speaking of her poverty trips to Kentucky, Huntsville, Alabama, and Wilkes-Barre, Pennsylvania. But it was clear that her own project was national beautification. A true Southern lady, she revered the land and its history, and her projects reflected it.

With the ballyhoo of her press secretary, Liz Carpenter, and her own love of beauty, Mrs. Johnson became the symbol of the national campaign to preserve the country's natural landmarks, mountains, rivers, and wilderness areas. She launched a struggle against billboards that blighted the nation's highways. Although it was not her style, she lobbied for a more beautiful America.

"Don't be a litterbug, Lady Bird will hate you," became a standard national phrase. Looking down from Air Force One, Johnson would say to us with some pride: "Lady Bird just can't stand those auto graveyards." She was so dedicated to her "America the Beautiful" campaign that a Republican politician grumbled at the time: "It's getting so a Republican can't even plant a geranium without feeling guilty."

The greatest testimony to her success was a cartoon showing a billboard which read: "Impeach Lady Bird." On her epitaph she said she wanted the words: "She planted a tree."

She had been born Claudia Alta Taylor, in 1912, in Karnack, Texas. Her nickname "Lady Bird" came from the family nurse-maid, who declared she was "as purty as a lady bird." In the White House, Mrs. Johnson trimmed down, shaped up, and wound up on the best-dressed list. Like predecessors and successors she had to spend heavily for stylish evening gowns, traveling clothes, and hairdos. Constantly photographed, she had to update her wardrobe, much more so than she would have by her own inclination.

She was not averse to wearing the same dress twice—and did—but she knew that one photograph could make an ensemble too familiar. "Sometimes I feel I am dressing the Washington Monument," an earlier First Lady, Mrs. Roosevelt, had said. Johnson would go on spending sprees, always wanting his wife and daughters to look their best. He prescribed bright colors, especially yellow, for her, and he was right.

I don't think I ever heard a snide remark about Lady Bird. Her total devotion to "Lyndon" guided her. Jackie Kennedy was once quoted as marveling: "Lady Bird would walk on cut glass for her husband." For all her loyalty, no one could say Mrs. Johnson did not know her own husband for his faults as well as his achievements. She soothed friends he had rode roughshod over and shielded him when he was boorish.

For example, irascible Johnson often treated his Secret Service agents as his lackeys. He made them do menial tasks, like cleaning the swimming pool at the ranch. All the Presidents used the agents for personal service—Jackie Kennedy would hand her wrap to her agent, for example—but they feared Johnson, or seemed to. One agent who was posted outside the door of his Oval Office was fired thirteen times. Johnson took out his rage at reporters because they were closest. He had a hovering suspicion that one of the White House policemen might accidentally "drop his gun." Just before he left the White House, Johnson assembled the White House detail on the South Lawn—many did not come—and publicly apologized for the way he had treated them at times when he was under stress and strain, but the apologies had come too late for many.

A secretary once said, "He doesn't get ulcers, he gives them." Johnson told such a story on himself, too. "I remember one day when a little Filipino boy brought me the wrong food for lunch. It was hamburger and I wanted something else. I shouted, 'Gol' dang it! I didn't want this!' He came back in a flash with some tapioca pudding." Laughing hard, Johnson said, "I guess he thought the tapioca pudding would save him."

I had been in the pre-White House Johnson home in Washington and at the Texas ranch when such hospitality was immediate and genuine.

When Johnson, who was constantly on a diet of low-calorie

foods, would complain, Lady Bird would chide, "If you can't run yourself, how can you run this country?" Diet tapioca pudding became as identified with Johnson's fare as cottage cheese and ketchup were to become with Richard M. Nixon.

Diet or not, Johnson was not averse to snatching a morsel off someone else's plate. When Australian Prime Minister Harold Holt and his wife were guests aboard Air Force One, Mrs. Holt raved to reporters about how much she liked American bacon. Johnson ate the bacon on his own plate, then speared a slice right off the plate of a startled Mrs. Holt.

Like Jackie, Lady Bird used to have breakfast in bed around 8:00 A.M. (Jackie, usually later) and read the newspapers. After that she might have a series of conferences with her closest aides, her personal secretary, then social secretary Bess Abell, and her press secretary Liz Carpenter.

She always saw herself realistically as a "very temporary tenant on a short-term lease." As for the eternal problem of living in a goldfish bowl, Mrs. Johnson said: "You have considerable privacy here. The walls close around you."

"My own feeling is that I get criticized for something I didn't think there was anything wrong in—I'm not going to worry about it," Lady Bird told me. "You must explore your own conscience on criticism to decide whether it's wrong or not.

"When you get here, you don't stop being yourself," she said. "I don't worry about privacy. I do worry about the lack of tranquility and serenity. I just like sometimes to lie in a hammock at the ranch. Perhaps I could do it out here under one of those trees . . . and look up at the sky. That's when you do your best thinking." When life became too much around her, her idea of heaven was "a datebook with a day blank."

She recalled that she asked Luci, "Honey, how do you feel about it, do you feel we have enough home life to suit you?"

"Well, mother, we have to," Luci replied. "There's just four of us and that's all we've got . . . there's only us who really understand."

"So if we turn inward in a way . . . ," Mrs. Johnson said to the press, not completing her sentence, but the meaning was clear.

We reporters found her candid but discreet. She was cautious, and sometimes needed to be. But she knew that, as First Lady, she was news, and understood what modern press coverage was all about. She had studied journalism when she attended the University of Texas and she successfully ran radio-TV station KTBC in Austin for many years. Because of her innate discipline, Mrs. Johnson went out of her way to study briefing books for state visits and for her own trips. I found her knowledgeable and tuned in when she traveled across the country or abroad.

Johnson's women were defensive when LBJ was criticized for turning out the lights at the White House or pulling his beagle's ears. "I think that's foolishness about beagles and lights," said Mrs. Johnson with a touch of irritation. "If you don't turn out the lights that aren't necessary, that's just plain neglectful." She recalled Oliver Wendell Holmes saying "a part of wisdom is to know what to treat with ignoring."

The lights incident arose during the 1964 campaign when LBJ was establishing the image of a man who believed in frugality. He demonstrated the point by turning out lights all over the White House. As a consequence, Lady Bird stumbled in the dark at the foot of a stairway, and White House police bumped into each other.

Johnson's obsession with turning out the lights in the White House had his staff in a tizzy. One evening Laitin left the press office to get a sandwich. He left the light on in his office. When he returned, Secret Service agents said: "Hey, don't go in. LBJ is sitting at your desk waiting to find out who left the light on."

"I grabbed a cab and went home," Laitin recalled.

"Light Bulb" Johnson watched wattage at the ranch too. One night he kicked open the guest house door demanding to know why photographer Bob Knudsen left lights on while viewing TV. When I interviewed Luci Johnson another time in the ground floor library of the White House, she went around after we were through and turned out all the lights.

I understood that a man who lived in Texas during the Depression would have a keen respect for the cost of electricity, but I did not like to see the White House darkened at night. I felt it should stand out like a beacon. When Mrs. Nixon moved in, she saw that the floodlights were turned on at night.

Lady Bird thought the Johnson daughters could maintain private lives, but she often quoted her daughters, especially Luci, about "the situation we're in."

Mrs. Johnson reveled in her daughters' adventures, consoled them when their romances ended, and was a tolerant mother confessor. "She listens to them like a judge," Johnson once said. She weighed their actions and never used a heavy hand.

Of her daughters she said, "Lynda Bird is delightful to me. She has so much ability. She speaks the same language and deals with many of the smart people around here in a way that I'm proud of and broadens her own horizons."

Of Luci, Mrs. Johnson observed she had an "almost painful sense of obligation to being our daughter and the role she is supposed to play. She hears she is supposed to be an American model for youth. She takes it seriously. She likes to be carefree. She is a very independent soul."

Romance and the White House marriages of Lynda and Luci were a happy relief to both Johnsons from the divisiveness that was shaping up over the war and the growing racial conflict.

Johnson had many worries, but none about his daughters. He observed that Lynda Bird, a top-notch student, would always be able to take care of herself, while Luci would "always have a man around to take care of her." Johnson commented that Luci could walk down the street naked and everyone would think "how cute."

He once told us, "The sweetest little civil rights speech you ever heard was one Luci made when she was twelve years old. She said, 'If my sister and I can look different, have different skins and mother and father look different but all live together as a family, why can't races live together?' "

Luci had heart. She was also a hip-shooter, and her mother often admitted: "When Luci begins a speech, I hold my breath." Lady Bird feared the girl would rattle off family secrets. She didn't. On her mother's campaign trip in 1964, just as Lady Bird would be winding up her speech on the back of the train, aides would push Luci out to do her bit. "You've got thirty seconds to make good," she would be told. If hecklers were out, and they usually were, carrying signs such as "Lady Bird—Black Bird," Luci would stare at them and, lisping slightly, say, "It's all right to disagree, but not be disagreeable."

Luci made great copy. I had an up and sometimes down relationship with her, but always rapport. To me, she personified the teenagers of the times; more than other first daughters, she seemed to stay in touch with her own generation. Luci was sitting in her Spanish class at the National Cathedral School for Girls in Washington when a usually giddy girlfriend approached her seriously and said, "The President has been shot."

In an interview I wrote for *Seventeen* magazine, Luci recalled:

"I thought she was kidding. I turned around and gave her a dirty look. I said 'I don't think that's a bit funny.' "

"Well, I heard it on the radio," the girl persisted.

"It's just a rumor," Luci thought. "Then the class began buzzing. The bells started ringing continuously. My teacher never said a word. The class stood up and walked to the chapel, four hundred girls, everyone so thunderstruck. Two or three who were my friends grabbed me in the hall. My principal, Katherine Lee, didn't know what the situation was. She said the best thing is to pray.

"My first reaction was I was the only one who knew President Kennedy. It never entered my mind that I was the President's daughter. Then a girl came up and said Miss Lee wanted to see me. With Miss Lee were two Secret Service agents. There was a knell from the Cathedral. I looked at Miss Lee and said: 'No!' "

She said, "We don't know for sure. They wouldn't do that if the President were alive. It's not right to do that. Then we found out."

"I told Miss Lee, 'I want Willie Day Taylor to come here.' " Miss Taylor was a close family friend and long-time assistant to Johnson.

"I remember sitting in the living room at the school, watching TV. I remember one of my friends, looking up at her and telling her, 'I'm not the President's daughter, I'M NOT.'

"Then my friend told me: 'Luci you have to accept these things as they are.' "

"But things like that don't happen," I said.

"My hair was filthy. I went home. I was waiting for my Daddy. I kept thinking what can I do for him. He calls us his pearls. One of the things that has meant a great deal to him has been for us to look nice, not all dolled up, but nice. If I can look pretty for Daddy, instead of crying. Then I thought this is ridiculous. This is horrible. This is the only thing I can do. The only thing I know about."

I liked Luci. She had spirit and she could even out-talk her father. In the newspaper business, you prefer outgoing personalities. As a seventeen-year-old, Luci complained bitterly that she was going to have to live in a "white elephant," that any new friends she made would be called "opportunists," that she would always be known as "President Johnson's daughter." She protested the loudest, yet of the daughters I have covered in the White House, she seemed to savor the life the most. Luci was the first of her family to arrive at the 1964 Democratic Convention in Atlantic City. She led the press on a run down to the beach and into the ocean. She sounded off about the Secret Service agents who went with her everywhere, even though she thought they were "great guys." And she made grand entrances into convention hall, sitting alone in the Presidential box.

Luci and her boyfriends gave us a merry chase and many good stories. My former UPI colleague Maggie Kilgore got an interview with Jack Olson, one of Luci's steady boyfriends, shortly after Johnson became President. "Heck," said Olson steadfastly, "I dated Luci when her father was only a Vice President."

Luci could not understand it when we all wrote stories saying she had changed the spelling of her name from "Lucy" to "Luci." "You can imagine how I felt when I picked up a newspaper and read on the front page that I had changed the spelling of my name.

"Big deal, hairy deal," she said, "and boys are dying in Vietnam. Besides," she continued, "I decided to change the spelling of my name when I was ten years old."

Luci did not let the White House inhibit her. She used to party in the East Room, much to her daddy's approval, and draw a circle around her when she went into a fast "frug," a "twist," or "the monkey."

There was obvious rivalry between Luci and her sister Lynda Bird, sometimes obscuring much love and affection. Luci said they were like "oil and water." When Mrs. Johnson took Lynda Bird to Greece, she expressed a wish that Luci was with them. "Oh, mother," said Lynda, "if Luci were here she would be looking for prehistoric bobby pins."

Luci was the first to admit that her schoolmarks were not anything to brag about to the President. She had trouble with her eyes, for one thing—she had to have her vision corrected by exercises. "Academically," she said, "I'm not one of the forerunners of today's youth."

She had a motto which pinpointed the dilemma of those who live in the White House. "You adjust or adjust," she explained.

The girl was strong-willed. "Luci," Mrs. Johnson once told us, "does not bend with the wind. She is not always flexible." Not even the President could deter her when Luci decided to marry Patrick J. Nugent at the age of nineteen, nor when she decided to become a Roman Catholic convert.

I picked up a tip that Luci was taking instructions in Catholicism and checked it out with Liz Carpenter. Liz said something about religion being a private affair but she did not deny it. That was enough for me. I wrote the story, which made headlines in every newspaper in the country.

Luci was baptized a Roman Catholic on her eighteenth birthday, July 2, 1965, at St. Matthew's Cathedral in a ceremony attended by her parents, her sister Lynda, and close friends. I had found out the exact date, but agreed to hold back the news so that she could have privacy. In return, she promised me an exclusive interview within an hour of her conversion. She gave me a moving story. "This is the happiest day of my life," she said. Luci was always deeply religious and obviously felt free to choose her beliefs. Her mother was Episcopalian and her father was a member of the Disciples of Christ, but was ecumenical at heart.

"I cried," she said of her baptism. "Just about everybody cried. Five years ago, I, like all young people, began to question and I began to wonder." Then she paused and said simply, "I found my answer in the Church." Many of her closest friends were Catholic. Episcopalians protested that she did not need to be rebaptized, but Luci wanted it that way.

The story brought me a little flack. Some White House newsmen teasingly complained that I had "canned interviews" about all phases of Luci's life. And certainly my breaking the original story had offended the Johnsons.

Luci had kept things lively at the White House. But after Pat Nugent stepped in, we saw a different Luci. He helped her reach appointments on time and teased her about her baby fat, so she dieted. He also helped her knuckle down to her studies as a freshman at the Georgetown University School of Nursing.

They had met on a blind date at Marquette University in Milwaukee, Luci escaping the press by using a blond wig and a false name. She had dated many young men, but once she met Nugent, Luci decided, "Pat is man enough to care about somebody from the beginning, and he has enough character to be concerned about me as an individual." He called her "Princess," sent her flowers, and took a job in Washington to be near her.

The President's greatest wrath toward me came when I filed a bulletin story saying that eighteen-year-old Luci and Patrick J. Nugent of Waukegan, Illinois, had called off their Halloween party to fly to the LBJ ranch to ask the President's approval to become engaged. Johnson, in Texas recuperating from gall bladder surgery, read the news on the ticker before Luci and Pat arrived.

They were supposed to land at Bergstrom Air Force Base near Austin, but the plane was diverted when the press converged on the airfield to interview the couple. There was no confirmation and no denial of the engagement story from the Texas White House, and the family holed up at the ranch, so I had to sweat it out. But the lack of denial was in a sense a confirmation.

Press Secretary Bill Moyers was out of town, so his brother Jim substituted for him at the first news briefing after my Luci story broke. When the inevitable question came, Moyers' prepared answer was, "Luci is a nice girl. Someday when she is twenty-one or twenty-two she may marry." His hedging was a good clue that I was right.

Later on a reporter came up to me in the Driskill Hotel dining room and said: "You're looking golden." But the Johnson family was seething. At a reception attended by the Johnsons and the entire traveling press corps, President and Mrs. Johnson barely bade me hello. I had been deep-frozen before but not that badly, and it was a jolt to be snubbed by the entire First Family.

On Christmas Eve, the picture changed. I went out to an Italian restaurant with some of my colleagues and Joe Laitin (it was always good to be with one of the White House press officers in the evening in case of a news break, and Laitin was the best in my book). During dinner, Laitin took a private call from Liz Carpenter. "We have to get back to the hotel for a briefing," Laitin announced. Then he whispered, "You're vindicated." The President and Mrs. Johnson announced Luci's engagement that night.

Afterward, Luci told me the story, starting with that sensitive Halloween weekend.

"It was a terrible thing to do to a man," she chided me. "Pat and I felt the pressures on him [her father] were so great we didn't even mention the subject all that weekend."

Luci said that after three weeks passed, "My father came to us and asked, 'What's all this I read in the newspapers?' That was when we sat down and reasoned together." That was what I loved about Luci. Whenever she sat down to "reason" with her father, she never lost a round.

"The rest of us may wobble about something, but not Luci," Mrs. Johnson said. "She is one person I know who makes up her mind and sticks by it."

I interviewed or chatted with Luci every opportunity I got. She was not afraid of the press and her insights were real. "It's unbelievable how much Daddy has become mellow since we've moved into the White House," she said. "We've all grown; he realizes he has to listen to lots of peoples' opinions.

"I talk to my mother. She's always said, 'Come to me; come to me, please.' But then when you go to her, you figure she's got enough problems."

As for dating, she commented, "My mother trusted me. I didn't want to disappoint her. I don't smoke or drink. I've got enough troubles without people saying Luci Johnson smokes or drinks."

Luci said that she admired Mrs. Kennedy very much. "She was always very kind to me. My judgments are not political." Incidentally, Mrs. Johnson had made every possible effort to accord Jackie all the rights and privileges due her. She named the East Garden the "Jacqueline Kennedy Garden," but apparently Jackie could not bear to return for the ceremony. There was a sense of a snub when she designated her mother, Mrs. Hugh D. Auchincloss, as her stand-in. Jackie, who had inspired the restoration of the White House to its "golden age" elegance circa 1800, remained on the Committee for the Preservation of the White House, but never showed up for a meeting.

Luci described her lot as, "this Presidency situation."

Although billed as a "simple family affair," her wedding on August 6, 1966, turned out to be the Washington extravaganza of the year and was televised live by all three networks. A modern girl with old-fashioned ideas, she decided to have the works: a 100-voice choir, twelve bridesmaids, a ceremony in the National Shrine of the Immaculate Conception, and a walk down the nave that was thirty feet longer than a football field. She topped it with a 300-pound, seven-tiered white summer fruitcake garnished with sugar swans, sugar roses, and lilies of the valley.

Johnson reluctantly agreed to wear formal dress—a cutaway coat, striped pants, a pearl gray vest, and a gray-and-black-striped ascot. The story I wrote for UPI that day began: "Luci Baines Johnson became Mrs. Patrick John Nugent Saturday in a splendid, tearfully joyous wedding ceremony that united the younger daughter of the President of the United States with the son of a small-town businessman."

Newswomen covering the nuptials were kept guessing on the honeymoon spot. We watched the gates, but through elaborate preparations Luci and Pat managed to leave the White House unobserved. They turned up in the Bahamas where the press caught up with them.

"She'll have a houseful of kids," her father said, and eleven months later there was a baby vigil in Austin. We newswomen never let each other out of sight. Ten days after we arrived, we learned that Luci was being rushed to Seton Hospital. Her son, Patrick Lyndon Nugent, was born on June 21, 1967, weighing eight pounds, ten ounces. Nugent's reaction was, "He's an elephant!"

"He's the only noncontroversial thing around here," said Mrs. Johnson. During Johnson's last year-and-a-half in office if there was any joy for him it was his blond roly-poly grandson who, Johnson said, looked like "Khrushchev." "I'm not daffy about babies," Johnson said one day, leading me into Luci's bedroom where "Lyn" was sleeping in his blue togs on Luci's canopied bed.

"You are his honorary godmother," Johnson said grandly. That was because I had been on the baby watch and had come to Austin, Texas, along with AP's Fran Lewine, Theo Wilson, of the

New York Daily News, and other reporters for Lyn's birth at Seton Hospital. We came to be known as the "midwives."

Even after her marriage, Johnson kept an eye on the news about Luci. When I wrote that Nugent was going to take a job with the Johnson TV station KTBC, LBJ was furious and had Luci call me up to complain. She said I was ruining her life and invading her privacy. I was remorseful but couldn't believe it was that bad. After all, the story was true.

Luci telephoned me often, and usually to upbraid me for some personal family revelation. I always sensed her daddy inspired the calls—and perhaps was even listening in.

Later she sent me a note which read "To Helen Thomas Cornell who filled our White House days with fair and frank reporting— and our lives with lasting friendship. Our love, Luci and Patrick."

President Johnson's elder daughter Lynda Bird gave the press fits most of the time she was in the White House. She was so much like her father that the First Lady's staff called her "Lyndon, Jr.," but later on, Lynda mellowed and took us in her stride. She also joined the journalist's club as a part-time writer for *McCall's* magazine and became more friendly. But she deeply resented our interest in her romances and like her father was not afraid to cut us dead with a look. Even when she married Marine Maj. Charles S. Robb, the first President's daughter to be married in the White House since Woodrow Wilson's daughter Eleanor was married to William Gibbs McAdoo in 1914, Lynda interrupted the happiest time in her life to glower at reporters for pressing too close.

Talking to photographers at Atlantic City, New Jersey, in August 1964, at the Democratic National Convention where her father won the Presidential nomination by acclamation, she snapped, "You always want just one more." She also refused to pose for a cover picture with Luci for a national magazine. "I'm not Luci Watusi . . . and I'm not a movie star," she said, stomping away. A movie mogul had seen Luci dance and made some approaches to the White House to put her in a movie, but there was none of the hoyden in Lynda. She was reserved, bookish, and wry, tall, pretty, but gawky.

While she was attending the University of Texas, a male student in one of her classrooms came up and said, "Say, I hear the President's daughter goes here and she's really a square."

Lynda managed a smile and said, "Oh, she's not so bad."

Lynda was demonstrative toward her father and thought nothing of running up to him in the East Room after a ceremony and throwing her arms around him. At the LBJ ranch, she shooed reporters and cameramen away when she decided the President had had enough. Her quick humor had a cutting edge. "Freedom of the press doesn't mean freedom from responsibility," she said.

In an interview with *McCall's*, Lynda, at the age of twenty-two, had this bit of advice for young people whose fathers might want to run for President: "Don't encourage him."

"I've always accepted publicity because I've grown up in it," she said. "But being the President's daughter had its drawbacks as well as advantages. It is not clearly defined as black and white. . . ."

When Lynda introduced Brent Eastman, whom she had met in Wyoming while on a beautification trip with her mother, around the Texas ranch, tart-tongued Cousin Oriole, a devout Christodelphian (a Protestant Sect), said, "I hope you're not Catholic."

Another beau, Hollywood star George Hamilton, transformed Lynda Bird into a glamor girl. Courtly and gallant, Hamilton took her to Hollywood's famous makeup artist George Masters and also had her hair restyled. Lynda, who had never had Luci's interest in fashion, suddenly turned up with a new, more sophisticated wardrobe. She began moving in jet-set circles, but always under the protection of the Secret Service. Hamilton's manners were impeccable, even when word got around that LBJ, for some reason, could not remember Hamilton's name and always called him "Charlie."

Hamilton's arrivals and departures in Texas were always hush-hush. Once AP's Fran Lewine and I rushed out to the San Antonio International Airport to find Hamilton with baggage and boxes of goodies from the ranch. He had arrived in LBJ's private helicopter owned by the family's Austin TV station and was going back to California.

Liz Carpenter had tagged me, "the most romantic reporter in town," and Lynda was furious with my reporting of her romance. In Texas, she was overheard ranting and raving about "that Helen

Thomas" to her mother. Mrs. Johnson tried to soothe her but only exasperated Lynda. "Oh, mother, you would see good in the devil himself," she said. Dirty looks from her were pro forma in those days. But I had lived through the Jackie era at the White House, and I saw a good deal of similarity between the two women.

Lynda showed up at a press reception her parents gave, amid a spate of rumors that she and George either had married secretly at the LBJ ranch or would wed quietly at Treasure Island in San Francisco the following weekend. As reporters closed in, Lynda held up both her hands showing they were bare of rings. "I am not married," she said. "And I am not at Treasure Island with Mr. Hamilton." She tried to walk away, then saw her mother and father watching across the room in disapproval, and she tried to contain herself.

"How do you like all the interest in your romance?" I asked teasingly.

"I don't like it," she shot back. "It doesn't give me any room to—"

By this time, Mrs. Johnson got the picture and waded through the crowd to get to her daughter. "Lynda," she said, "let's do have our picture taken together."

It was clear that Mike Howard, Lynda's chief Secret Service agent, was keeping Johnson fully informed on Hamilton's conduct. Her guards thought he was a fine fellow.

"They're having a sparkling time," said Mrs. Johnson fondly.

Suave, handsome Hamilton sent her 365 roses on Valentine's Day with a note: "You are my Valentine today and every day of the year."

Lynda was blossoming as a glamor girl, surrounded by "social aides," young officers from the military services, all of whom had to be bachelors. Hamilton faded, and Lynda first turned her attention to Marine Lt. David LeFevre who began escorting her to the theatre and to parties. Then serious love came along, and she kept it a secret for some time. Word finally leaked out. It was Charles S. Robb, Marine captain and career officer, who also served as a White House social aide.

"Lynda and Chuck" became engaged one Sunday while they were in Texas. I had covered the family at St. David's Episcopal

Church in Austin a few hours before their engagement was announced. Lynda wore gloves concealing her diamond ring, but she glowed with happiness.

Johnson was pleased. Robb's ancestry was rooted in the French Huguenots and his grandfather, Robert W. Wolley, had served in Woodrow Wilson's administration. Still more pleasing to LBJ was Robb's military career and his desire to serve in Vietnam. I was reminded of Mrs. Johnson's crisp remark to a friend who was trying to assure her that a young Texan who was engaged to Lynda for a brief time came from a good family. "I know the stud line," said Mrs. Johnson.

Before the wedding, Robb had held a news conference at the Marine barracks and captivated reporters with his deft handling of hot questions. He said that he expected to be sent to Vietnam the following March, and as a professional soldier he expected to be treated "precisely the same way" as the other fighting men. He also admitted to some fear. And he said a good marriage is a "partnership and takes love and understanding." As for children, he wanted a family, but "the time or number we may leave to a higher authority."

Like Luci's, Lynda's nuptials involved near-royal preparations, and we plumbed all sources for every detail. On December 9, 1967, Lynda Bird married Captain Robb in the gleaming beauty of the White House at Christmas-time with candlelight, green garlands, and white flowers.

Johnson escorted his twenty-three-year-old daughter to the improvised white satin altar in the East Room. Robb wore his dress uniform, and Lynda wore a heavy pearl-white satin gown and a small coronet to support a fifteen-yard train. Her hair was combed back in a regal pompadour.

Looking on among the guests in the historic room was George Hamilton.

Reporters later asked Johnson if he was nervous during the ceremony.

"Not as nervous as I was thirty-four years ago," he said, meaning when he and Lady Bird were married.

Johnson confided to friends that no father can see his daughter going down the aisle "without getting a catch in his throat."

"It's like going under for the third time when you are drowning
. . . everything is gone . . . all the scenes of the past are vividly
recalled in those brief moments . . . the report cards she brought
home, her first date, the evening she wore her first prom gown when
she was fourteen."

The wedding was not free of Vietnam demonstrators: they were
across the street in Lafayette Park, just as they had been for Luci's
wedding.

Again there was the chase to find out where they would spend
their honeymoon. We didn't find out until the Robbs arrived in the
Virgin Islands.

Lynda said good-bye to her husband four months later when he
flew to Vietnam from Norton Air Force Base, California, with 164
other Marines. She told him he was going to be a father. When she
flew back to Washington on an overnight "red-eye" special, she
was greeted at the door by her anxious parents. Lynda, who had
been crying, burst out, "Dad, why do they have to go to Vietnam?"
That night Johnson stunned the world by announcing he would not
seek reelection so that he could build a better world for peace. He
had discussed his decision with Robb before he left.

Johnson was proud to have Robb in Vietnam and carried his
letters around in an inner coat pocket. Having his son-in-law under
constant enemy fire near Danang gave him a new personal sense of
urgency about the war. Both Johnson sons-in-law returned home
safely after he left office.

When I asked Lynda during a reception at the National Gallery
of Art if she were pregnant, her eyes flashed and she said: "Oh,
Helen, you have been trying to find that out since December 10,"
the day after she was married. I have always admired Alice
Roosevelt Longworth, "Princess Alice," who was telephoned by a
UP reporter when it was rumored that she was pregnant. She
floored him by answering the question directly: "Yes," said the
daughter of President Theodore Roosevelt. "Isn't it wonderful?"
Always go to the source, if you can.

When Lynda Bird went to Bethesda Naval Medical Center to
have her baby, Johnson played the role of father and grandfather.
We got the word that it was "a girl" and he came by to pass out
cigars. He was in a great mood that night.

Lynda Bird brought her daughter back to the White House amid much joy, with Lynda and the family posing for news pictures. The baby had a yellow ribbon in her hair and wore a long white gown that had once belonged to her mother. Both Luci and Lynda left the White House soon afterward. On the trip back to Texas on Nixon's inauguration day, both were to confide that they regretted calling the historic home a "white mausoleum."

There is no question that Mrs. Johnson was the powerful persuader in helping Johnson decide not to run for reelection. She thought it was time that the man who had always lived as though there was no tomorrow should live more peacefully till the end of his days. Perhaps she feared that Johnson's heart might not last another term. He had suffered a massive heart attack in 1955 but even under White House tensions he did not have another heart attack until he was out of office. My personal speculation is that she felt Johnson's burdens had become unbearable. She helped draft his valedictory statement and said after Johnson made it: "I felt ten pounds lighter, ten years younger, and full of plans." She smiled and her voice had a lilt. As the days dwindled down, she counted the hours.

She said later that she found her role as First Lady had been taxing "physically, emotionally, and spiritually." She welcomed the chance to be a private citizen again.

When I had heard her say, "*We* never wanted to be President," I thought she was really saying "Now I can at last live my own life."

The Johnsons were in the White House some ten months after his renouncement. Reading all the stories about the demise of their era, Mrs. Johnson said: "I'm tired of being buried."

She said that her grandson Patrick Lyndon was going to take the move back to Texas the hardest. Lyn, she observed, would pick up the telephone and would not find a White House switchboard operator on the other end.

"Life," she said, "is richer and fuller because I tried harder and did things I never thought I could do and was scared to do. I'm glad for all the things I did and only regret some I did not do."

Years later at the LBJ ranch, Mrs. Johnson told me that "the saddest times for him [LBJ] were when he thought he was going to get the Viet Cong to the peace table . . . the whole network of enemies to the peace table for constructive talks and then like mercury it would slip through your fingers. . . ."

Mrs. Johnson said that she would talk to her husband about all the possibilities and "sooner or later we would come around to the same way of thinking. Sometimes there is no clearly visible right way. There are two dark roads and you grope your way down one."

When Johnson died in January 1972, she said: "I've had thirty-eight wonderful years; what more could I ask?"

She was best described by their old family friend Marvin Watson, former Postmaster General, who said: "Lyndon Johnson loved a woman, and she was his greatest joy and his greatest comfort."

Chapter 5

Renunciation

On Sunday evening, March 31, 1968, Lyndon B. Johnson, wearing a blue suit, a hazy light gray shirt, and a red tie strode purposefully into the Oval Office and took his place at his barren desk. Off camera to his right sat Lady Bird and Lynda. Luci and her husband, Pat, stood behind them.

AP's Doug Cornell, Cliff Evans, veteran broadcaster and vice president of RKO, and I were permitted to stand in the doorway for what we knew was to be Johnson's most momentous address to the nation on Vietnam. Word had spread through the press room that Johnson might add some closing thoughts to the advance text of his speech. A reporter in UPI typed out a flash just on a hunch: "Johnson won't run again."

Standing in the doorway of the President's office, I scanned the room. Flanking Johnson were a portrait of Andrew Jackson and Gilbert Stuart's famous painting of George Washington; nearby was *Eastbound Mail Stage* by Peter Hurd (who had painted a portrait of Johnson that he had rejected as "the ugliest thing I ever saw"). Over the fireplace was a dashing portrait of Franklin Delano Roosevelt in his dark blue cape. There were groupings of couches, armchairs, and a long low coffee table. One drawer of the table was open. In it was a telephone console like the one on the President's desk. Photos of his daughters were propped up nearby. Lynda's was autographed: "To the No. 1 man in my life." The wooden floor was still nicked from President Eisenhower's golf cleats.

Johnson sipped from his water glass as technicians signaled that cameras were rolling. Johnson said that the United States was prepared to go anywhere, any place to discuss bringing the "ugly" war to an end and announced he was halting the bombing raids against North Vietnam. He called on Ho Chi Minh to respond to this bid for peace. Johnson looked up at his wife as if to signal her, then read: "I shall not seek and I will not accept the nomination of my party as your President."

"My God," Doug gasped. For a moment none of us believed the electrifying announcement. Johnson, consummate politician, stepping aside? Impossible!

Mrs. Johnson had written in her diary three years before that her husband would not run again. She had helped him draft the statement he had just delivered, but only when he read the words on nationwide television was she certain he would go through with it. Their daughters' eyes were full of tears. Luci said later mournfully that she would not be able to cast her first vote for her father. She was to celebrate her twenty-first birthday that year.

Later in the evening, reporters were invited to the elegant yellow Oval Room in the family quarters to chat with Johnson. On a table we spotted a book: *The Inauguration Addresses from George Washington to John F. Kennedy.* The inscription read:

Dear Mr. President,
  Jack was going to give you this for Christmas.
  Please accept this from me.
                    (signed), Jackie, December, 1963

Reporters, scrambling into the room, filled the sofas and chairs and eased onto the oval rug waiting for Johnson. He appeared, wearing a blue Mao-style shirt over gray slacks spooning chocolate pudding from a goblet. He did not offer us any.

As we pressed our questions, Johnson kept stressing this decision was "irrevocable." Finally, exasperated, he silenced us: "My statement speaks for itself. I don't see any reason why we should have these high school discussions about it." I felt sorry for this proud, vain, tough, stubborn man whose main goal in the Presidency—to unite the country—had eluded him.

Some time earlier, Johnson had showed friends a live oak tree at the family's cemetery on the ranch and had said: "This is the tree I expect to be buried under. When my grandchildren see this tree, I want them to think of me as the man who saved Asia and Vietnam and who did something for the Negroes of this country. Yet I have lost popularity on Vietnam and on the Negro question."

Johnson's speech culminated a reevaluation of the chances for victory and peace. It followed the shocking Tet offensive in South Vietnam and an urgent request for 240,000 more troops by Gen. William C. Westmoreland, U.S. military commander in Saigon. Johnson, who had previously committed half a million men, knew that that would escalate a war that was growing more unpopular each day, with no solution in sight. It had become "Johnson's war" even though he had inherited it from Kennedy and Eisenhower who, like him, believed that unless South Vietnam was defended against the Communists, Laos, Cambodia, Thailand, and other Southeast Asian nations would fall. (Ironically, they did fall like dominos when the 1973 Paris peace agreement negotiated during President Nixon's administration was ignored by Hanoi and neglected by Secretary of State Henry Kissinger.) Johnson had hoped Hanoi would come to the negotiating table once he ended the bombing and his own political ambitions.

The morning after his poignant capitulation, we flew with him on the Presidential jet. We knew before takeoff that we would return to Washington the same day, but when we were airborne we learned that his first destination was Chicago where he had a long-time commitment to address the National Association of Broadcasters. "I don't make commitments and break them," he told reporters.

Johnson looked weary and physically spent, but he also appeared exhilarated and warmly expansive on the trip to Chicago. Long months of indecision were over and thousands of telegrams were already urging him to reconsider. The bombshell announcement seemed to lift a cloud from Johnson, and his detractors became, for a brief time, at least, admirers who praised his courageous decision.

In his restrained speech to the NAB, Johnson made a humble confession: "I understand far better than some of my severe and perhaps intolerant critics would admit, my own shortcomings as a communicator."

On the flight back, the President invited Doug Cornell and me, RKO's Evans, Jack Sutherland of *U.S. News and World Report,* Dan Rather of CBS, and Max Frankel of *The New York Times,* to join him in his cabin for a lunch of sirloin steak. As Johnson devoured two bowls of his favorite Pedernales chili and two helpings of ice cream, he reiterated he would remain President until January 20 and basked in the well-wishes of the public.

Johnson, in that off-the-record conversation, which I now feel free to disclose, revealed much of the motivations that prompted his decision to step down. We asked if he felt relieved, and he replied: "Yes, I think so. I don't think there's anything unusual about it or noteworthy. When you're speaking to a TV audience that size on a subject of that consequence . . . there is always a certain tenseness. Grant or Lincoln said that they never addressed more than one person that their stomachs did not feel like a rolling ship.

"I don't feel frightened when I speak. I did when I was a little boy. I came to believe that what I said there was the best thing under all the circumstances."

Johnson told us that he had striven "to get the right phrase to convey my thought." It had been a long evening, he said and he had talked by telephone with friends from all over the country until 2:30 A.M.

Johnson also told us he had used Truman's statement of withdrawal from the Presidential race on March 29, 1952, sixteen years and two days before Johnson served his own notice to the world, as a model for renouncing his position. As he neared the end of his speech at a Democratic fund-raising dinner, Truman, who like Johnson delighted in surprise, had said simply: "I shall not be a candidate for reelection. I shall not accept a renomination."

Johnson said that on his inaugural day, he and Mrs. Johnson agreed he would serve only one full term. She said at that time, "We have about fourteen hundred days to go."

"When it reached a thousand days to the end of his term, Mrs. Johnson reminded me. Then eight hundred. And so it's gone.

"It seemed to me that I am becoming more of an object of contempt and controversy than I thought to be in the interest of men and women I have to serve. It was getting to the point where a man could no longer be President. Yes, I feel I made several errors in the past. I came to the conclusion if I signed the Lord's Prayer it would be objected to.

"This division hurts our men a great deal. They don't understand draft card burners saying that it's being done in the name of free speech and dissent.

"I grew up in the school where I had to be prudent but there was a time when you had to put the whole stack in and let everything ride on it. I did that on the civil rights bill.

"Only last week Senator Robert Kennedy introduced me at a dinner in New York. He said I had been elected by the greatest plurality in our country, but I would never hesitate to spend the popularity to do what's necessary for the country." Johnson complained about those who charged he was "power hungry."

He said, "I don't think Mrs. Johnson believed I was going to say it until I actually read the line. But I knew it. George Christian knew it." Christian was his Press Secretary.

Grasping our arms and poking our shoulders, Johnson insisted, "I've had a very good life. A full life. A productive life. The rest of this year I'll unleash a lot of talent. I'll give others hell. I'll try to shake them up. In the war. In the cities. To get things done . . . without anybody saying he's trying to win the primary in Wisconsin or he's trying to win in California.

"As long as I live, I'll find plenty of satisfaction. My feelings are not hurt. People have been better to me than I deserve. Life, too. Remember I had three operations last year. I've been happy doing everything I've done in my life. I'm not a cry baby."

Johnson continued nonstop and we wrote furiously as he rambled on in a stream of consciousness that at times was heartrending.

"John F. Kennedy said I was the best one for him. He wanted me. Mr. Sam [Rayburn] said, 'Let's give the people of this nation a chance to vote for a man from Texas. We can't do a thing for the country if Nixon is President.'

"I said, yes, I would run as Vice President. When I became President, what did I do, fire everybody? No. I had the feeling I was the trustee of President Kennedy's administration.

"Friends came to me and said Arthur Goldberg would go from

the Supreme Court bench to be our Ambassador to the United Nations. It was not my idea. I wouldn't pull him off the bench. You don't do it to someone as able as he is."

I thought of how dejected Goldberg and his wife looked when they came to the White House when Johnson announced that he had resigned his lifetime Supreme Court position to go to the UN after Adlai Stevenson's death. Reporters had written that Johnson had done some "arm twisting" to get Goldberg off the bench and replace him with Washington lawyer Abe Fortas. In reality, LBJ gave Fortas no choice but to take the high judicial post.

"I think the dissension within the administration has been kept to a minimum," Johnson told us on the plane. "Certainly nothing like the fuss between Harry Hopkins and Harold Ickes during the FDR era."

He also confirmed that much-rumored report at the time that some people had pressed him to appoint staffer Bill Moyers as Secretary of State to succeed Dean Rusk. Johnson thought of Rusk as a "giant" but White House reporters also knew Rusk as a major "hawk" on the war who insisted he was open to a "whisper" from Hanoi or a telephone call from Ho Chi Minh. As it turned out, there were soundings through diplomatic channels to which the White House apparently chose to turn a deaf ear.

With mimicking gestures, Johnson gave an intimate picture of the Presidency that few of his predecessors could have captured. "Sometimes you have to carry things on your shoulders. This one is hurt because he felt slighted. This man's wife is piqued. This man didn't get invited. A man [a reporter] who has one of the biggest circulations in the country. He once complained 'You greeted my competitor first.' "

Johnson grabbed reporters' lapels, fixing his eyes on ours, seeming to plead and cajole us into understanding the situation. We were transfixed.

"I have no vindictiveness in my blood [toward his foes]. No hatred. No vituperation. I hear talk about us Texans. How uncouth we are. Sometimes the people you talk to are the people who know the least. For a boy who came out of Johnson City—the Presidency! But if I could, I never would have left the Senate.

"I know what the powers of the Presidency are and I exercise them. I asked Congress to come in and if they don't, they can go to hell. We're playing with fire these days. Maybe we need a Churchill to wake us up. We act the same way today that we did in the 1930s and the 1940s.

"I feel that if we lose Vietnam, in a matter of hours we lose Thailand, Burma, Laos, Cambodia . . . the other countries in Southeast Asia. Then, of course, we're no longer the Number One nation in the world, we're Number Two or Number Three or whatever.

"When Ho Chi Minh says: 'Stop bombing and all other acts of war,' he is actually saying 'Surrender!' If Ho would say 'Good Morning' we'd not only stop the bombing, but other things, too. If he'd say anything," Johnson added plaintively.

Johnson said he not only consulted with his top advisors, including eminent men from outside the government, he also demanded to be briefed by those who had briefed them.

"We concluded we'd stop all bombing if they'd sit down and talk. I'm going to protect our men at Khesanh. I've got to. I don't care what you say."

At that point he reached for a small pad embossed with gold letters in the upper left-hand corner "Aboard Air Force One" and sketched a map. He drew the supply route from North Vietnam to Khesanh.

"There's always someone disruptive. Is criticism and carping inherent in the Presidency in the future? I suppose after a time you develop barnacles. If we had listened to the columnists years ago in the thirties and forties . . . today we'd be slaves.

"I think we are unjust to our Presidents. Truman. Living out there, quietly, unnoticed. Things that I did came out of Truman's basket. Medicare is one example.

"I think Eisenhower is very much underestimated. He's done things without regard to self or political party. He said, 'On domestic issues, I'm a mean Republican. But when the nation is involved in a war, the people should be together.' When Eisenhower was President and I was Democratic Leader in the Senate, he said, we won't divide the country if you won't. We communicated. Today, we communicate through the Associated Press and United Press."

Johnson continued in his effort at catharsis. He told us that he did not agree with Kennedy on the Bay of Pigs or his tax bill but felt he should go along.

"Franklin D. Roosevelt was slandered as much as anyone could be," Johnson said. "They said he had a disease. That he was Jewish. They said he was of German origin.

"I don't need the job . . . the salary. I don't need your approval. I'm going to live a full, happy life. I don't give a particular damn what you think. But I do think that this country is going to be better for y'all, for the things I've done.

"If I can remove myself from the line of fire. If I can get somebody . . . *Republican or Democrat* . . . to unite the country. Because united we stand, divided we fall . . . !"

Johnson berated us for saying he had a "credibility gap."

"I never believed we had a credibility gap," he said. "I don't think we've lied to you and I don't think we're incredible. If you make others believe your President is a sly, slick wheeler-dealer, others will believe it. It hurts his men.

"Most people want their President to do well. That's true of both parties, particularly when he's learning to walk."

He was cagy when we asked for his choice of successor from the Democratic Party—Vice President Hubert H. Humphrey, and Senators Robert Kennedy and Eugene McCarthy. He told us off the record he thought that Nelson A. Rockefeller, then Republican Governor of New York, would make the best candidate. A week after his renunciation speech, I understand Johnson summoned Rockefeller to Camp David and told him so.

LBJ once said, privately, "I'm pretty strong for the Rockefellers. They work for the people."

When Air Force One, bearing the seal of the President of the United States, landed in Washington, I asked Johnson to auto-graph a copy of his NAB address. He added a personal note for me, and for other reporters who handed him similar documents. Then he shook hands all around before strutting down the ramp.

I think all of us felt then that there would never be another Lyndon Johnson. I can still hear him saying, "I'm the only President you've got," and I was not sure whether he was trying to remind himself or convince the country.

This fascinating, hypnotic man still was completely absorbed in the Presidency; denying, defending, explaining, until his last day in office. He longed to be classed with his choices of great Presidents —Lincoln, Jefferson, Franklin D. Roosevelt.

Reporters spent much time psychoanalyzing Lyndon B. Johnson, especially his mania for secrecy and his feeling of inferiority which he could not overcome. "I'll never be given credit for anything I do in foreign policy," he complained, "because I didn't go to Harvard." He used to point out with pride, however, that he had a Rhodes scholar (Dean Rusk) and Ivy League graduates in his Cabinet.

During the tense months of 1967, Johnson had seemed to feel cornered. He derided the "nervous nellies" and men of little faith; the "cussers and the doubters," the war critics and the flag burners. "If the nation's young people provide the proper leadership and bear their full load, then the cussers and the doubters will be relegated to the rear; the doers and the builders will take up the front lines," Johnson had said in a speech to the members of the Junior Chamber of Commerce in Washington. He exhorted the enthusiastic gathering: "It's not required that you tear our country down—tear our flag down—in order to lift them up."

Very few reporters had suspected Johnson would not run again. He valued secrets and kept the best until the last. In June 1967, he said in a speech at The President's Club dinner in Los Angeles:

"We can now begin to marshal the resources that we need to carry our case to all the people in the election of 1968. . . .

"When I read about my decline and defeat, I look over the problems that other Presidents have had and I don't seem to remember many of them that the American people turned their backs on in time of crisis in a time of war."

As war stepped up, he had slid deeper into the quagmire. Soon it became impossible to distill rhetoric from truth and the American people were treated to a daily recital of kill ratios, captured documents, terrorist attacks, and villages destroyed to save them from the enemy. The time came when Johnson could travel only to military bases to be free of antiwar demonstrators. On one trip, he boarded an aircraft carrier off Georgia and when he was leaving a sailor reported to Johnson that his helicopter was waiting. "Son," drawled Johnson, "they're all my helicopters."

Despite such hauteur, LBJ identified with the people. On a walk with reporters around the South Lawn, leading his yapping dogs, Johnson described, with strong emotion, terror tactics by the Viet Cong who had bombed the United States Embassy in Saigon "killing little secretaries at their desks" and forty to fifty people in the street.

"Why should we stop our bombing if they won't stop this kind of thing?" he asked. "For sixteen months I didn't bomb but I knew they shot at our destroyers and we answered after the Pleiku attack. I did the only thing I could do without being impeached." Johnson insisted that he was hitting only steel and concrete. He said the targets were roads and bridges, not people in cities or embassies or political targets. "But I wouldn't be much of a commander-in-chief if I didn't strike back when they are attacking my brother," he insisted.

Johnson took that role seriously and literally. He ran the war, even to the point of picking the targets. "They can't hit an outhouse without my permission," he would say. A cartoon of the period depicted a GI in the jungle in Vietnam picking up a field telephone and hearing LBJ on the other end barking an order. During long nights, Johnson used to telephone the twenty-four-hour "situation room" (the secret communications center in the White House basement) to find out how "my boys are doing."

On June 29, 1966, Luci had come home after a date with her fiancé, Patrick Nugent, and found her father pacing the floor, deeply worried, his face gray. He told her that he had ordered the bombing of the oil dumps at Haiphong and rails near Hanoi. "Your daddy may have started World War III," he said in distress. "You may not wake up in the morning."

Luci told her father that whenever she felt alone and afraid, she would visit the Benedictines at St. Dominic's Roman Catholic Church in downtown Washington.

"Would you like to go see my little monks, Daddy?"

Johnson agreed to go and Luci's "little monks" opened the church at midnight so the President of the United States could pray. After that he went there often for solace and spiritual comfort; sometimes he complained that the kneeling benches were too hard for him and should be padded. I went there with him the Sunday morning several hours before he renounced a desire to run for reelection.

In late November after the election of Nixon, Garnett Horner of the *Washington Star* and I were summoned to Johnson's small hideaway office off the Oval Office where the walls were filled with photos of Johnson, photos of Johnson with past Presidents, and with Lincoln quotations. The interview was "on background," meaning we could not quote him directly but could express his feelings.

On December 1, 1968, I wrote: "President Johnson looks back on his five years in the White House in a mellow mood these days, proud of his accomplishments in promoting the general weal, philosophical about some of his keen disappointments. Some things he would do differently if he could do it over again.

"He hopes that his successor, Richard M. Nixon, and his family will not have to endure what he feels were unfair attacks and ugly things said about him and his loved ones."

Johnson did not live long enough to see the ordeal of his successor's last months in office. Nixon, too, was to leave the White House feeling that he had been treated unfairly by the nation.

Johnson seemed to have made peace with himself, yet he could not help but turn back to the old hurts. He said he did not feel that he had been treated objectively and that there is a tendency in the country to heap unnecessary abuse on any man who is President. He also felt that the press simply refused to accept his Texas "style."

In contrast to the hostility of the changing of the guard when Eisenhower took over from Truman, Johnson moved mountains to make the transition to the next administration as smooth as possible. After he announced he would not seek a second term, he told aides to prepare to pack. He wanted to leave the White House and become the elder statesman with all the rights, privileges, and trappings that he had accorded Dwight D. Eisenhower, a man of whom Johnson always stood in awe. Eisenhower had reciprocated by totally backing his Vietnam War stand, and LBJ had often gone to see him for private support.

Several weeks before they moved out of the White House the Johnsons entertained the leaders of the national veterans' organizations. He was at his best—nostalgic, sentimental, tolerant. There was obviously a great story here, and I was trying to figure out how to lead it off, but Johnson said it was off-the-record, and I was almost relieved.

The outpouring was so overwhelming he was in an ebullient mood. He had spent several hours visiting with Humphrey and as he later told a group of newswomen at a get-together in the family quarters, an episode discussed in an earlier chapter, Humphrey was "just so cheerful" and had justifications for everybody concerning the election campaign defeat.

As he sipped on a low-calorie drink and munched on hot popcorn, Johnson spoke of his visit with Vice President-elect Spiro T. Agnew and their talk about the problems of the office. "You never know what it's like to be a father until you are a father. I feel that way about the Presidency and the Vice Presidency," he said.

Johnson went on to say that there could be only one pilot on the plane when the plane is in trouble. In terms of Agnew, he said, "He's the copilot and I'm not going to beat him on the head either."

He said some people "think of the Vice President sitting like a nut on a log, having no authority; he has no power; he is bound by the decisions the President makes. If he's independent that means he is disloyal. If he's not independent, they say he's a stooge, a puppet. President Kennedy worked so hard at making a place for me, always saying nice things, gave me dignity and standing. But back in the back room they were quoting Bobby, saying I was going to be taken off the ticket. You never know if it's true if you're not there. The last thing he told me in Dallas was 'Lyndon, we're going to carry two states, if we don't carry any. I'm determined that we do that.' [Kennedy was referring to their native states of Massachusetts and Texas.] That was the last thing he said to me the last time I saw him."

"It's difficult to come from a state where you are 'Mister It,' 'number one' . . . and all the power that went with it, to the Vice Presidency. I was trying to tell him [Agnew] things that would excite him, like the space program, the Governors. I'd just take one of those jobs and be happy. There's just more than you can do . . . help them with their programs, and help the President, why it's wonderful."

As for his own feelings as his term was drawing to a close, Johnson told us, "If the good Lord didn't take me by the hand and help me—that would be it. What good would it do if I scored a few points on Nixon [on Vietnam] if Pat didn't get back or Chuck got killed." He referred to his two sons-in-law, Patrick J. Nugent and Maj. Charles S. Robb.

Looking back, Johnson always remained in awe of the destiny that catapulted him into the Presidency. He boasted that he had "no Bay of Pigs" like Kennedy. But his own Waterloo was Vietnam and he knew that he could not rally the people for what he called a "time of testing" in view of the protests, the violence in the cities and on the campuses, the general disenchantment of the people, and even of some of his closest advisors.

"Here Comes 'Mr. Stop the Bombing,' " he used to say when Moyers would walk into the Cabinet room for a meeting when the Hawks versus Doves controversy was beginning to rage.

In covering the White House I had always been taught to project rather than to look backward. Today's story is important. Yesterday is for the ages. Nevertheless when Nixon's inauguration day rolled around I decided it would be a great human story to take LBJ back to his beloved Texas hill country to live—back to his roots where his friends called him "Lyndon" and where he could finally be relieved of the awesome burden he had so long coveted and carried for five years and two months. So it was arranged for me and AP feature writer Saul Pett to cover LBJ on that sentimental journey.

There had been the traditional ride with the new President to the Capitol for the swearing-in ceremony. For Johnson and Washington, it was the end of an era between a master politician and a city that embraced, then devoured his kind of men. I knew Johnson must have been wondering how history would judge him.

Several hundred friends had gathered at Andrews Air Force

Base for a fond, sometimes tearful farewell. The Johnsons trooped the line, hugging, kissing, shaking hands with old friends, party leaders, and political comrades-in-arms. On board the plane his wife, Lady Bird, and his two daughters, Lynda Bird Robb and Luci Nugent (their husbands were in Vietnam), stayed close to him when we became airborne. Saul and I had asked to talk to Johnson and his family for their impressions of the White House.

"At what moment did you feel that you were no longer President, after Nixon was sworn in?" Saul asked Johnson as we sat together in a back cabin. Johnson looked at his gnarled hands a moment and said, "Four seconds afterward, I felt differently."

Mrs. Johnson was smiling contentedly, but Luci and Lynda had been crying. When Lynda took off her dark glasses I could see that her eyes were red. Luci said that she cried when she was leaving the White House earlier in the day and looked out of the windows of the car and saw some of the maids peering through the windows dabbing their eyes. The two girls disclosed that they had both slept in the seven-foot-long Lincoln bed their last night in the White House, for history's sake.

When the Johnsons left the White House, I recalled Luci's first impression of it when she was sixteen years old. "It's a very big place," she said. "It's a very dark place. You can be just as happy as you want to be in it, or you can be miserable."

Few Presidents have put it as profoundly or as well, I thought.

In the plane was a bouquet of yellow roses from the Nixons. Luci Johnson Nugent handed me a note of thanks:

ABOARD AIR FORCE ONE
(January 20, 1969)

Helen—

I'm truly glad to see you here—you have really gone all the way with the LBJs—and it means a lot

(from Luci Johnson Nugent,
signed with drawing of
a smiling face)

A day or so later we were invited to the ranch for an interview with Johnson. He said he was glad to get that "sack of cement"—the Presidency—off his shoulders. He said he would be able to be sick on his own time. "It's hard when you think of being sick on 200 million people's time." He was going to walk in the sunshine, ride horseback along the range, and view his retirement "like having a day off."

His hair now a silvery gray, Johnson looked handsome in his favorite ranch outfit—khaki-green gabardine slacks and matching jacket. But as he described his life in retirement in his Texas hills, he looked glum.

I asked him if he was happy. "Yes," he replied, "I think so."

Several weeks later I had lunch with Liz Carpenter and as we were walking back to the White House, I stopped at the gate to say good-bye to her. She was going on to her office in the National Press Building.

"Liz," I said. "What do you miss most about the White House?"

"Power," she replied.

That is it, I thought. That is what LBJ misses.

Chapter 6

Nixon:
The Fortress Presidency

Nixon's life-style came into focus within days after he joyously took over the Presidency in January 1968. Formality was to prevail at the White House. No more were we to enjoy that freewheeling Texas "Y'all come" atmosphere. The Nixons, who had traveled abroad extensively during the Vice Presidency and the years he was out of national office, enjoyed the royal trappings and palatial surroundings of foreign heads of state who thought the leader of the free world should have similar accoutrements.

The President was ridiculed in the press when he tried to outfit the White House police in tunics and helmets straight out of *The Student Prince*, and they had to be abandoned. He settled for a Marine guard in full dress uniform at the door leading into the West Wing, which housed the official offices.

Nixon at first also decreed "white tie" for State Dinners. Presidents Kennedy and Johnson earlier had realized that few guests relished wearing such stiff attire, and neither did they. Nixon soon yielded and went back to black tie.

Nixon, like his predecessors, ordered extensive redecorating in the West Wing, and Mrs. Nixon helped him transform the Oval Office into a bright blue and yellow showcase, with a portrait of George Washington over the mantel. Ceremonial touches thrilled him, yet paradoxically he worked best in the peace and quiet of his hideaway office, "out of the line of fire." He did his "thinking time" there.

His hideaway reflected Nixon's sentimentality, with family album pictures of his wife and two daughters, Julie Eisenhower and Tricia Cox, mementos of his political wars, GOP elephants, and, after 1973, a map of the United States sans Massachusetts and the District of Columbia, the only two places where voters turned him down in his landslide election in 1972.

His top aides spent lavishly ordering plush new rugs, French provincial furniture, and ordering a new paint job for their offices. The word was, "This is our White House now."

The press room off the West Lobby had grown more congested as the ranks of the White House reporters swelled. Photographers had to stow equipment on the South Lawn in a shed known as the "dog-house." Cramped as we were, we cherished our squatter's rights because we were as close to the seat of power as possible. Presidential visitors who came through the door, which was the official entrance, were fair game for interviewing.

To my surprise Nixon walked in late one Sunday afternoon when I was working in the press room alone. He took one look around our tight little island with its empty pop bottles, wadded paper from bad starts on stories, the messy disarray. It was a typical press hangout but Nixon was appalled. "This is a disgrace," he told me. When he departed I picked up the telephone and called in the story of the President's impromptu visit.

Soon afterward, construction of a new press center began above the indoor swimming pool in the West Wing, and months later we moved into quarters with a lounge and briefing room in the style of an English club with Currier and Ives prints on the walls; $574,000 went into the renovation project, which was described variously as an Elizabethan pub or a high-class funeral parlor. During the Nixon years we were asked not to carry paper coffee cups from the press room into the briefing room.

The layout was much grander than we had had before and we could spread out more. But UPI's White House staff of three still found the booth where we had our telephones and typewriters a tight squeeze.

More important, we were at a greater disadvantage in keeping an eye on the President's callers since we had no freedom of movement beyond the press center, or even the grounds in that period. Our access to the news was, therefore, more limited. We began to see the renovation of our offices as a subtle part of the Nixon war against the press. Our press room became Henry Kissinger's office.

After the project was complete, Lyndon Johnson came to call on President Nixon, and the two Presidents took a tour of the new press room. Johnson looked over the briefing room, took in the straight-backed chairs, tufted sofas, the hidden platform for cameras, and said, "This is a wonderful improvement. Is there the same improvement in the stories?"

As cameramen snapped away, Nixon shot back with a smile, "Not in the pictures."

"There's no excuse now for mistakes," Johnson said.

Both Presidents had had their troubles with the press, but in the Johnson administration, the name of the game was manipulation of the press; in the Nixon era it became outright hostility. Nixon's troubles with the press began, of course, long before he entered the White House. From the beginning of his political career he had viewed the press as a major adversary. After Nixon's devastating political setback in the 1962 California gubernatorial contest against Democratic Governor Edmund Brown, he had lashed out at reporters in an emotional outburst: "You're not going to have Richard Nixon to kick around any more. This is my last press conference."

His triumphal political comeback in the 1968 Presidential contest after the bitter defeat against Kennedy in 1960 bolstered his belief in himself, and like other Presidents before him, he got a "honeymoon" with the press. Even the *Washington Post* cartoonist, Herblock, who had drawn scathing caricatures of Nixon with a five o'clock shadow reminiscent of Senator Joe McCarthy's in the fifties, now gave him a clean shave. A clean start.

In the early months of his administration, Nixon's stock was high with the public. Luck was with him, especially when astronaut Neil Armstrong stepped on the moon. But the plaque the *Apollo 11* spacemen left there had only one name on it—that of President Richard M. Nixon—yet it was Kennedy who had made the commitment in the early sixties to land a man on the moon within the decade, and it was Johnson who had proudly spurred on the space program as Vice President and then as President. Nor did the names of astronauts who had pioneered in the program appear on the plaque. It was as if space history had begun with the Nixon administration. Some clerics took umbrage when he described the advent of the moon landing as "the greatest week in the history of the world since the creation."

In the same spirit, from the beginning, the Nixon press office seemed determined to program the news. I was shocked when I first heard we were being labeled "the enemy" in the back offices. It seemed a strange way to proceed in the aftermath of Nixon's success with the press in his 1968 campaign. They had labored to make the press happy with creature comforts while providing a controlled flow of news. Perhaps we should have seen the new Currier and Ives press room as an omen.

We had heard, as we always did with the advent of each new official family, that this was going to be an "open administration." But Nixon belied that during his first year in office when he told reporters he would hold news conferences only when they "are in the public interest." He rarely thought they were, averaging about seven a year during his first term, sometimes going four or five months without holding one. He had won high marks for his early press conference performances, but they were an ordeal for him. He complained that press conferences required preparation that made him neglect the nation's business.

When he did hold a press conference, Nixon did his homework well. For two or three days before the scheduled conference he would study briefing papers and instruct his staffers to quiz him so that he could practice answers. It often galled him when his careful preparation went for naught. We were accused by White House Counselor Ehrlichman in a speech of asking "soft, flabby questions." We realized that the criticism came from Nixon, who complained to his aides that we never asked "hard" questions, although he always prepared himself for the worst. I am sure that in the last year of his Presidency he did not feel that way since an air of hostility pervaded those news conferences.

I was flattered when Nixon told me during an interview, "You always ask tough questions, tough questions not in the sense of being unfair, but hard to generalize the answers."

Unlike Johnson, who had four press secretaries, Nixon had only one, Ronald Louis Ziegler, from the moment he stepped into the White House until his emotional farewell to the troops six years later. So no one in the press corps was surprised when the Watergate tapes revealed Nixon telling Ziegler, who was about to conduct a news briefing, "Go out there and be your usual cocky self." Ziegler's stock was high with the press at first. He was quick, bright, and personable. He could joke and banter with the reporters and he tried to ingratiate himself.

In contrast to other and better liked press secretaries, such as Johnson's George Reedy and Ford's Jerry terHorst, Ziegler was not originally a newsman. A protégé of H. R. (Bob) Haldeman, he had worked for him at the J. Walter Thompson advertising firm in Los Angeles, Ziegler was a public relations man and, like Haldeman, thought of the press as a tool to be used to further the goals of his employer, President Nixon. I saw him several times before he actually took over as the "voice" of the White House. He came with Nixon to look over his new surroundings and met with the man he was to succeed, George Christian, LBJ's Press Secretary. Ziegler seemed to be champing at the bit. He kept the traditional office of the Press Secretary a few paces from the Oval Office, and furnished it with a deep royal blue rug, a sofa, comfortable arm chairs, bookshelves, and a telephone with a silver receiver.

Once settled in the White House, Ziegler sounded out for advice such pros as the UPI White House Correspondent Merriman Smith who simply told him, "Never lie." In the last dark months of the Nixon administration, it became more and more clear that the advice had not been heeded.

Ziegler was in awe of Nixon in the beginning and later, in the dying days, became a trusted lieutenant. He memorized the views of the "boss" and repeated them to us authoritatively. He remained under the watchful eye of the all-powerful Chief of Staff, Haldeman, who gave him daily instructions on what to say at his press briefings.

When we were in our old press room, before we moved to the spacious new quarters, Smitty, who sensed danger from the Nixon coterie, used to say: "Some day they are going to wall us in."

In the good first days, Ziegler worked to stay on good terms with the reporters. He could and did occasionally blow up or upbraid a reporter, but he was usually quick to apologize later. Once I phoned him at seven in the morning. He answered my questions as best he could, but before he hung up he chided me for calling at that hour. I fluffed up the pillow and settled back in bed, waiting for him to call back. Sure enough, he did.

Ziegler was the personification of cool self-assurance at the podium. Though he mangled the English language, reporters listened intently because they knew he had daily access to the isolated President, and probably accurately reflected the President's views.

He became a master of artful circumlocution and of the delicate business of not answering questions. He had several techniques, and "zieglerism" and "to ziegle" entered the vocabulary of the White House press corps. He constantly refused to comment on stories that he labeled "speculation." One day in 1972, I asked him if the President had delivered an ultimatum to end the war to North and South Vietnam, threatening to bomb the one and withhold funds from the other. I pointed out that news stories had used that word, "ultimatum."

"Helen," Ziegler replied, "that word had come about by the source stories and the speculation stories. I have no comment on those stories."

I remembered Pierre Salinger's observation to us in the Kennedy administration that "no comment" is tantamount to "yes."

Vietnam had caused both Johnson and Nixon to be less than candid and the people had been shortchanged. "Let the people know the facts and the country will be safe," Lincoln had said. But then Ron Ziegler said, "I can only be as factual as the facts permit."

Secrecy and surprise are afflictions of every President I have known. Everyone has become proprietary about information and how it is dispensed—many times only to protect their own image. I remember Ziegler telling us at a news briefing that the United

States would not provide tactical air support to the Cambodians. Later when I confronted him with reports from correspondents in the field that the Air Force was flying low support missions, he looked at me and said: "Why don't you focus on what we're doing today."

Reporters do not get all their news from the Press Secretary, of course. Often the big stories come from Presidential aides who are willing to speak "on background" as "administration" or "White House" sources. One of the best reporters I have ever known at the White House, Alan Lidow of Golden West Broadcasting Co., never asked a question at a Ziegler briefing, but he came up with an exclusive story nearly every day. He had developed trustworthy sources.

In the spring of 1973, during a joint press conference I inquired who, if anyone, had reported the results of the so-called John Dean investigation to President Nixon, and I asked for Nixon's reaction. The reply, featuring Ziegler and Special Consultant to the President Leonard Garment, was a showcase example of zieglering:

Garment: Helen, I followed a number of the briefings on this, and I think that they do accurately describe the situation that took place at that time.

Q: You are not giving me an answer.

Garment: I think you have had answers on this subject.

Q: No. Who?

Garment: Well, I think you have from Ron.

Q: Tell us again what you know.

Ziegler: The position is stated in the previous briefings.

Q: It was not stated in previous briefings.

Ziegler: We went through this, Helen, in a briefing when you were on vacation.

If they had, no one knew it. Throughout the early days of the Watergate unraveling, Ziegler was the point man, sent out to accuse the *Washington Post* of printing hearsay and innuendo. Later he apologized publicly to the *Post*. He explained that he had been "overenthusiastic."

When it became clear that Ziegler was in the bull-ring and would remain so, many of Nixon's friends and advisors urged him to get rid of his highly vulnerable Press Secretary. But Nixon refused.

Nixon defended him as a man who could wear "two hats," serving both the President and the public. Ziegler was the last of the original entourage that had accompanied him to the White House.

During the infighting, Ziegler was closer to the President's ear than former Treasury Secretary John T. Connally and former Defense Secretary Melvin R. Laird, who had come aboard at the White House to help resurrect its prestige in the wake of the resignations of Haldeman and Ehrlichman. Both urged Nixon to dump Ziegler. As a compromise, Deputy Press Secretary Gerald L. Warren was tapped to do the briefings, getting Ziegler out of the line of fire. Warren rarely saw Nixon and saw him not at all for briefings in the last two or three weeks Nixon was in office.

When reporters complained that Warren was not getting his information directly from Nixon while speaking daily in his name, Ziegler marched Warren to the door of the Oval Office, opened it slightly, shut it and said, "There, now go tell them you have seen the President." At best, Warren was in a caretaker role. At the same time he was a loyal believer in Richard Nixon, but admits he did not know him intimately. He expressed "shock" when he saw the transcript of the June 23, 1972 tape, the evidence that spelled out the culpability of the Nixon Presidency.

From the start of the Nixon administration we soon became used to Nixon's penchant for citing historical "firsts." It led one reporter to quip: "Someone should write a book entitled 'the making of a precedent.'"

When we traveled to Indonesia, Nixon said in a toast at the Presidential Palace in Jakarta: "I realize that the position I'm in is a unique one, one that will not come again. Since I am the first President ever to pay a state visit to Indonesia, the next American President who comes here will not be in the position I presently find myself."

He told a Republican rally in New Jersey in 1970: "This is the first time that a President of the United States has spoken in Morris County. I'm glad to be the first President to do that."

Nixon's strong suit was foreign affairs and his interest span in domestic programs was minimal. He wanted to dismantle the

"Great Society" programs such as anti-poverty, the Job Corps, Head Start, even the school milk program on the ground that the federal government under the two previous Democratic administrations had usurped responsibility that belonged in local hands. Instead he initiated "revenue sharing" and stressed his desire to return "power to the people."

Nixon always seemed happiest when he was getting on a plane, preferably one on the way out of the country. He loved the pomp and ceremony that accompanied such tours. But they were hectic trips. Sometimes we would be in a country only twenty-three hours, and often in the sweltering heat of Asia in the dead of summer. In New Delhi, when Nixon spoke of the warmth of the welcome, Indian Prime Minister Indira Gandhi sensed he was also thinking of the thermometer. She was quick on the draw and replied testily: "Well, sir, you came at the wrong time of the day and the wrong time of the year."

When we traveled to Yugoslavia, President Tito took Nixon to his birthplace. He led the way into his ancestral cottage and pointed to a mahogany cradle. "My bed," he smiled. I listened to the byplay between the two leaders in amusement.

"Do you remember when you were born?" Nixon asked.

Tito beckoned Nixon to come sit with him on a bench around an old concrete furnace that used to keep his family of nine "very warm." Pointing to a rifle over his bed, he told Nixon he had used it to protect the family vineyards.

"Against animals," Nixon asked.

"No," said Tito, "against people."

But it was the wall with pictures from the family album that attracted the attention of both men. Tito pointed out a photograph of himself as a "Partisan" fighter in World War II and showed Nixon a "most wanted" poster with his picture. The Nazis had put a price on his head.

"One hundred thousand marks!" exclaimed Nixon.

"Gold marks," corrected Tito.

"Were you worth it?" Nixon asked. Tito looked at him, smiled slightly, and walked away.

The President signed the guest book: "Richard M. Nixon, President, USA, Oct. 1, 1970," with his souvenir pen. Then he handed the pen to the museum keeper and said: "See, it has my name on it and the White House—you can keep it."

Nixon was uncomfortable making small talk, and whenever he approached young people his patter would cover: "Where are you from?" and "Do you like baseball?" I have observed him often in such situations. Even when we flew to South Vietnam in July 1969 for a few hours and visited the base at Long Binh where the soldiers were lined up to meet the President, he never asked one of them how the war was going, possibly because he feared they would tell him.

I had been tipped off on the Nixon secret trip to Vietnam and UPI had a big beat on the story. We were able to alert our Saigon bureau to man the barricades for a Presidential visit. During the fast-moving tightly-guarded five-hour trip, Mrs. Nixon was praised by Madame Nguyen Van Thieu, wife of the South Vietnamese President, for "disregarding the dangers to come here. She and her husband have intensified our morale by coming here."

"I was protected," said Mrs. Nixon simply. And she was, by bomb demolition squads and jeep-loads of rifle-carrying soldiers. During a tea party at the Presidential Palace, the Vietnamese VIP ladies told Mrs. Nixon how much they missed their children but said they had sent them away to school "because of the danger."

"Did the women talk about peace?" we asked. "No, I guess the men did," she answered. She avoided references to the deprivations of war. We were constantly ringed by convoys and troops and we knew men were dying in the bush. The atmosphere of safety seemed incongruous.

At Nixon's first press conference as President I had asked him to elaborate on his peace plan. Lyndon B. Johnson, who had grappled unsuccessfully with the burning dilemma of war and peace in Vietnam and was watching the televised conference back at his Texas ranch, told friends: "Helen asked a good question."

Nixon's strategy was to get out of Vietnam "in an honorable way," but it took a lot longer than the country expected. He followed the groundwork already laid by Johnson, who had spoken of a Vietnamization program that would gradually turn the war over to the South Vietnamese to defend themselves. Once he was in the White House, Vietnam became "Nixon's war" and as he rallied a "silent majority" to stand with him, he chose to ignore the reviving peace movement.

I remember walking into the Oval Office in the fall of 1969 as a half-million anti-Vietnam War protesters were staging a peaceful "moratorium" on the ellipse behind the White House. I was in the "pool" of reporters and photographers who were permitted in for a couple of minutes for picture-taking. In a statement that was obviously intended for us to hear, Nixon raised his voice and told his visitors pointedly: "I'm going to watch football this afternoon."

Nixon was signaling his lack of concern over the demonstrations, but I thought the remark rather bizarre at the time. A few years later I was to hear President Ford discuss "soccer" with a caller at the height of the crisis over the Cambodian seizure of the American merchant ship *Mayaguez* in the spring of 1975.

Nixon, like other Presidents before him, liked to view himself as the coolest man in the room. Nixon thought of himself as being tough and able to withstand the struggle, no matter what. He spoke often of the Quaker philosophy of "peace at the center." But his personal behavior did not indicate that he was unflappable or really had peace of mind. When he made the stunning decision to invade Cambodia in May 1970, he obviously did not realize that it would tear the country apart. It caught us all by surprise and was to heighten the activity of the peace movement that had quieted down during the early months of his Presidency.

I got to bed very late the night after Nixon announced the "incursion" into Cambodia had already begun and was roused around 7:00 A.M. by my office asking me to get to the White House in a hurry because Nixon was going to the Pentagon for a briefing. I dashed out of my apartment minus makeup and grabbed a cab to the White House, getting there just before the motorcade began to move. The others in the pool looked equally disreputable. The newsmen, apparently, had not had time to shave.

Nixon had only had a few hours sleep himself. He wanted reassurance from the generals that at last the headquarters of the insurgents, COSVN, would be smashed. While he was being briefed in a chalk talk by the military, we waited in the corridors and moved outside just ahead of him as he was leaving. Nixon stopped to talk informally to a group of Pentagon workers who had waited to see him. When a young woman complimented him on his speech of the night before, her kind words touched a human chord in him, and he poured out his response: "When it got down to the conclusion, then you say, well, the usual thing, you ask for support for the President and all that guff. Then you finally think of those kids out there. I say kids. I've seen them. They're the greatest.

"You know, you see these bums, you know, blowing up the campuses. Listen, the boys on the college campuses today are the luckiest people in the world—going to the greatest universities— and here they are burning up the books, storming around about this issue. I mean—you name it. Get rid of the war and there'll be another one.

"And then, out there, we got kids who are just doing their duty and I've seen them: They stand tall and they're proud."

He had dark circles under his eyes, and he looked like a man in a daze. I felt that he was beseeching that small crowd for support to offset the burgeoning charges that antiwar groups were already mounting.

A couple of days later, four students were killed during a protest demonstration at Kent State University in Ohio, and the White House issued a callous statement that "this is what happens" when protests get out of hand. This so jarred the public and some White House staffers that Nixon's press office felt compelled to put out a more compassionate revised version.

A week later, in a televised news conference, Nixon paid tribute to my friend and mentor, Merriman Smith, who had committed suicide in a deep depression a few weeks before. I worked late that evening and went to an Italian restaurant in the early morning hours to hash over with friends the shocking events of the past two weeks, and missed one telephone call from the President. Nixon called thirty-eight people that evening including two calls to my home, I found later from his logs, after his news conference.

I was in bed and still wide awake at 3:45 A.M. when the telephone rang again. The White House signal board operator was on the line announcing a call from the President. I still do not know why I did not think it unusual to be getting a call from the President at that hour, but then those were unusual days. When Nixon got on the line I thanked him for the nice things he had said about Smitty. We talked a while, and Nixon said something about "a bomb here or there." Clearly he was disturbed about his Cambodian action and the nation's reaction. A mass march on Washington, D.C., was underway and students were pouring in from all over the country.

After Nixon hung up, I called my office and dozed off, not knowing until I got to the White House a few hours later that Nixon, after ending our conversation, had summoned his startled valet, Manolo Sanchez, who in turn alerted the Secret Service, and they all drove to the Lincoln Memorial.

At the Lincoln Memorial, Nixon stood on the steps as dawn was breaking and rapped with several hippie students. He told them of Churchill and his decisive leadership in World War II ("we will fight them on the beaches") in contrast to the appeasement policies of Neville Chamberlain. He tried to explain why it was necessary to fight North Vietnam's aggression against her neighbor.

He weathered that crisis, but more and more like LBJ, he preferred to withdraw to the shelter of the White House, to avoid hostile encounters with protesters. Candlelight vigils became commonplace as the White House was picketed day and night. When massive picketing in front of the White House was prohibited, demonstrators were moved across the street to Lafayette Park. From the Watergate testimony we now know how the protesters upset Nixon. One man with an antiwar placard so disturbed Nixon that one of his aides offered to go across the street and beat him up. They settled for getting the picket to move along to a spot where he, the President, would not see him.

My one other personal telephone call from the President came out of the blue on a Sunday afternoon when I was in the press room after covering worship services in the East Room. It was at a time when a Middle East ceasefire had expired. (A couple of years later the October 1973 Arab-Israeli War broke out.) Nixon told me that he was optimistic that the United States and the Soviet Union would be able to exert enough influence to restrain both sides. "Neither side will gain and both will lose" if hostilities resumed. His prediction that the ceasefire would hold was correct at that time.

Although Nixon's National Security Affairs Advisor, Henry A. Kissinger, became identified with the historic diplomatic breakthrough with China and détente with the Soviet Union, Nixon was the innovator and it was his policies that Kissinger implemented. Both Nixon and Kissinger seemed to equate diplomacy with secrecy. They went to elaborate lengths to cover their tracks and to keep all policy planning under wraps. The bold stroke of reopening relations with Red China was accomplished in total secrecy. The news, when it was announced, electrified the world and sent shock waves through our Asian allies, Japan and Taiwan.

I was in the White House press room in Laguna Beach, California, when we suddenly got word that the President was flying to Burbank, a suburb of Los Angeles, to broadcast a nationwide address from a television studio. As we sped down the highway to pick up a press helicopter to accompany Nixon on the trip, we speculated that the announcement would probably concern some new development in Vietnam. When I saw Nixon getting off the "chopper" with Kissinger, I knew it was going to be a "good news" announcement. He was smiling broadly, Under his arm was a red folder with his speech typed in huge block letters for easy reading.

We were getting "vibes" that this would be a big one. The news of the China visit was a bombshell. When Nixon emerged from the studio he looked elated. A crowd had gathered and he shook hands and basked in their praise. We were sure that he had made a popular move and that people now welcomed a friendly gesture toward mainland China.

We motored to Perrino's Restaurant, an elegant dining spot in Los Angeles, and Nixon, Kissinger, Haldeman, and Ehrlichman celebrated their diplomatic victory with a gourmet meal and a $40 bottle of Chateau LaFite Rothschild. Reporters sat in a booth some distance away, but kept an eye on the Presidential party. We also ordered an expensive continental dinner but had to devour it quickly when it arrived about the time Nixon was preparing to leave. White House Deputy Press Aide Bruce Whelihan got stuck with a whopping bill as we barged our way out of the restaurant when we got the signal to get back to our cars.

On the trip to China in February 1972, we were allowed to be much more subjective than in all our years of newspaper reporting. Both my bosses, Julius Frandsen and Grant Dillman, taking heed

President Truman and the author outside the White House on one of his famous walks. (*UPI*)

Jackie Kennedy and John-John coming
from church, Helen Thomas at left.
(*White House photograph*)

President Kennedy teasing Helen Thomas in the Rose Garden in 1961
after she lampooned Jackie at the Women's National Press Club show;
the inscription reads "For Helen Thomas—with admiration and warm
regards, John Kennedy." (*White House photograph*)

In the Oval Office. ABOVE: President Kennedy with Helen Thomas and others. BELOW: President Johnson and Helen Thomas; the inscription reads "To Helen with affection, Lyndon B. Johnson." (*White House photographs*)

To Helen
with affection
Lyndon B. Johnson

LEFT: Luci's baby, Patrick Nugent, playing with the author's type-writer on Air Force One. (*UPI*) RIGHT: Helen Thomas bending the President's ear. (*UPI*)

LBJ and his grandson, Patrick Nugent, greeting the author; the inscription reads "To God Mother Helen. With love from both us—Lyndon B. Johnson." (*White House photograph*)

Tricia Nixon at the wedding shower at
the White House given for her by
Helen Thomas and other reporters.
(*White House photograph*)

Mrs. Nixon greeting a friend. (*UPI*)

ABOVE: At a White House party for AP's Douglas B. Cornell, the Nixons surprise the author and her fiancé by announcing their engagement. (*White House photograph*) BELOW: Mr. and Mrs. Cornell after their wedding, with Martha Mitchell. (*UPI*)

With Secretary of State
Henry Kissinger. (*UPI*)

President Ford on the run to escape reporters' questions; Helen
Thomas at left. (*UPI*)

President and Mrs. Ford with Helen Thomas; the inscription reads "To Helen Thomas, with congratulations on your superb professionalism and total integrity and with appreciation for your friendship. Best wishes. Jerry Ford. P.S. *What* a photo! J." (*White House photograph*)

from Ziegler that we would be getting little substantive news out of China until the final communiqué, told me to concentrate on the human interest stories—to tell the American people what Communist China was like after a twenty-year hiatus in relations with the United States.

I will always remember the press plane on which I flew into Peking in February 1972 as a flying library. I had never before seen reporters, including myself, on such flights immersed in piles of books and abstaining from booze. All of us were determined to bone up so that we would not fly completely blind on such a momentous story. Wearing a heavy fur-collared storm coat, I was one of the first off the press plane. The Chinese had limited our number to eighty-seven and we were handpicked by Nixon. I was sympathetic with those who could not make the trip and I felt helpless because of the restrictions. There were three women on the trip, NBC-TV's Barbara Walters, Fay Wells of Storer Broadcasting Company, and myself.

Everywhere we went on the trip Mao sayings were emblazoned on billboards. Many of my colleagues had managed to memorize some of the sayings in the little red book of Mao's thoughts. But I must say I was startled when Nixon not only recited Mao in his toast in the Great Hall of the People, but used one of Mao's expressions in speeches later at the White House. Nixon's favorite among the Mao sayings was: "So many deeds cry out to be done, seize the day, seize the hour."

Met by Chou En-lai, the wise statesman and China's Premier, Nixon rode into Peking in a limousine with lace curtains on the windows hiding him from public view. I trailed them in the press motorcade, feeling as alien as if I had landed on the moon. Few people were about, and those that were either turned their heads or slowed their bicycles as we passed. Nixon in Peking was at times like a little boy, wide-eyed in wonderment, hardly able to hide a look of triumph.

I must say I never thought I would see the day when I would be sitting around with friendly Chinese communist revolutionaries drinking to the health of Mao Tse-tung. The trip was a cultural shock for all of us. Our hotel rooms were YWCA-style, spare but with a comfortable chair and a desk. On the desk were Chinese stamps, a painted canister of tea, a thermos of hot water, fresh fruits, and a dish of chocolate and hard candy. I dropped my bag and checked into the press room at the Hotel of the Nationalities. Afterward we were to pick up Nixon's motorcade for the start of his talks with Chou, but we waited and waited. No Nixon. Much later we were told that Nixon had slipped off for a secret meeting with Mao at the villa of the Chinese revolutionary leader at the edge of the Forbidden City.

The sensational Nixon-Mao meeting was a galvanizing ingredient for the historic journey. Nixon's top staff members were euphoric. From any standpoint, Nixon had scored a diplomatic coup of far-reaching dimensions. He also won the admiration of Americans, who want their Presidents to go that extra mile for peace. I remember how struck I was by the cleanliness of Peking and its puritanical environment. I carried tangerine peelings around in my bag for three days, not wanting to be a litterbug in such pristine surroundings but not knowing where to discard the debris.

We were in never-never land. There was no crime, no muggers, no beggars, and no tipping. One newsman who tried to jettison his thermal underwear in a wastebasket in his room kept getting his longjohns back, laundered.

The Chinese men and women marveled at the pace we set, and how hard reporters worked on two hours' sleep at night. I think they viewed the operations of the press corps as a very strange exercise.

In the evenings, we were always invited to the banquets in the Great Hall, to dine on unforgettable delicacies and down successive Mao Tais, a lethal Chinese drink, for the frequent "Gambei" toasts. "The Chinese version of white lightning," we called it. Everyone quickly got in the spirit of the new relationship.

Throughout the China trip, Nixon and his staff seemed to be posing. Certainly they were playing to mass television audiences back in the states. Ziegler's amateur stage managing attempts reached new heights when we toured the Great Wall with President and Mrs. Nixon. While we loitered outside a tea house where the

Nixons and their hosts were relaxing, Ziegler came up to the "pool" and prompted us: "If you ask the President how he likes the Great Wall, he will be prepared to answer."

Programmed as we were, this was viewed as a golden opportunity. At last one could speak to the President we had been covering from afar. One correspondent, Charles Bailey of the *Minneapolis Star*, was selected to put the big question to the President: "How do you like the Great Wall, Mr. President?"

Lifting his eyes toward the magnificent sight, Nixon recited: "I must say that the Great Wall is a great wall."

Reporters began to grow restive over the official news blackout. We were kept occupied visiting the People's Commune, the People's Liberation Army camp, and socializing at banquets with Nixon and Chou En-lai in the evening. But secrecy shrouded the talks. Later, Nixon semi-apologized to us at a gathering at his guest house, saying that it was the price we had to pay because of the delicacy of the negotiations.

The Chinese were true to their word about freedom of the press. There was absolutely no censorship. I am sure that dealing with a free press was an eye-opener for them. We would send our cable copy at ten cents a word, and they did count the words. Telephone calls were $14 for the first three minutes. I ran up an astronomical bill, but no one complained. The story was the thing.

We saw Nixon and Chou only for picture-taking sessions or when they marched around the mammoth banquet table, bowing and clinking their glasses of Mao Tai. Once when Chou asked reporters if they were having a good time, Nixon in an off-stage whisper said: "More than they deserve."

When we were in a government guest house to witness the start of a meeting between Chou and Nixon, the Chinese Premier urged photographers to take more pictures of Nixon. "If they do take them, they will only burn them," Nixon said with a bitter smile. It was a reflection of his growing resentment of the press.

The trip was a diplomatic coup for the President, and Mrs. Nixon also scored a personal triumph in China.

Nixon was sequestered in meetings, so Mrs. Nixon led the way for an entourage of correspondents. The three women correspondents on this breakthrough trip went along and when my male colleagues found that the First Lady was going to exotic places, they tagged along, too. Walter Cronkite, William Buckley, and James Michener were among those in our group.

In her magnificent beaver-fur-lined red coat, strikingly proper for color television, Pat Nixon was seen by millions of Americans watching the exciting saga. She was in her glory as we visited the Great Wall, the Forbidden City, and lovely Hangchow. I saw Chou En-lai paying a lot of attention to her and teased her about it. I remember following her on a shopping spree in Peking. When she picked up silk beige pajamas for her husband, her eyes twinkled and she asked if I was going to buy a gift for Doug. I was too busy covering her shopping then to do my own, but later I did buy Doug some silk scarves and pajamas.

When we went to one of the communes, Mrs. Nixon commented on her own childhood on a farm. As we looked into a pigpen, she said, "I wonder what kind of pigs they are." "Male chauvinist, of course," I wisecracked. She was startled, but everybody guffawed except the Chinese, who were not au courant with women's lib jargon.

When Chou escorted the Nixons on a tour of an enchanting park at West Lake in Hangchow, he stopped in front of a cage of lovebirds. When the birds entwined their necks and beaks in embraces, Chou began to giggle and looked at Mrs. Nixon, somewhat embarrassed.

She broke the awkward moment, "Lovey Dovey," she said, with a grin.

So she kept her remarks on the light side, but then she always shied away from political observations on foreign trips.

On the long trip home from China in Air Force One, we were all exhausted. It was Kissinger's habit to stroll to the back of the plane, where the press sat, to chat for a while. His insights were fascinating but were always "on background" and we would have to attribute them to a "high-ranking American official."

After every foreign trip I took with Nixon and Kissinger, I would pose one question to Kissinger: "Were there any secret agreements?" With an expression I interpreted as "how can you ask such things," Kissinger would give his absolute assurance that there were no secret understandings, that nothing would be kept from the American people.

The first summit trip to Moscow in 1972 also had mystifying overtones. The Russian people were kept blocks away from the Nixon motorcade. If ever I saw a government operate in fear of its people, it was in Moscow. The Nixons were well aware that the Soviet leaders were not about to have admiring, or even for that matter, curious crowds turning out on the streets near the Kremlin to see the American President. In Leningrad, it was a different story, and the natives were less submissive. Held back by police at intersections of the main boulevards, they strained to get a look at the capitalist visitors.

The Nixons were guests at the Kremlin. The President's suite of several rooms was worthy of a Czar. Nixon and Soviet Communist Party Leader Leonid S. Brezhnev hit it off and the days and nights during nearly a week-long visit were completely filled. One night, as the Nixons sat in the box with the Brezhnevs at the magnificent red-and-gold Bolshoi Theatre, and I was in an orchestra seat, the wife of an Italian newspaperman shouted from high in the gallery, "FREE-DOM FOR VIETNAM." The Russian secret police, with whom the reporters had many confrontations during the trip, rushed up and grabbed her. I jumped from my seat to try to find a telephone to call in the story. I was very concerned about the woman, who was forced to leave the country the next day.

Sometimes the U.S. Secret Service agents accompanying the President and the members of the press would bark at each other and I know the agents thought of me as an enfant terrible. But in the Soviet Union, where the agents were bullied as much as the press by the KGB, we had that feeling of comrades-in-arms. We were all in it together. When our plane lifted from Moscow airport we applauded in relief.

Twice I was on planes in the Soviet Union which developed engine trouble. During the 1972 summit I was one of the two reporters permitted to fly with Nixon and Brezhnev. The plane sat on the ground for a long time before a stream of Soviet dignitaries got aboard with their apologies over the engine trouble. An embarrassed Brezhnev and Nixon, along with the pool, then boarded Air Force One, which was standing by.

Nixon's Press Secretary, Ronald Ziegler, demonstrated to us that Nixon had the capability of instant communications both in Russia and China with a highly classified telephone apparatus he carried in a briefcase. Unexpected information sometimes came to the press from the walkie talkies carried by White House staffers and Secret Service agents, who talk into their sleeves where their microphones are hidden. Reporters sometimes picked up their messages. On a trip to Brussels in June 1974, when Nixon's Watergate troubles were reaching their crescendo, I was sitting in a "pool" car in front of the American embassy when I overheard a conversation concerning a mysterious "Mr. Christopher."

A voice came over the radio: "How shall we play it with the press?" It was decided that a "Mr. Christopher" should be secretly let in through the back door of the Brussels Hilton Hotel. When we later asked Ziegler: "Who is Mr. Christopher?" he blanched. Later he told us it was Charles G. ("Bebe") Rebozo of Key Biscayne, Florida, Nixon's best friend, who had been traveling in Spain and had just happened to come by.

The complexity of Nixon's personality was a constant source of debate in the press room, as we probed his psyche to find out what made him tick. We had theories galore.

But, I for one, believed that few of us understood what really motivated him. Certainly his need to demonstrate strength over weakness, his constant reiteration that the United States "has to be No. One" in the world were not difficult to analyze. He had his bedroom decorated in red, white, and blue, with the spread on his four-poster bed matching the drapes. On the wall was the painting, Hassam's *Flag Day*. From the moment he assumed the Presidency, Nixon wore a small American flag in his lapel. So did his button-downed staffers who all copied "The Boss." The need to win also ran through his speeches. I remember one late summer afternoon when the "pool" was summoned to go with Nixon to the Redskins' football practice. After the players put on a calisthenics show for him and romped like children around the President, Nixon delivered a brief lecture on how "important it is to win."

Oftentimes, we attributed this obsession with victory back to the young Nixon at Whittier College in California who had sat on the bench too long at football games before he went on to Duke University Law School. He never made the first team, but he tried hard.

Nixon loved to watch sports; in fact, he watched television only to see football or baseball games. He could not bear to watch replays of his own speeches or news conferences. When he moved into the Oval Office, he promptly had Johnson's console of three TV sets removed, along with the UPI and AP tickers, and pulled out all the rest of the Johnsonian gadgetry in the Presidential bedroom, including push buttons to open the windows.

Nixon's image of himself was aptly described in his interview with AP's Saul Pett in January 1973, when he said: "I believe in the battle, whether it's the battle of a campaign or the battle of this office, which is a continuous battle. It's always there wherever you go. I, perhaps, carry it more than others because that's my way." After the battle, he experienced a let-down feeling.

It was acutely painful for Nixon to present the Metal of Honor to the parents of American soldiers who had died in Vietnam. Once he was photographed smiling as a mother was crying. The news shots of that episode upset him and the White House. Actually, he was very sensitive and the smile was a reflection of his nervousness and awkwardness at that emotional moment. After that incident the press was barred from covering such events, and most ceremonies of that kind were assigned to Vice President Spiro T. Agnew.

Nixon staffers grew more and more wary of encounters with critical outsiders.

After Nixon ordered the B-52 round-the-clock carpet bombing of North Vietnam during Christmas 1972, he went into hiding. He made no public appearances for about three weeks and skipped Christmas worship services while the White House remained silent on the subject amid worldwide criticism.

But not all public encounters were in the President's control. When nineteen-year-old Debra Sweet of Chicago came to the White House to accept the "Young American Medal" for organizing a thirty-mile march by high school students to raise money for American Indians and for earthquake victims in Nicaragua, Debra told him softly:

"Mr. President, I won't believe you're sincere about this award until you get us out of the war."

Nixon mumbled something about, "We're doing the best we can," and sped up the ceremony. He was furious with his chief photographer, Ollie Atkins, for arranging for a group picture of himself with Debra and her parents.

At times, Nixon's antipathy toward the press came through even in his attempts at humor. Once, with a horde of reporters and cameramen, I walked into the Cabinet Room near the Oval Office for a picture-taking session of Nixon and his Cabinet. Nixon looked up at us with a grin and said, "It's purely coincidental that we're talking about pollution when the press walks in."

Long before the growing crises of the acceleration of the war in Vietnam and Watergate, I recall happier times when I was one of the few reporters invited for a New Year's Eve drink in Nixon's hideaway office. He boasted that he mixed the world's finest martini and offered his "secret formula": six parts gin to one part vermouth. As he sipped a glass of white wine, and we, his potent martinis, we asked if he believed in the polls, which were then favorable. Nixon replied that he did not keep close tabs on polls, that it was like "taking your temperature every day," he said.

Nixon wanted to win big in 1972, and he was determined to leave no stone unturned to do it. The trips to China and Russia were part of the strategy.

I was covering Nixon while he was at Key Biscayne, Florida, the weekend of June 17, 1972, when members of the Committee to Reelect the President broke into the Democratic National Committee headquarters at the Watergate. At the news briefing on Saturday, June 18, White House Press Secretary Ronald Ziegler described the break-in to us as a "third-rate burglary" and denied any White House involvement. Later, I could see the pattern of his programmed denials every time there was a new development in the Watergate affair.

Among other things, Ziegler said that E. Howard Hunt and G. Gordon Liddy, the break-in henchmen, had left the White House payroll as consultants with an investigative unit working on "declassification" of top secret documents, in early March. Actually, I later learned that in June, White House telephone directories still carried their names and when this was discovered the directories were quickly grabbed up and shredded.

We failed to confront Nixon with the burning questions of Watergate during the election campaign for several reasons. He held very few news conferences and Ziegler blocked reporters from any contact with Nixon at airfields and other public places. Nixon was as protected as an imperial monarch. Also, we had been focusing on the Vietnam peace negotiations.

At San Clemente in front of his villa, "La Casa Pacifica," Nixon told a news conference that, based on an investigation conducted at his direction by White House counsel John Dean, he could state "categorically" that "no one in this Administration, presently employed, was involved in this very bizarre incident."

Only after we got back to the press room at the Surf and Sand Hotel in Laguna Beach and read the transcript of the conference more closely did we notice his phrase "presently employed."

In April 1972, Ziegler came into the press room and told the reporters that his statements on Watergate during the ten previous months were no longer operative.

"You mean they are *in*operative?" he was asked.

"Yes," said Ziegler, whose credibility was forever shattered after that.

On November 7, 1972, Nixon won a second term and vanquished Senator George McGovern in the greatest landslide in United States history. McGovern had campaigned on the theme that the Nixon administration was "the most corrupt in history," but the public believed that to be preposterous.

As I watched in the White House press room, the news ticker showed one state after another—49 in all—going to Nixon. Nixon had finally won an overwhelming mandate. But I was struck more by the atmosphere in the Executive Mansion that night. It was without joy.

There was no White House celebration; the air was somber.

There was no unconstrained rejoicing among staff members. Nixon was upstairs in the Lincoln sitting room in the family quarters, alone and nursing a toothache. Every once in a while, members of the family would bring him the latest returns.

For the victory statement, the Nixon family went to the hotel where the Republican National Committee was celebrating. Nixon called on Americans to put aside politics and "to get on with the great tasks that lie before us."

The following morning at 8:30, Nixon summoned his Cabinet, most of whom had acted as his surrogates on the campaign trail, making speeches two and three times a week, and he thanked them. Then he turned the meeting over to Haldeman who demanded their resignations by nightfall. "You're all a bunch of burned out volcanoes," he told them. The same message was delivered to about 2,000 federal department and agency heads, some of them new appointees who had just relocated in Washington and had bought new homes. They were shaken and bitter.

Nixon, wanting to tighten his control over the federal bureaucracy, a feat that had eluded him during his first term, decided to create a Super-Cabinet. He seeded his White House aides into top or number two positions in agencies all over town, where they would be immediately responsive to conservative White House direction.

In an interview with Garnett Horner of the *Washington Star* at that time, Nixon likened the average American to a "child in the family" saying, "if you give him too much, you spoil him." But the average American had put him in office.

We would have thought that Nixon would be exhilarated after the electoral victory. He was not. He may have had a sense of doom. The first Watergate trials of the burglars were about to begin (in December). Perhaps he feared that the secrets of the White House could not be kept much longer. Or perhaps it was the familiar letdown after a crisis he had spoken of in his book, *Six Crises.* He always felt joy in the struggle but an anticlimax after the struggle was over. He was now a lame-duck President. Nixon became more and more isolated, more and more remote. After his reelection, Nixon put out word that he was going to spend much of his time at Camp David, the Presidential hideaway in the Maryland mountains.

Chapter 7

The Nixon White House

Until the summer of 1973, a year before Nixon's resignation, White House aides were still trying valiantly to create noteworthy parties that would build the President's reputation as a gracious host and benefactor of the arts. "Social events during the second Nixon administration should contribute strongly to establishing the President's place in history—to the way and to the atmosphere in which he will be remembered," said one last diehard memo for Haldeman from Ms. Winchester, Mrs. Nixon's social secretary, regarding future White House social plans.

Robert Goulet, Peggy Lee, Beverly Sills, Peter Nero, Pearl Bailey, Eugene List, the American Ballet Theater, the Modern Jazz Quartet, Al Hirt and his New Orleans Band, Roberta Peters, Rudolf Serkin, "The Fantasticks," The Young Saints (a multi-talented troupe from the ghettos of Los Angeles), the Harkness Ballet, the Folklorico Dance Company from the University of Guadalajara, and the Broadway musical *1776*—to mention but a few, came to the Nixons' parties.

Entertainers usually rehearse in the historic East Room before their performance before the President and his guests, and I don't think anything in show biz or politics produces more goose bumps than these White House "matinees." The rehearsals are usually staged before a large and appreciative audience of White House and military aides and other government workers who seldom get into a formal White House affair—plus, of course, a few White House reporters like myself who waltz in from the press room because we could interview the performer and enjoy the entertainment, in advance.

I've known of only one performer who showed total contempt for the press at the White House. And that, of course, was Frank Sinatra. Most entertainers appreciate the fact that reporters are there to record their White House appearance for the public and for posterity. And if they don't, their public relations people do. Sinatra (who does things his way), to the surprise of reporters was invited by the President to perform at his State Dinner for Prime Minister Andreotti of Italy. During the inaugural party months before, Sinatra had confronted columnist Maxine Cheshire at a Washington party and had hurled a barrage of obscenities at her because he didn't like a story she had written about his friendship with Agnew. He was persona non grata thereafter with many Washingtonians. But Nixon introduced him at the Andreotti dinner as an American institution, "akin to the top of the Washington Monument."

Other entertainers over the years have made guests and reporters alike feel welcome. Four artists from the White House marquee stand out in my mind as warm and masterful performers: Pearl Bailey, Sarah Vaughn, Beverly Sills, and Peggy Lee.

Pearl Bailey became a White House regular during the Nixon years and she and I formed a fond friendship with each other. Her appearances were always show-stoppers. Pearl has a genuine love for people and since her near-fatal heart attack she has tried to spread it around as much as possible. She brought out the best in President Nixon, who was always somewhat reserved at formal White House parties, when she had him accompany her on the piano during the dinner for Chancellor and Mrs. Willy Brandt of Germany. Later, hamming it up for the audience, she admired one of the gold chairs in the East Room and pretended she was going to walk away with it. Nixon wound up giving her the chair. I'm sure no other performer ever walked out of the White House with a piece of the President's furniture tucked under her arm.

Pearl performed at the White House again early in the Gerald Ford administration at the President's dinner for the nation's Governors. On this occasion I saw her walk over to Governor George Wallace, lean down over his wheelchair and kiss him on the cheek. It was apparent they liked each other. The black singer-actress and the crippled Southern segregationist Governor were both showing that they could bridge the gap. Pearl and I both bent over the Governor's wheelchair. "Helen, Ya Habibe!" Pearl exclaimed, tossing a few Arabic words at me. "What the hell are you doing down here?"

What I was doing down there was the ultimate in eavesdropping. I wanted to hear what the Governor said to the singer, and it was "Say a prayer for me." "I'll do that," Pearl promised. When Pearl danced with President Ford later, the several hundred guests in the East Room gathered round for the performance. Pearl kicked up her heels as if she was back in *Hello Dolly* while the President did his old dependable 1940s two-step—with all the style and enthusiasm he could muster. The audience of VIP guests clapped in tempo.

Even President Nixon's comparatively conservative parties occasionally took on a festive flavor. When Duke Ellington came to dinner at the White House on his seventieth birthday, he—like Pearl—loosened things up by getting Nixon to play the piano, and the President loved it.

Perhaps it was mere bravado, but Nixon also seemed to be in his glory at the State Dinner for Soviet party leader Leonid I. Brezhnev. Held in June of 1973, it was one of the last major White House social functions of the Nixon era. Watching President Nixon at this party, I felt that he was clinging to some last high hope that his association with the Russian leader would so illuminate his success in the foreign policy field that the public would forgive and forget Watergate.

Brezhnev played his part to the hilt. A big, jovial chain-smoker, Brezhnev was in his element at a later glittering social occasion. For Nixon's black tie dinner, he wore a dark suit decorated with two shiny medals that dangled from a red ribbon pinned to the jacket. I asked Secretary-General Brezhnev to tell me about his medals, and he answered proudly, albeit cryptically, "I have a right to wear these."

I remember a kaleidoscope of scenes from the White House parties, I recall how Beverly Sills recovered when the strap on her formal broke as she was singing for President Nixon and some 200 guests in the East Room. With one graceful gesture, she swept her cape over her bare shoulder and never missed a note. I remember a Washington society reporter who addressed the black man next to her when she spotted a napkin on the floor of the State Dining Room. "Why don't you pick that up?" she asked. The man she had addressed was the ambassador from Ghana and a shock wave spread through the room as the story made the rounds. I remember Christina Ford, dancing so energetically that I thought she would twist right out of her lovely strapless white sheath. And Spiro Agnew fending off reporters at a White House reception in his darkest days while his wife, Judy, looked on, the strain reflected in her face.

One of the most memorable toasts I heard was given by the seventy-five-year-old Duke of Windsor, who surrendered the British throne to marry "the woman I love." At the end of a white tie dinner given by the President in honor of the Duke and his seventy-three-year-old wife, the former king delivered this tender toast: "I have had the good fortune to have a wonderful American girl consent to marry me. I have had thirty years of loving care, devotion, and companionship—something I have cherished above all else."

Late in the Nixon years, in May 1973, a magnificent dinner was held in the White House to honor the 600 recently returned Vietnam prisoners of war and their wives. Nixon was swept up in The-Boys-Are-Back victory celebration, so exhilarated that he threw open the entire mansion—even the family sanctum—to guests during the cocktail hour. The POWs, restored to health and readjusting to American life, were awed to be in the White House, the symbol of the nation they had suffered for, and their wives were lovely in new specially-bought gowns and carefully coifed hairdos.

Bob Hope, John Wayne, Edgar Bergen, Phyllis Diller, Roy Acuff, Joey Heatherton, Jimmy Stewart, Sammy Davis, Jr., Les Brown and his Orchestra, among others, entertained and hailed the heroes.

Dinner was served outdoors in an enormous yellow-and-white striped tent at organdy-covered round tables, decorated with bouquets of fresh flowers. The Nixons had pulled out all the stops to make it a memorable evening. They were served All-American roast beef, vegetables, and apple pie. It had rained the previous day and we were all ankle-deep in mud. I was glad I had worn old shoes. But no one minded too much except for the waiters who stepped carefully with the big silver platters in hand.

The POWs and their wives were open and demonstrative in their adulation of President Nixon and members of his administration, particularly Secretary of State Henry Kissinger. There was much hugging, kissing, and back-patting; everyone present was caught up in a spirit of celebration and gratitude. The guests of honor clearly gave the President and his Secretary of State personal credit for their freedom. Nixon and Kissinger, plagued by a number of mounting crises, loved being cast as heroes, and were more relaxed and casual than they usually were with outsiders.

I was caught up myself by the drama and meaning of the night. I was also aware of the other news of the day—as a reporter must be when assigned to a White House party. The Watergate scandal was breaking wide open and prominent in the headlines that day was a story that Kissinger had turned over to the FBI a list of his top aides who were suspected of leaking government secrets to reporters.

When I saw Kissinger early in the evening, surrounded by a group of admiring POW wives, I had to approach him. At his side was Helmut Sonnenfeldt, one of his closest friends and one of his top assistants on the National Security Council. Kissinger had submitted Sonnenfeldt's name to the FBI, as we had just learned.

"Oh, I see you speak to those you wiretap," I said to the Secretary of State.

Kissinger's face turned red; he glared at me as though I had committed the ultimate sacrilege, and he blustered, "Can't we have one night of peace?"

I tried to tease him out of his tantrum and he was soon in high spirits again, exuding charm and affability. The wiretapping issue, I later realized, struck his most sensitive nerve. I had kibitzed with him many times before and he seemed to enjoy the badinage. Further, he knew, as every seasoned Washington politician knows, that the conversation at a White House party will almost certainly center on the nuances and ramifications behind the day's headlines. A party at the President's house serves a multitude of purposes. It is often a more relaxed extension of the conference table, as well as an exercise in communications. It brings together decision- and policy-makers and other VIPs and socialites and allows them to exchange views and information, along with snippets of local and international gossip, in an elegant, convivial social setting.

I never hesitate to approach a guest at a White House party with a reasonable question or quip when the opportunity presents itself. I wouldn't be a worthy newsperson if I didn't because some of the best features and news stories break when the President is entertaining. Further, I believe the press should cover every official White House function as a matter of routine so that the public can share vicariously in these historic events. The White House, after all, belongs to the people. That's what President Kennedy and each of his successors always told us.

The hosts, guests, and entertainers come to a White House party to be seen—and quite often to be quoted, to the chagrin of most Presidents, their families, and their aides. But the purpose of a White House party is never fully served unless reporters are there to cover it. We are an irritating but necessary element. The White House is loath to invite us because it is afraid we won't behave, but its concern is always offset by a desire to see the party reported in the papers the following day.

There are unwritten rules covering a White House social function we try to follow. When the champagne is passed, I sip lightly. If a guest says, as many guests do, "Now, this is off-the-record, Helen," I abide by that. I also carry my notebook because I want guests to know I am a reporter. I don't think it is fair to sneak up and talk to a guest anonymously. In laying down the ground rules for our party behavior Connie Stuart, Mrs. Nixon's former press secretary, once teasingly accused us of carrying tape recorders in our bosoms.

Every President regards White House entertainment as a reflection of his administration and culls newspaper columns for reaction to his fetes, but none was more aware of this than Nixon. By 1969, the second Nixon year, top Presidential aides like Haldeman, Ziegler, and Dwight Chapin, the Deputy Assistant to the President —as well as the President himself—were heavily involved in arrangements for White House social functions. They were concerned with rituals, entertainment, guest lists, food, wines, and music.

A memo from Constance Stuart to Lucy Winchester of November 18, 1969, indicated that RMN was becoming a most anxious host: ". . . the President believes that the guest list for the Bob Hope show should be developed in conjunction with Ambassador Mosbacher (Emil Mosbacher, Jr., then chief of protocol) and Peter Flanigan (an assistant to the President) in order to get swinging people," Ms. Stuart reported. "He wants swinging people for this Evening at the White House. Can do? The President and Bob Haldeman also believe Carol Harford and Nancy Hanks (of the Arts Endowment) are a source of artsy-craftsy people for evenings at the White House. . . ."

Plans for press coverage of White House parties were of great concern to Haldeman who always seemed to fear that we reporters would commit some grievous social faux pas. He stood, arms crossed like a bouncer, and glared at us as if we were potential rowdies. Once he suggested that we cover a State Dinner while standing behind velvet stanchions in the foyer of the first floor. Mrs. Nixon vetoed the suggestion.

Haldeman's interest in White House entertainment extended to the thorny question of who was to foot the bills, always one of Washington's better-kept secrets. Congress gives the President an entertainment allowance each year, but this is embellished in many ways. Entertainers at White House parties always donate their talents; they are *never* paid. At a State Dinner, the State Department picks up much of the tab for food and drink. The military flourishes at every public and private White House party, and the music provided by service bands is paid for by the Pentagon. The handsome young military social aides who act as escorts at White House functions are also there, courtesy of the armed services.

A memo to Dwight Chapin from Constance Stuart, dated February 18, 1970, states:

In meeting with Bob Haldeman yesterday, we discussed the question of payment for dinners such as the William McChesney Martin dinner, the Hershey dinner, and the National Center for Voluntary Action dinner.

Where possible, we need to get the agency, the Department or the organization involved to pay for the dinner, rather than dip into the official White House entertainment account. The discussion as to "who pays" needs to be made at the time the dinner is scheduled. Bob suggests your office should be responsible for determining who will assume costs and negotiating this with the group involved.

Once the decision has been reached, would you please let me know so that I can inform Rex Stouten [then the chief usher] and fend off the ladies of the press when necessary.

These intrusions by the West Wing—the President's side— diminished the contributions of Mrs. Nixon and her aides to the White House social scene.

At these festivities Pat Nixon always looked impeccable and lovely in her white and pastel gowns. She never wore black. The Nixons, once they said good-bye to their honored guests, always left the party promptly for the family quarters upstairs. Pat would sometimes glance back wistfully. She loved to dance, but I don't think her husband danced with her at a White House party on more than two or three occasions. When she went upstairs to the family quarters she could still hear the band playing. I remembered how JFK and LBJ would sneak back to the party after the guests of honor had left. I think they were afraid they would miss something.

The President devised two new social events: Evenings of Entertainment and Religious Services at the White House. Under the first format, the Nixons were able to entertain, in one big gesture, some 300 persons who might never be candidates for a formal dinner. Guests for these Evenings at the White House arrived at 8:00 P.M., and were seated in the East Room for a performance by some noted artist or artists. President Nixon introduced the entertainers, without benefit of a microphone, speaking softly and almost reverently, and clasping his hands, somewhat unctuously. All Presidents are actors, but Nixon especially loved the role of master of ceremony. Drinks and a buffet dinner were served after the show.

The format for the religious service was similar. Guests, or worshippers, between 300 and 400 in number, assembled in the East Room on Sunday mornings and President Nixon introduced the minister, rabbi, or priest who was to conduct the service. After the services, guests were served coffee and pastries.

I covered nearly all the worship services. President Nixon wanted the White House to represent a spiritual rallying point for young people especially. The Secret Service was happy to be able to protect him inside the White House rather than in church. But I always felt that George and Martha Washington, whose full-length portraits dominate the East Room, were looking on questioningly, wondering, as I did, about the separation of church and state. When Teddy Roosevelt called the White House a "bully pulpit" this was hardly what he had in mind.

It was clear to me, from observation, that the services served a social and political as well as a spiritual purpose. My sense that President Nixon wanted the Sunday congregation to be composed of the "right" people was substantiated by a memo dated September 30, 1969, which H. R. Haldeman sent to Rose Mary Woods, the President's personal secretary:

The President still feels that we have too many non-VIPs at the Sunday worship service. His estimate is 40% non-VIP this past Sunday. I have no idea whether he is right or not. In any event, he wants the balance to be 80% VIP and no more than 20% non-VIP. Can we shift the list to that type of balance for future services?

Ms. Woods, never a great Haldeman admirer, appended an indignant and sarcastic note to the memo:

For my part, we will try but all I do is add the friends of the President—and when we don't know about the service until the middle of the week it is not easy to get the VIP friends.

Incidentally, the actual percentage for the Sunday in question was 72.11% VIP and 27.89% non-VIP. (That is counting the guests of Congressmen and Cabinet people as VIPs—because we have to.)

I always wondered who was represented by the eighty-nine-hundredths of one percent in Ms. Woods' calculations.

Another incident showed me just how closely guarded were the invitation lists to the Nixon worship services. It involved a Marine sergeant who was stationed at Camp David, the Presidential retreat in the Catoctin Mountains. The Marine Corps patrols Camp David and in those days the Corps provided wire service reporters with an "escort" whenever they headed for the duck blind. This was a

three-sided outdoor wooden enclosure, equipped with two telephones, for UPI and the AP, where we watched and waited, in all
kinds of weather, for the Presidential helicopters to arrive from
Washington. Doug Cornell and I struck up a slight speaking
acquaintance with one personable young sergeant who was our
frequent companion in the Camp David barricade. Obviously, he
had been ordered to keep quiet around reporters but he once
confided to Doug that he would like to attend a White House
religious service. The request seemed harmless enough and the next
day Doug made a call to the White House social office to see if an
invitation for the Marine could be arranged. The answer was a curt
"no" and the sergeant was shipped out. We never saw him again
although we were at Camp David often in future months. Doug felt
miserable about this unhappy outcome.

I covered the White House religious services in much the same
manner that I covered other White House events, and always gave
big play to the sermon. Most guests were approachable and
enjoyed being quoted, particularly John and Martha Mitchell, who
attended the services regularly. Norman Vincent Peale looked
uncomfortable but expressed his faith in the President when I
asked his views about the Watergate coverup, then rapidly
unraveling. I felt it was important to ask the widely-respected
clergyman and close Nixon friend to impart some of his philosophy
about this moral issue that was dividing the country.

Peale and evangelist Billy Graham were prominently featured
clergymen at the worship services. Graham, whom I first saw when
he played golf with President-elect Kennedy in Palm Beach,
Florida, then frequently with Lyndon B. Johnson, had an intimate
relationship with Nixon. Like comedian Bob Hope, who was a
friend of all the Presidents, he was a welcome White House visitor.

Ziegler used to reprimand me for asking questions of substance
during the post-worship coffee hour. "Don't ask me those questions
at a time like this," he said sternly. When veteran social reporter
Dorothy McCardle was barred from covering the service at
Christmas-time as well as other parties during the yuletide season, I
wrote a story about the ban. The ban was meant as a slap at
Dorothy's employer, the *Washington Post*, for its extensive and
relentless Watergate coverage. Dorothy, as it happened, had never

been assigned to the Watergate story. But that's not the point. White House aides had prevented a reporter from doing her job because her paper was uncovering a major political scandal. Other Presidents had put reporters in the doghouse by excluding them from the "pool" assigned to cover a particular party, but no social "ban" had been imposed in recent times against a newspaper in such blatant retaliation.

Ziegler called me at home after my piece ran on the UPI wire. He sounded excited and irritated. "Why didn't you touch base with me before you wrote that?" he asked. "You saw me at worship services."

"Because you told me not to discuss official business at the Sunday services," I answered, "and I could not track you down later."

Ziegler ignored my answer and said he had a statement. Three times he read a short, noncommittal blurb he had obviously just written, changing a word or a phrase with each reading. Then I heard him ask, "Is that all right, Bob?" Haldeman apparently had been listening in on an extension. The story, complete with Ziegler's statement, was printed in a number of papers and Dorothy was soon "reinstated" as a regular reporter at White House social functions. Mrs. Nixon had the grace to write her a note expressing her regrets over the incident.

The Nixon worship services were discontinued when the Watergate scandal began to overshadow everything else in Presidential politics—and so, ultimately, were all other social events at the White House. Watergate was taking its toll in breaking the spirit at the White House.

Oddly enough, Mrs. Nixon told me that the Nixons decided to hold worship services in the White House as a way of sharing the Executive Mansion with more people. There is no doubt that Mrs. Nixon viewed the White House as a home she could happily share with the American people. Sharing, she said, "is something that gives us great pleasure. We love this house. Everybody in America loves it. What people want to do most is to see the White House." She recalled that Leonard Firestone, a wealthy friend from Los Angeles, said he and his wife would rather come to a worship service than a State Dinner "because it's more intimate."

"I'm a very religious person," she said. "It isn't exactly the praying. I follow the golden rule. I taught it when I was young and I never lost it. I also have great faith and live a life based on this philosophy."

Mrs. Nixon always said she did not drink or smoke. Certainly she did not in public. I once saw a tray of sherry aperitifs being passed around. She reached out for a glass, saw the newswomen looking at her, and pulled her hand back. I wanted to say go ahead and take it. But she had been brought up in the old school that First Ladies have NO "bad" habits.

The White House took on a new elegance under Pat Nixon's tutelage. Visitors may always be grateful that she turned the lights back on after Johnson's era of frugal darkness. The decisions to add floodlights on the mansion at night and to keep the flag flying were her innovations. Inspired by the many palaces she had visited abroad, she also replaced the early American lighting in the Grand Hallway with shimmering crystal chandeliers. Many times I heard that she felt that she was never properly credited for the decorative changes she made in the White House.

When she knew her husband's chances of remaining in office were fading, she cancelled plans to order a new set of Lenox china with a cobalt blue-and-gold border and an eagle in the center. The design was a cross between the china purchased in the Harrison and Wilson administrations.

"Clem," she called Conger, the White House Curator, her voice tense and sad, "I think you'd better call off the porcelain. I don't think it's the time."

Conger later said, "It was very traumatic because we all loved and admired Mrs. Nixon." Conger had helped her refurbish the White House. He said it was "threadbare" when the Nixons moved in because Mrs. Johnson had been afraid to alter "Jackie's project."

A few months before Nixon resigned, the famous portrait of Lincoln by George P. Healy, which hung over the mantel of the State Dining Room was replaced with a landscape of the Hudson River in autumn. It was lovely but hardly as striking or as magnificent as the important painting of Lincoln. "It was too brooding," Conger explained. "The Nixons preferred a landscape in the dining room." He agreed that portraits were not proper for dining rooms. But one of President Ford's first moves was to bring the Lincoln portrait back to what I thought was its rightful place.

Mrs. Nixon had the family quarters painted a bright yellow and she had Lyndon Johnson's telephone removed from the dining room table. The Nixons felt that mealtime was not the time for official telephone calls. Nor, as mentioned earlier, did she enjoy the Revolutionary battle scenes on the antique wallpaper Mrs. Kennedy had chosen. But since the government had paid $12,000 for the paper, which was painstakingly removed from an historic room in Thurmont, Maryland, Mrs. Nixon dared not rip it out.

Early in February 1971, New York artist Aaron Shikler had completed the full-length, ethereal (some said eerie-looking) portrait of Mrs. Kennedy for the First Lady collection in the White House. Jackie passed the word that she did not want a formal ceremony as was the tradition for such occasions. She had not returned to the White House since she left it in December 1963, although she had been invited on many occasions.

Mrs. Nixon then arranged for Jackie and her two children, Caroline and John F. Kennedy, Jr., to come to the White House for dinner and a private viewing. If the Nixons had planned on a secret visit by Mao Tse-tung, the arrangements could not have been more hush-hush.

The two First Ladies had known each other since their husbands had served together in Congress. The only time there had been friction between them was during the 1960 campaign when Pat said she bought her clothes "off the rack" and much was being made of how much money Jacqueline Kennedy spent on her wardrobe.

Mrs. Nixon told Clement Conger to hang the Kennedy portrait where he thought it would be most suitable. He placed it on the wall next to the entrance of the diplomatic reception room, flanking a portrait of Lady Bird Johnson. Most portraits of First Ladies hang on the walls of the ground floor of the White House.

Nixon sent his pilot, Col. Ralph D. Albertazzie, to pick up Jackie and her children in New York in a jet plane. Orders were given for her car not to be stopped at the gate. White House corridors were blocked so that no one was allowed to walk through, not even Conger, who found himself peeking out of his ground floor office door when Jackie passed. "No one was to leave their offices so she [Jackie] would not feel anyone was looking at her and she would be free to roam to her heart's content," said Conger. "It was an historic, unparalleled visit."

The entire Nixon family was present and they were overjoyed that Jackie had chosen to return to the White House for the first time in their era. In the family quarters, a dinner fit for Jackie's gourmet tastes, was served: seafood American, roast tenderloin of beef, artichokes, hearts of palm vinaigrette salad, and Soufflé Grand Marnier with strawberries. The wine was Pouilly Fuissé 1967, Chateau La Tour 1959, topped off with champagne, Dom Perignon 1962.

Julie and Tricia took Caroline and John on a tour of the house and Nixon later escorted them to the Oval Office where John sat in the President's chair. By all accounts Jackie was "extremely pleased" with the way the portrait was displayed and she approved of the changes Mrs. Nixon had made in the mansion. According to Conger, she told Pat, "Don't be afraid to change, always upgrade." John F. Kennedy's portrait, painted by the same artist, was ultimately hung in the Grand Hallway, as was the portrait of Lyndon Johnson. It pleased Johnson that he was given a prominent spot in the house, Conger said.

I was working late in the White House press room when I got a tip that Jackie was coming. I confirmed my information with Mrs. Nixon's press secretary Helen Smith, who was, in my opinion, one of the few pros who ever held that job. She never lied. Mrs. Smith knew what news was all about. When she confirmed the story, she asked if I would hold it off the ticker for a certain time to give Jackie a chance to leave. I agreed, as long as I could have the story exclusively. I knew that when I hit the wire with it, it would cause a sensation. The White House switchboard lit up with calls from reporters all over town. Jackie still aroused great excitement in blasé Washington.

The following day I covered a reception Mrs. Nixon was giving and she made it clear that she was unhappy that the Jackie story had broken. "I don't know how it leaked," she said. "There were only four of us who knew she was coming. We were going to announce it today."

Whereupon I delivered a brief lecture on what is news. "Mrs. Nixon," I said, "there is no such thing as a leak. There is legitimate news which governments or people want to suppress. But news, fortunately, does not always break at what you think is the proper time, and it cannot be managed or programmed."

She took it well. The visit had gone smoothly, Jackie did have the privacy Mrs. Nixon had promised. I think Mrs. Nixon feared Jackie might have thought the story was leaked by the Nixons.

All I know is that there were a few missing faces around the White House after I got the story. I should have realized the capacity the administration had for revenge against news sources.

Mrs. Nixon got back at me in a pleasant way with a leak of her own. Doug Cornell of the Associated Press and I became secretly engaged and planned to marry after he retired on October 1, 1971, after thirty-six years of White House reporting. We had decided it would not be seemly for two wire services to operate under the same roof. A few days before Doug's retirement, Press Secretary Ronald Ziegler told me the President wanted to give a surprise farewell party for Doug. He asked for the names of Doug's friends and I was happy to supply them.

It was to take place on Thursday evening, September 30, just before Nixon departed for Key Biscayne, Florida. I was thrilled and hinted to Doug that he should wear his best dark suit for a party at the White House. I told Helen Smith she would be getting a wedding invitation shortly. She said she was happy about the news and asked if she could tell Mrs. Nixon. "Sure," I told her, "if she can keep a secret."

Well, I found out that Mrs. Nixon can't keep a secret, and I'm glad of it. During the reception for Doug in the State Dining Room, I tried to stay in the background, not wanting to get into the act. Soon I found myself being pushed up to a platform where Nixon asked me to read his citation. I was very touched and emotional as I began to read the citation:

The President of the United States of America to Douglas B. Cornell, Reporter extraordinary, White House correspondent with six Presidents, and friend of many years:

As you retire after more than four distinguished decades in Washington journalism, you take with you the abiding respect and admiration not only of your colleagues but also of those whose activities you have chronicled— including especially that House freshman from California whom you began covering twenty-four years ago, and who has prized your fine reporting ever since. Associated Press readers, newsmakers, and news professionals across America will miss the Cornell by-line. So will I. All of us join in warm tribute to a consummate professional.

It was signed "Richard Nixon" and dated "The White House, Washington, D.C., September 30, 1971."

When I reached the last two words "consummate professional" I said "Richard Nixon" all in the same breath. Nixon was quick on the uptake. He went to the microphone and said that he had often been called a "consummate politician." Everyone laughed, especially Nixon. He has rarely been seen more relaxed or comfortable with the press. He had always liked and respected Doug.

Then Mrs. Nixon stepped forward and announced our engagement. The tears began streaming down my face as I took notes. The room erupted with good cheer and there were sentimental tears in a lot of familiar eyes that night.

Then Nixon said, "They say marriages are made in Heaven, but the best press marriages are made at the White House."

The headlines read that Pat Nixon had "scooped" Helen Thomas.

And when Doug was asked what the high point of his career had been, he said: "This is it. No President ever gave me a party before."

Nixon once told an interviewer that he was not comfortable with many people, and sometimes not even with his own wife, but he counted on her to be there and she was, always. He was never demonstrative with her in public and it seemed sometimes that they moved through life ritualistically, but I felt they were very close and became much more so when they left the White House.

They had lived a lifetime together and she always expressed true love and genuine pride in him. Nixon often used to say at friendly gatherings that he realized he had married "above himself." Once when she was asked whether she would want her daughter Tricia to marry a politician, she replied, "I would feel sorry for her if she did."

"Well, you married one," countered a reporter.

"Yes," she said, "but I don't tell everything."

President Nixon said once about the role of his wife in his career, "I remember through all of our campaigns, whether it was a receiving line or whether it was going to a fence at the airport, she was the one that always insisted on shaking that last hand, not simply because she was thinking of that vote, but because she simply could not turn down that last child or that last person."

She described her principal attribute as "personal diplomacy," calling it "my only claim to fame, both at home and abroad. . . . It's Dick's life. I think a man needs that a great deal."

Because we look for the human side, I think women reporters were particularly interested in the Nixons' relationship with each other and the detached way they treated each other in public. I am sure this was not because of a lack of love, but because of Nixon's introverted nature and a lifetime of hiding his deepest feelings until moments of crisis.

On the other hand, I have seen Mrs. Nixon rush up to her husband, her arms opened wide, to hug him. It was easier for her to display affection. I will always reject the concept of a "plastic Pat" or "Barbie doll" that others mistook to be the "real" Pat Nixon. She was the warmest First Lady I covered and the one who loved people the most. I think newspeople who covered her saw a woman who was sharp, responsive, sensitive, and instinctively protective of her loved ones. It irritated Mrs. Nixon to be described as shy, and frankly I never thought she was. Cautious perhaps, but not as much so as some of her pre-Kennedy-era predecessors, and she could stand her ground fearlessly. We learned that many times.

Once tawny-haired, Pat Nixon became a blonde. Her Marlene Dietrich high cheekbones made her very photogenic and she had a model's figure. Like other pretty California girls of her era, she had played a few bit parts in the movies. She rarely took an unflattering picture. She quickly made it clear that she would wear American designer clothes and she was always impeccably groomed, every strand of hair always in place. She eventually paid for (from her personal funds) a full-time hairdresser who also did other chores for her and her daughters.

Like other members of the family, she enjoyed the prospect of living in the White House. "I don't think anyone could ever drive past it without being impressed," she said. "I never take it for granted. It's always a thrill."

She relished the 1968 triumph. It had taken time for her to recover from the "truly shattering moment" in 1960 when her husband was defeated by John F. Kennedy. I had covered many "Pat for First Lady" events that year. I always felt that she may have considered the vote a personal repudiation, although of course it was not.

Millions watched the totally disciplined Pat Nixon break down that election night as her husband conceded defeat. Tears streamed down her face and she ran down the hotel corridor alone, heartbroken. She broke down, she said later, when she saw the faces of the party faithful who had worked so hard for a Nixon victory.

Several months after that election, I saw Mrs. Nixon lunching with a friend. She looked like a suburban housewife, happy to be out of public life. "I'm beginning to live again," she told me. When Nixon began to get political fever again in 1962 and decided to run for Governor of California, she was adamantly opposed, but campaigned again at his side. After that second devastating defeat, he confessed that "as usual" his wife was right and he promised her he would quit politics.

When I met Mrs. Nixon again in 1968, I saw a much more sophisticated, confident woman. She was clearly not gung ho about campaigning and would solo stump as little as possible. Her daughters took over where she had left off. Mostly she went along for the ride, while Nixon's bright young public relations men ran a smooth campaign with much flare and little substance. They did not seem to care whether she was around or not. Women had no place on their high-powered team.

August 11, 1970

MEMORANDUM FOR BOB HALDEMAN
FROM: CONSTANCE STUART

The spirit of détente and cooperation between the President's staff and Mrs. Nixon's staff seems to be sagging a bit, and I hope you might be able to work with me to remedy the situation.

The problem area is in the planning of trips.

I am operating under a directive from Mrs. Nixon that says she would like to accompany the President and be with him when he travels and makes a public appearance in this country or abroad.

There are several valid reasons:

1. Her presence enhances the "dynamic family" image.
2. She receives good local press coverage (a subject that is very much on her mind these days).
3. She can highlight some of the President's programs.
4. She can contribute to the campaigns of local candidates.

The first two reasons need no explanation. On the third and fourth points some explanations may be in order. When Mrs. Nixon travels with the President and he has a meeting on a particular subject, she has chosen to visit projects that emphasize the work he is doing in the meeting. When the President went to Chicago in February to discuss the environment and water pollution, Mrs. Nixon went out to see projects on conservation, land reclamation, and thermal pollution. When the President stopped in Fargo to deal with agrarian problems, Mrs. Nixon visited a state university laboratory emphasizing the development of grains and cereals. In Denver, while the President was talking with law enforcement officials, Mrs. Nixon visited a juvenile home to see what was being done with young offenders and the drug problem.

On the fourth point, the local candidates have been most receptive to being seen with Mrs. Nixon. In Denver the candidates had the option of staying in the meeting with the President or getting much more visible exposure by moving with Mrs. Nixon. They both chose to go with Mrs. Nixon and were extremely enthusiastic about the value of their association with her with respect to their campaigns.

My problem is that we are not informed about these trips until the 11th hour[1] and it is very difficult for us to put together a decent schedule for her. No one from my staff is advised of the trips or invited to attend any of the planning sessions to get an idea of the nature of the trip. I have to sulk around with secretaries, aides and friends who, at least, are sympathetic to our plight.[2] Mexico has been scheduled for over three weeks and yet I have received no information on this trip, sat in on no planning meetings, received no tentative schedules. Mrs. Nixon would like to know what her involvement is.[3]

On the Denver trip it was with great reluctance that Mrs. Nixon's advance man was allowed to sit in on a planning session in California and no one understood why he had to go out and advance her stops.

On the New Orleans trip, which I found out by way of the grapevine on Monday, Dwight Chapin was greatly perturbed that I had knowledge of this trip four days prior to its happening. I was treated as a spy in my own camp.

Two irritation factors develop. Mrs. Nixon, who doesn't understand why she finds out about things so late, and the President's staff who doesn't understand why we are late with schedules and scenarios for Mrs. Nixon when it is finally accepted that she is to be a part of the trip.

My requests are simple:

    1. I or a member of my staff should be included in the initial planning meetings on trips.[4]

[1] Marginal notation by Haldeman reads: "Not True."
[2] Marginal notation by Haldeman reads: "Usually call right off."
[3] Marginal notation by Haldeman reads: "Once we have official schedule—ask for ideas—."
[4] Marginal notation by Haldeman reads: "Not."

2. Mrs. Nixon's advance man or advance woman should be accorded the same privileges and information as the President's advance staff.

3. Mrs. Nixon's advance personnel should receive some amount of cooperation from the advance team out in the field.

If there is some logical explanation as to why my requests cannot be met, I would be more than happy to have it spelled out to me. I am a reasonable woman and would be happy to hear your dulcet tones on the telephone.

My I.O. is 206.

cc: Dwight Chapin

THE WHITE HOUSE
WASHINGTON   8/11/70
(handwritten letter)

Connie—

If you are having this many problems suggest you speak up. HRH is not the person to hit with them—I am! Your memo speaks with some truth—some semi-truths and is vague in other areas.—But you're basically right.

It is not the kind of thing H should waste one minute on. If you are having this many problems let's solve them.—My I.O. is 408—I called 206 but you were out—

Chuck Colson

Haldeman particularly discounted Mrs. Nixon's role before and after she moved into the White House. He tried many times to control her side of the White House, but every once in a while she put her foot down and called a halt. In retrospect, Mrs. Nixon probably should have stepped in more often and been more alert to the way he tried to ride roughshod over her staff. His memos were brutal and her aides feared him. There was little respect between Mrs. Nixon and Haldeman, and he prevailed too many times.

I heard often that she felt she was not given enough credit for her contributions. When Haldeman tried to curtail press coverage, she often countermanded him. She was so much more sophisticated than the Palace Guard I wondered why her husband did not listen to her more often.

Much as she blossomed in the glow of people, she could be as reclusive as her husband. She disliked having her aides hover about during a reception. She rarely had personal contact with her secretaries although they could get her on the telephone promptly whenever there was a problem. As with Jackie Kennedy, papers and letters were sent up in folders.

Mrs. Nixon had a private life in the White House that we were never quite able to get a fix on. For one thing, she was a loner. Her closest friend was Helene Drown of Rolling Hills, California, with whom she had taught at Whittier High School at Whittier, California, and if she shared her innermost joys and despair with anyone it was with this woman who was 3,000 miles away.

But with reporters, she maintained an image of contentment. She would tell us she never argued with her husband and she never got tired. We took it all with mild skepticism, realizing that she felt that a First Lady must always appear competent and serene. She had come up through a stoic school for Presidential wives and she may have been the last one to think it necessary to hide her feelings completely.

Many women reporters who covered Mrs. Nixon through the years in the political arena felt they had rapport with her. I know I did even when I angered her. I felt happier when she expressed her feelings; it made her all the more human. She gave one bit of advice to Connie Stuart on handling the press: "Treat them with kid gloves and butter them up."

In her early days as First Lady, Mrs. Nixon rarely, if ever, had a "no comment." When we traveled with her, she would chat cheerily with her press entourage. She was "good copy," as we say in journalistic jargon and had firm opinions, with breezy and slangy comments like "kiddo" and "righto."

In those days when the Nixons felt beleaguered Mrs. Nixon entertained a group of ministers' wives. We had a brief colloquy with her during which she told me that the wives told her they were "praying" for her husband. "I told them I pray for the press," she said raising her fist, her eyes flashing.

"Why? Do you think they need it?" I asked. She replied something to the effect, "Don't you?" In that brief moment, I caught the unrepressed Pat Nixon I had often wished would surface more often. But she took issue with my reportage, insisting that her words were not said in defiance. Nevertheless, she got a flood of mail, more or less telling her "right on."

No First Lady was as solicitous of visitors, sometimes seeing thousands at one reception. She took time to shake hands, would pause to chat, always kept an eye on name tags, and went out of her way to put an arm around a well-wisher or to sign an autograph. It came from her heart and many a woman went away starry-eyed from the personal touch which became Mrs. Nixon's hallmark while she was in the White House. Meeting people was her forte, and she felt best traveling abroad as a goodwill ambassador. Before 1968, she had traveled around the globe five times with her husband.

"It takes heart to be in political life," Mrs. Nixon once observed. "I don't think I would have chosen politics for my life. But there it was. It was what my husband wanted and there was a part for me to play. So I dug in and played it. I found I really liked it. . . . I think if you really put your whole heart into something and work for it, you generally end up liking it."

Mrs. Nixon's personality was best expressed when she was able to travel on her own.

Flying back to Washington from a Western campaign swing in 1972, she was in a great mood, confident that her husband's reelection was assured, and exulting in the outpouring of affection for herself, particularly in crowd-drawing appearances in Oklahoma.

"I don't think in such a short period, we ever had such a change in our history and I think the days ahead, and the years ahead under this great President—I don't take any credit, but listen, I kinda love him—and I think he's just going to do a great deal for our country." She was speaking about her husband.

A reporter teased Mrs. Nixon that we had never heard her speak publicly "so eloquently and movingly" about her husband. "I've done so much for twenty-five years, but I've never boasted," she said. "I cannot boast for my family."

There were many touching moments on Mrs. Nixon's tours that took us to forlorn homes for juvenile delinquents and other institutions that seemed to offer more hope. During a West Coast tour in 1969, I covered Mrs. Nixon at a center for blind children where they performed scenes from *The Sound of Music* in her honor. As they moved haltingly to the stage, one sightless boy said: "Isn't she beautiful." We were deeply touched. Tears fell on our note pads, but we jotted on. Mrs. Nixon felt the same way and with great emotion she rushed up onto the platform to hug and kiss the children. They could not see her, but they knew she was the First Lady.

In 1958 in Caracas, Venezuela, when rioters spat on the Nixons and threw rocks at their motorcade, Nixon aides marveled at her lack of fear. She went readily when her husband dispatched her to Peru following the devastating earthquake high in the Andes in 1969. We flew in a cargo plane that landed on a dangerously short runway. On the way back, she climbed into the cockpit for the takeoff. I rode in the back on a bucket seat, holding my breath. I also had the dubious privilege of flying over the Andes in a small helicopter. I was strapped in but the doors of the press chopper were open and when I looked down I thought a reporter's life can be treacherous indeed.

But seeing Mrs. Nixon bring food and blankets to the thousands of refugees made us proud. She symbolically represented the massive emergency aid the United States was pouring in and she was welcomed with open arms. "You know who your friends are when you are sick," an officer told her, quoting a Peruvian proverb. From the chopper we saw an entire village wiped off the face of the map. Only one small tree remained as a marker.

She snapped at a group of Red Cross women who urged her to

take a rest stop in a tent. "I didn't come here to sit." The grateful Peruvian government later gave her their nation's highest decoration for her humanitarian mission.

She learned a lot about the country through the hundreds of letters that poured in for her. She also tried to answer an incredible amount of mail and to sign the letters personally, often devoting as much as four hours a day to the task.

At times Mrs. Nixon felt cooped up in the White House and she began to enjoy her weekends at Camp David. "We are shut in this house," she said. "There's no place to walk on the grounds." For her to go out shopping would cause too much "hubbub," she said. I remember in one of the first interviews with Mrs. Nixon, she gave the most definitive explanation of Charles J. ("Bebe") Rebozo's very close relationship with the family. " 'Bebe' is a good friend," she said. "One reason he is so good for all our family is that he never brings up anything political, distracting or negative. He's just our good friend. If Dick has to work, Bebe understands. Dick has other friends, too, very close friends. He is like an uncle to our children."

She admitted "We don't have time for a lot of close friends," adding, "that's why I enjoy the girls so much."

"We're a very close family," Pat Nixon told us. As reporters, we were not privy to those cherished family moments. But we got glimpses at times. We got to see the family Christmas tree with decorations saved since the Nixons' newlywed days and red stockings made when the girls were young. The family had always been close-knit, partly I think because the parents had few intimate friends. The Nixon home was a closed circle so the members centered their love on each other.

Julie and Tricia Nixon had moved into the White House as if they themselves had won it. In a sense they had. They campaigned vigorously for their father in the 1968 campaign, each bearing the scars of his defeat by John F. Kennedy in 1960. For support in all things political, Nixon had only to look to his two devoted daughters. In the White House they scorned their generation and thought as he did.

They considered Mrs. Nixon a disciplinarian and in interviews always complained that their mother was not getting enough credit for her contributions to enhancing the White House and encouraging volunteerism.

Not once during his years in the Presidency did Julie or Tricia indicate publicly—and there is strong evidence that they did not privately—that their father could be deeply questioned about his Vietnam War policy or the Watergate scandal.

Both of the Nixon daughters had lived with the ups and downs of politics since childhood. Tricia was born on February 21, 1946, nine days after Nixon began his first campaign as Republican candidate for California's Twelfth Congressional District. Julie was born during his first term. In an interview in the Oval Office attended by nine newswomen in connection with Mrs. Nixon's fifty-ninth birthday, President Nixon spoke fondly and intuitively in his sometimes rambling way, about his two daughters.

Julie is an extrovert, warm and very outgoing, gregarious. She has always got to be in motion, and she is doing something all the time. And Tricia [whom Pat Nixon nicknamed Dolly] on the other hand, is more introverted. Tricia is a curious combination. She is extremely effective whenever she has to do anything publicly, but she doesn't like to do anything publicly.

In other words, she is not one who enjoys the spotlight. I am not saying that Julie enjoys it either. But if Tricia had her druthers she would prefer not to go out on campaign trips. But she does them extremely well.

And I think Julie does them extremely well, too. So they both have the ability, and that, I think, probably was acquired from their training and the rest, namely their mother, and they both have the ability to be gracious and I think dignified and charming as they go out in the public positions.

But one, Tricia, would prefer a life which was far less in the public spotlight. I am not suggesting Julie likes a life or wants a life in the public spotlight, but to Julie, it is not as much of a problem.

Asked why his daughters had contrasting personalities, Nixon said: "I think people are born different."

Tricia was the loner in the White House and seemed as aloof as Jacqueline Kennedy. Called "Little Princess" and "Mystery Girl," Tricia protested, "I don't think I'm mysterious at all."

She was the least understood of any of the Presidential daughters

I covered because of her reclusiveness and her apparent feeling that she did not need to explain herself. Intelligent and articulate, Tricia sometimes seemed to be to the right of her father politically. She was proud to be a conservative and took strong positions in the inner family circle. Nixon assured one reporter that Tricia was "not on the kooky right." But I was always impressed that when she did decide to speak up, she did so with passion.

I was one of the few reporters to interview her personally when she lived in the White House, and then it was by telephone. Her answers were extremely revealing and showed she had a mind of her own. Tricia was recovering from a long and severe siege of the measles at the family's villa at Key Biscayne, Florida, when I arranged through the First Lady's press office to call her on her twenty-fourth birthday. I asked her about a letter she had written at the age of eighteen to Governor Lester Maddox of Georgia. Maddox had chased blacks out of his restaurant with an ax handle, and Tricia congratulated him for closing his business in Atlanta rather than serve blacks because of a court order. She based her endorsement of Maddox' action on a firm belief in the right of "private property."

But in the interview she said she regretted sending the congratulatory note and explained, "I don't want to think anything I did would promote segregation. But I'm a firm believer in the strict construction of the Constitution. I'm not pro-segregation. I really believe people should be equal. Some would say it's racist. But that's the farthest thing from my mind." In fact, Tricia had already begun a project in Washington tutoring three grade-school children from the black ghetto area. She found it "very rewarding" and said, "It gives me an ear to young people. There's no generation gap."

The interview took place at a time when Vice President Spiro T. Agnew was already well launched into a campaign of scathing criticism against the press, and particularly against television network commentators for what he called their "instant analysis." When I brought up his branding of the press as "effete intellectual snobs," Tricia told me approvingly, "The Vice President is incredible. I feel I should write him a letter. It's amazing what he has done to the media . . . helping it to reform itself. I'm a close watcher of newspapers and TV. I think they've taken a second look. You can't underestimate the power of fear. They're afraid if they don't shape up."

Her comments raised eyebrows in broadcast circles, since many believed that Tricia's comments might have come straight from the Nixon family dinner table. From developments in the White House later on, they undoubtedly did.

As for criticism, Tricia said, "I think you have to divorce yourself from what people say about you; you have to believe in what you're doing."

Whenever reporters cornered Tricia, they got a "good story," as the saying goes. When she reluctantly agreed to go through the Norfolk Azalea Festival ritual, after her father persuaded her that Virginia was politically friendly, she gamely answered reporters' questions and gave us a glimpse into her interests.

She expressed her love of working with children and confessed that the childhood story she loved best was *Cinderella.* Her hobbies, she said, were sailing and collecting Dresden and Meissen China. Tricia definitely was not the athletic type, and when she would meet her boyfriend Edward Finch Cox for weekends at his family's Westhampton, New York, estate, he would play tennis and as she jokingly put it: "I would wave the pompons."

She is petite, weighing under 100 pounds, with long blond hair, she has a fragile complexion, and is always carefully groomed. I thought Tricia was a real beauty. For a long time she did, however, dress very jeune fille, and affected an "Alice in Wonderland" look. It was that image that made reporters split with laughter in San Clemente when we learned the Nixons had given visiting Soviet Premier Leonid Brezhnev Tricia's old room. The hearty Russian padding around in dainty Tricia's pink and white flower-strewn setting was an incongruous image.

Tricia's blue eyes can sparkle with fire when she is angry, but she also had the ability to remain cool under pressure. None of the Nixons found the White House "the loneliest place in the world" as so many Presidents had. Tricia said, "I never feel alone in the White House," and "if I want privacy, I go to private parties and I don't tell people. I can't go out in crowds, people always recognize you, but I've really found it possible to have a private life."

Reporters were constantly trying to find out what Tricia was up to and even where she was. Once when Mrs. Nixon was asked Tricia's whereabouts, she smiled and said, "If you find out, you're better than I am." Live her own life she did, seldom showing up when singer Pearl Bailey or other memorable stars appeared on the White House stage at Nixon's Evenings of Entertainment.

Her father told *New York Daily News'* Paul Healy, who wrote in a *Ladies' Home Journal* article that when the President suggested, "Let's go to church, sometimes Tricia says, 'No.' And she doesn't go." Healy reported that when Mrs. Nixon said at the dinner table that she had agreed to discuss Tricia in an interview, Tricia kicked up a fuss, but Mrs. Nixon shot back, "twenty-four-year-olds don't rule the world."

When Tricia wanted to shine she could. She gave a televised tour of the White House for CBS-TV that rivaled a similar hour-long show Jackie had given during her heyday in the Executive Mansion. The reviews marveled at Tricia's poise and articulateness.

On two social occasions she blossomed as a hostess for contemporaries. Her Masked Ball had overtones of a Mardi Gras in New Orleans, with multicolored circus balloons bursting from every wall of the White House and flickering lights and small topiary trees lining the way into the state rooms. She wore a beaded white lace gown, the one she had worn as Queen of the Azalea Festival in Norfolk, Virginia, and carried a lorgnette-type mask of feathers and crystal beads that dangled from her wrist as she danced. Her escort was Representative Barry Goldwater, Jr., a bachelor at the time, and rumors coupling them romantically swept the capital.

Her second big party was for royalty when the Nixons pulled out all the stops for Britain's Prince Charles and his aloof, pouting sister, Princess Anne.

When white-gloved Anne shook Mrs. Nixon's hand in the welcoming line, her first comment was "Why so much press?" She proved to be a difficult girl, and when Tricia and the Eisenhowers took the royal siblings on a nighttime tour of Washington sights, the press motorcade had to follow at a distance. While Charles read the *Emancipation Proclamation* and other speeches at the Lincoln Memorial, Anne scurried up the steps and down again. I caught up to her as she was leaving and asked what she thought of the monument. "I don't give interviews," she snapped and huffed off. I had expected her to say "It's very nice," or make some other typically innocuous comment, so I figured she had misunderstood me. I went up to her again, and said, "There must have been some mistake. I simply asked how you—" A burly Scotland Yard man hushed me. "You have been told," he said sternly. For such impertinences, my sister journalists and I were titled "The Witches of Washington."

When the British press labeled several of us "The Witches of Washington," Tricia Nixon Cox signed my White House guide-book: "To the most bewitching of all witches."

Tricia smoothed it over at a glittering ball on the South Lawn with thousands of little lights and bouquets more elaborate than any I'd seen at the White House before.

Tricia interrupted her quiet, sedate life mainly to slip up to New York on weekends to see Cox, nicknamed "Fast Eddy." His lineage went back to Chancellor Robert Livingston, who swore in George Washington as President.

I was covering President Nixon at the Western White House during the yuletide holidays in January 1971, when we got the word that he was going on a jaunt to Catalina Island for an afternoon outing. We flew by helicopter on the two-hour excursion, forty miles across the Pacific from his San Clemente home. Nixon was accompanied by his daughter Tricia, and his best friend, "Bebe" Rebozo. It was a joyful, sunny day. The President signed autographs as the kids on the rocky island tagged along behind him and the wary agents. Nixon was never in a better mood. He invited some of the local youngsters to take a look inside his private jet helicopter.

Tricia looked like a schoolgirl in her purple sweater and skirt with her long blond hair held by a braided headband. I noticed that she kept looking at a ring with a large sapphire flanked by diamonds on her wedding finger. As soon as I could maneuver close enough, I asked her bluntly, "Tricia, are you engaged?"

She was furious and countered, "Are you?" Immediately after her show of temper, Tricia ran away, with Rebozo and the Secret Service agents in pursuit. I had obviously touched on the truth. It was one thing to know that in my heart, but a reporter has to go on more than a hunch or even observation. Pat Nixon was protective. When I asked about Cox, she said, "Tricia has boyfriends in every port."

As Tricia later told a news conference, she and Cox had been secretly engaged for two years. Cox finally broached to Nixon the subject of his daughter Tricia's hand while the family was spending the Thanksgiving holiday at Camp David. Tricia recalled, "Eddie was white as a sheet when he went in to see the President. We had been watching the *Greatest Show on Earth* and we got so nervous we had to go out and take a walk around the grounds. Then he talked to my father. I don't think he was really surprised."

Tricia said, "I think he was speechless for a moment, but you know how fathers are." There had been rumors that Cox, who had been a member of "Nader's Raiders," was too liberal for Nixon. There were also reports, that were denied, that Cox's blueblooded parents thought he was marrying beneath himself.

The engagement was formally announced on March 17, 1971, at an "Irish Evening at the White House," a joyous occasion combined with a celebration of Pat Nixon's birthday. Singer Dennis Day warbled "Danny Boy" and "When Irish Eyes Are Smiling" to the accompaniment of actor Fred MacMurray on the saxophone.

Tricia wore a low-cut white gown with a hemline of feathers; she risked showing much more decolletage than she had before at the White House. When a guest asked if she was going to convert Ed to the Republican Party, she smiled and said, "I don't think I need to do any proselytizing."

Cox's family and social register friends were very much in attendance. His mother, Mrs. Howard Ellis Cox, who lives in the Gracie Mansion neighborhood of New York City, said she was delighted with her prospective daughter-in-law.

"Tricia's good at a lot of things," she said. "Not many people realize what a splendid sense of humor she has. She's very quick and witty, but never makes a sharp retort. It's always well thought out."

Meeting the press the next day in the Map Room on the ground floor of the White House, her hair pulled back into a braided chignon, Tricia captivated the reporters with a charm and sophistication she had rarely displayed in her two years in the White House. There was none of the appearance of being a "Miss Muffet" which her detractors had dubbed her.

She fielded the questions with exceptional deftness and style. She showed off her heirloom ring, confessing, "I think Eddie's more intelligent than I am. Eddie's very athletic." She said that her future husband, then a Harvard University Law School student, was good at word games. He was so "incredibly esoteric," she said, that he knew the spelling and meaning of "infracaniophile." "It means underdog lovers," she explained. "All Americans are basically underdog lovers."

"Ed is my first and last love," she said softly. In the hubbub that followed, I held an off-the-record wedding shower for Tricia and invited the women reporters who regularly covered her to attend. It was the fulfillment of a joking promise that I'd be hostess at a celebration if she would confirm rumors of her engagement. It was held in the Decatur House, an historic home a block from the White House. Tricia came with her mother, sister, and Mrs. Cox.

Some of the gifts she received were gags. We gave her a red wig and huge oversize sunglasses so she could get around "in disguise," and potholders, aprons, and cookbooks. All the gifts were examined by the Secret Service, which put all gifts under a fluoroscope before they could be opened.

Pat Nixon had no mother-of-the-bride jitters. "Anyone who can't plan a wedding in a month," she said, "just was not worth her salt." The prewedding buildup had all the fanfare of a royal coronation. Reporters had several days of copy when the White House put out the recipe for Tricia's wedding cake. When *The New York Times'* food department attempted the pound cake, it reported it "mush on the outside and soup on the inside . . . the oven was a mess." The cake fiasco swept across the country, and the White House was not amused, especially Swiss-born Chef Henry Haller. The cake tasted fine to me if a little on the dry side.

Reporters flew in from across the country, but Julie Eisenhower, who still bore a grudge over the crashing of her wedding reception by Judy Martin of the *Washington Post*, had Judy barred from Tricia's wedding.

Julie Eisenhower had banned coverage altogether of her wedding in December 1968 in Marble Collegiate Church in New York, even though her father was President-elect. She simply did not want reporters to descend on a sentimental occasion. I had stood outside the church in the cold that day and rode in the motorcade from her Fifth Avenue apartment to the church and waited at the Plaza Hotel for details of the reception.

Tricia chose the Rose Garden of the White House as the setting for her June 1971 wedding, the first outdoor wedding at the White House in the 171-year history of the mansion.

The guest list was limited to 400 select friends and government officials. I was one of the small pool of reporters who attended the wedding ceremony. Martha Mitchell arrived wearing an orange sherbert flouncy garden party dress with matching parasol. "Everyone else checked their umbrellas," grumped Defense Secretary Melvin Laird as he sat behind Martha and her husband, John.

Rain delayed the nuptials a few hours before the ceremony. Nixon dropped by the huge tent on the South Lawn where the press was ensconced, sheltered from the downpour. He revealed that Tricia had been advised to move the wedding to the East Room, but had decided to gamble on the weather clearing. Reverend Billy Graham told reporters he would pray for the rain to stop.

The site of the wedding was now touch and go. At 12:30 P.M. Connie Stuart, Mrs. Nixon's staff director who had been bringing weather bulletins, announced to cheers, "Tricia has decided the ceremony will be in the Rose Garden."

The seats were still damp when the guests sat down for the brief ceremony. Washington's dowager, "Princess Alice" Roosevelt Longworth said that she felt as if she had been "sitting on a wet sponge during the ceremony." Someone asked her if she were reminded of her own White House wedding in 1906, and she replied, "Good God, not a bit. I was married twenty years before Hollywood. This wedding was quite a production."

Tricia was petite and exquisite in white lace as she came down the aisle on her father's arm. Nixon, who wore a cutaway, told her she looked "beautiful" as they started down the path to the altar.

The wedding was traditional in all respects, except for passages from *The Prophet* by Kahlil Gibran, requested by the bride and groom: "Stand together, but not too near together, just as the pillars of a temple stand apart yet stand together."

Dr. Edward Latch, the Chaplain of the House of Representatives, who performed the services, addressed the couple with "Love gives and forgives, accepts and adjusts. . . ."

President and Mrs. Nixon looked happier than I have ever seen them before.

When Nixon danced with his wife, lovely in a pastel lace short party dress, she threw her arms impulsively around him. Guests applauded.

In fact, this was the first time the President had danced publicly. "My parents were Quakers. They didn't believe in this sort of thing," he said, setting off with Tricia to the tune of "Thank Heaven for Little Girls."

Lynda Bird Robb, who also two-stepped with Nixon, told him that her father, who loved to dance, was a "backsliding Baptist."

Later when Nixon was asked if he would ever dance again at a White House party, quipped, "Never again."

I tried to get Nixon to reveal where the couple would spend their honeymoon and he gave a couple of hints. "Well, they are not going out of the country. We have taken care of that." He said they would not need a passport. "We promised them that they could have privacy all by themselves, not even Secret Service."

Tricia and Ed were escorted to their limousine by their parents as guests crowded onto the portico and Bill Harrington's society band played, "Toot, Toot, Tootsie Goodbye." A few days later I spotted Tricia's number-one Secret Service agent near the White House, and I figured the newlyweds could not have gone far. Indeed they had not. I got the scoop that they were honeymooning at Camp David, the Presidential retreat, where their privacy was insured by the military.

The following day, on June 13, 1971, next to the wedding story in *The New York Times*, was the sensational revelation about the "Pentagon Papers," a story that would lead eventually to the White House plumbers and, in the end, to Watergate and disaster.

Tricia and her husband settled happily into Cambridge, Massachusetts, where Edward was finishing his law course at Harvard.

Tricia had flattered reporters on occasion, saying she envied us in our profession and would like to be in journalism. She received several TV offers but never seriously got with it, and decided she should enjoy the life of White House daughter while she could.

Although the family apparently had no doubt that Nixon would win reelection in 1972 after his journey to China and the steps toward détente with the Soviet Union, they decided to work for a big win. Tricia and her husband, along with Julie Eisenhower, hit the election circuit. David Eisenhower, who was fulfilling his Navy commitment, was barred by law from campaigning.

Tricia traveled extensively, expressing this view of her father's administration:

In his search for a generation of peace in the world and a new emphasis on human resources and community stability at home, it seems to me that my father stands for ideals that an overwhelming majority of Americans support—and want their government to continue. I believe he has transformed America since 1969, moving it back from the brink of breakdown and back to its traditional principles and progress. I believe my father's reelection will be a step toward a positive future—not only for our own country, but for the aspirations and opportunities of all humanity.

Julie, the younger daughter, was always the Nixon daughter to be reckoned with. When her father lost the Presidential race to Kennedy in 1960, she had cried and had remained unreconciled. It has always seemed to me that Julie believed her father was infallible. She never followed her contemporaries in any convictions that ran counter to the parental views. During the Vietnam War, she was a loyal defender, and the price was high in terms of her personal life.

Knowing there would be campus disturbances after he decided to invade Cambodia in May 1970, Nixon forewarned the young Eisenhowers before the public announcement. Julie left her classes at Smith and David left Amherst. Both flew to Washington to be with the President and Mrs. Nixon to avoid campus heckling.

Julie closed herself off socially from the majority of the students, who disagreed with the war policies and she had to forego Smith College graduation ceremonies to forestall pickets. It was painful for the Nixon family to skip Julie's graduation from Smith. When I asked Mrs. Nixon at a White House reception whether she was going to pass up the commencement, she snapped, "Oh, Helen, you sound like a broken record." I realized that it must hurt her very much not to be able to enjoy that parental prerogative, but I have a firm belief that a reporter has to be able to bear rebuffs just as a public servant must be able to bear tough questions. I always know that when I pry into people's lives they may slap me down, but that's their prerogative, and it is a human reaction.

David had many verbal jousts with antiwar protesters all the same. Demonstrators gathered in front of the Eisenhowers' Northampton, Massachusetts, apartment when the Nixons visited them for dinner on the President's birthday. Afterward, while the Nixon motorcade zoomed away toward the airport, David came down from his apartment and confronted the demonstrators in a not so friendly dialogue.

David displays strong conservative views at times. Once he said he agreed with Attorney General John Mitchell's description of the "May Day protesters" as "Brown Shirts." A Navy ensign at the time, he said in an interview at Virginia Beach, Virginia, "The group in Washington last week was certainly of the same cast of mind as the Brown Shirts. The Brown Shirts were attempting to destroy democracy and succeeded because democracy was weak in their country. I think it is a tribute to the United States, at least to our constitutional form of government, that we have been able to withstand these assaults."

Asked what the alternatives were for the protesters, David said the only way to really get anything done is to work "through processes of government which are open and which this country has long believed in and worked through. . . . I think their cause will forever be set back for as long as they choose to carry out these charades."

Julie's support of her father's Vietnam policy drew jeers during the 1972 campaign. In a Cleveland news conference, she defended her dad's Vietnam policies and said she would gladly give her life "for the Thieu" government. The *Los Angeles Times'* brilliant cartoonist Paul Conrad drew a sketch of a mother sitting at a writing desk with a framed photograph of her young son in uniform. The caption underneath read, "Dear Julie, thank you for offering your life to save the Thieu government. Unfortunately, it comes too late for my son who . . ."

Mrs. Nixon was on a tour in Los Angeles when the cartoon appeared. That day she was scheduled to hold a news conference with the "ladies of the press," but it was cancelled.

Julie received her master's degree in education, but taught only briefly. Instead, like most Presidential daughters, she chose to enter journalism and became the Washington editor for the *Saturday Evening Post.*

Julie believed that part of her role as the President's daughter was to work at humanitarian projects. She took on a summer job as a tour guide at the White House and was specially solicitous to blind children, leading them through the historic rooms and explaining the surroundings.

I enjoyed interviewing Julie immensely from time to time because she was honest and, like a mirror, reflected her own feelings and the feelings of her family. She called them as she saw them, fearlessly. She was a believer. Much of her irritation with the press, and there was a lot of that, displayed a deep frustration in not being able to convince reporters what in her own heart she felt to be true. When Julie took up the cudgels and became her father's Number One Public Defender, she did it on her own initiative. "It was something I took on myself," she told an interviewer.

Around Christmas-time 1971, I arranged to interview Julie at Camp David in the western Catoctin Mountains. I was quite thrilled at the thought of finally seeing the mountaintop Presidential retreat created originally for Franklin Delano Roosevelt. I had been checking Presidents in and out of Camp David since the Kennedy era, but only from just inside the gate where reporters could make certain that the Presidential helicopter landed and took off safely. At times it seemed that covering Presidents was simply a matter of arrivals and departures.

Julie herself arranged for me to talk to her there, but that idea was scrapped at the last minute by White House aides, much to my unhappiness. As a compromise the White House set up the interview at a Ranger station a few miles down the mountain in Catoctin National Park. Camp David was ruled out of bounds for the press. I later learned that President Nixon had ordered extensive construction and renovation at his favorite hideaway and did not want the press to know about it.

It was a cold snowy day and Secret Service agents drove Julie down. I was waiting and the park superintendent was on hand to greet her. She wore a red pants suit she had received for Christmas and a heavy pea jacket. Her short soft hair style gave her a vivacious gamine look.

Over coffee and cookies, with a tape recorder on the table, Julie answered a wide range of questions about herself and her family. She was so appealing, sincere, and definite that she reminded me of Jo in *Little Women.* My UPI story began: "Julie Nixon Eisenhower says she is certain her father will seek reelection because the 'country needs him.' She also is sick of 'justifying the fact that he is warm and human.' "

Julie conceded that some reporters think she and her sister, Tricia, are "terribly boring and square," but said she personally felt they were on the same wavelength with other young people "except for the hippie element."

I asked her how both Nixon girls could echo their father's thoughts without a generation gap. Julie's answer was that "the main thing is that we just think so much of our parents—it's not that we're not able to branch out on our own, because I think we have, but I just admire what my parents have done with their lives so much."

When I told her that "many people say your father is not warm and does not relate to people, what do you think?" Her hackles rose.

"I don't agree," she said emotionally. "He's a very warm, warm person."

As for criticism of her father, Julie said, "Sometimes it's very irritating because I can see that they're all wrong."

She also commented that her husband David, also then twenty-two, would be great if he ran for the Presidency someday," but added, "I just can't envision it."

January 6, 1971

MEMORANDUM FOR: HERB KLEIN and RON ZIEGLER
FROM: JOHN R. BROWN III
SUBJECT: Julie's UPI Interview

On reviewing the UPI interview with Julie it was noted that it was a waste not to have had this on Television. In addition, you should note that the key note to this was the enthusiasm—not the facts.

cc: H. R. Haldeman
     A. Butterfield

THE WHITE HOUSE
WASHINGTON
January 9, 1971

MEMORANDUM FOR JOHN BROWN
FROM: RONALD ZIEGLER
REGARDING: UPI Interview with Julie

I agree it is unfortunate that an interview such as the one Julie gave to Helen Thomas was not on TV. However, I think when the story appears in the Sunday papers on January 10, as you will agree, the interview will have good impact.

I am suggesting to Connie Stuart that she attempt to arrange a TV interview with Julie along the same lines as the Helen Thomas interview.

cc: Connie Stuart

CONNIE:

Attached is a memorandum from John Brown and above is my response to it. Would you talk to Julie about the possibility of doing a TV interview similar to her UPI interview?

January 11, 1971

MEMORANDUM FOR RON ZIEGLER
FROM: CONSTANCE STUART

I was rather surprised by your memo concerning Julie Eisenhower's interview with Helen Thomas. There is nothing "unfortunate" about an interview that runs in both the *Washington Post* and *The Evening Star* on the same Sunday. The story will receive wide national and international distribution as you well know.

The fact that Julie granted a UPI interview certainly does not preclude her giving such interviews to other media. Julie's TV interview with Nancy Dickerson early this fall was along the same lines as the UPI interview. Julie has agreed to an interview some time this month with Clare Crawford of WRC. This interview would then run on the evening NBC News shows as opposed to the morning shows where Julie has already appeared. I've also talked with Herb Klein about doing an interview with Julie for the Captain Kangaroo show. Herb thinks this would be a good place for Julie to make an appearance.

In addition to the UPI story and the television, an interview with Julie will appear this month in Family Weekly, the Sunday supplement, including a cover photograph, and Mrs. Nixon, Tricia, and Julie are on the cover of *Good Housekeeping* this month with an inside story by Jessamyn West.

Julie has accelerated her graduate school program and has little time to spare, but she has been most cooperative in giving what time she has and we will try to make as much use of her as possible through March when David graduates and we may loose Julie to some far-flung Navy post.

cc: Bob Haldeman
     Herb Klein
     Alex Butterfield

Julie had many more friends than her mother and sister. An activist, she made extemporaneous speeches easily. Sometimes she appeared to dominate the Eisenhower menage. When reporters would corral her husband David for comments on the issues of the day or the scoop on what was going on inside the White House, Julie would gently but firmly pull him away. She felt she could field our questions better than he could and that David might volunteer more information than she wanted him to reveal.

David had been serving in the Mediterranean during Nixon's 1973 Christmas saturation bombing of North Vietnam. He and some of his Navy buddies began to waver and display doubt over the wisdom of Nixon's war policies, but when he came home to Washington, his wife and father-in-law reimposed their beliefs about Southeast Asia on him and got him back in line.

David's tour of duty over, the Eisenhowers moved into a $125,000 home with a swimming pool, in Bethesda, Maryland, owned by "Bebe" Rebozo. He reportedly leased it to them, but Julie would never disclose their rent. The Secret Service installed security equipment about the place, and the Nixons used it as a haven from the White House. Such visits were never announced in advance, and enterprising photographers were shooed away from the street by agents. The President and Mrs. Nixon would bring dinner from the White House kitchen, and David would build a fire. Sometimes Mrs. Nixon, who dearly loved David, would come early and garden, a hobby she had been denied during her years in a New York apartment and at the White House. David could not bring himself to call her anything but a formal "Mrs. Nixon" and the President, "Mr. Nixon."

Later, Julie and David gave up the house and moved into a new apartment building a few blocks from the White House.

The Nixons were clearly a strong presence, but in making major decisions directly affecting his own life, David followed Eisenhower advice. He was very close to his grandfather, Dwight David Eisenhower, a five-star general before he became President, and remembered his words: "If you want a military career, go into the army, but if you are only fulfilling a service commitment, join the Navy for the shorter haul."

After the Navy, David decided to study law. All the Nixons opposed it, but he accepted the counsel of his father, retired Army Col. John Eisenhower, Ambassador to Belgium, who told his son that it was important to have a profession. In an interview I had with David for UPI, he said that the President "doesn't like the idea of my going to law school; my wife doesn't either; Mrs. Nixon doesn't like it either, but my Dad likes it very much. My Dad is the one who wants it. The thing is, lawyers seem very blasé about their credentials which are very powerful in my opinion."

One summer David worked as a sports columnist for the *Philadelphia Bulletin*. When editor George Packard was asked about his work, he said, "He writes as well as any President's son-in-law does." David had been semi-interested in becoming a journalist, but once involved was less intrigued. Besides, because of the White House, he felt there were "certain limitations" to his ability to write.

Both Julie and David had at different times expressed delight in living in the White House. David regarded the White House as a second home. When his grandfather left the White House in January 1961, David had hidden a note reading, "I shall return." Asked to compare the advantages and disadvantages, Julie said, "If you don't appreciate living in the White House, I think there's something wrong with you . . . the opportunities you have. So many great things happen to you and I feel proud because I am helping my parents in a way that makes me feel I am making a small contribution."

In the ensuing months, Julie threw herself into her father's reelection campaign and was much in demand as a speaker at rallies and Republican fund raising. She worked closely with the Committee to Reelect the President and was on the road more than her father.

His immense victory was hers also in many ways.

In those days neither Julie nor Tricia nor their mother apparently had the foreboding of the tragedy that was to mar their last two years in the house to which they had given so much of their own personal lives to win. It was clear that they believed that the landslide election would ensure four more years of happiness in the Executive Mansion.

Chapter 8

Resignation

On the evening of his sixtieth birthday, January 9, 1973, Nixon granted AP's Fran Lewine and me a tandem interview. When we arrived Ziegler warned us that questions on Watergate and Vietnam were verboten. That was a jolt since they were the most significant topics of the time.

The setting again was the hideaway office where Nixon sat surrounded by symbols of happy times; he proudly pointed out photographs chronicling his marriage and childhood of his daughters and symbolic GOP elephants.

Since the two burning questions were off limits, Nixon gave us a monologue on his philosophy on aging. Sitting in an easy chair, he observed:

"Boredom is likely to cause health and emotional problems. You never get bored in the Presidency." He continued, "When a man or woman gives up, then he is finished. He's old before his time. When he's constantly recharging he never gets old."

As he talked, he looked fit, but his black hair was beginning to gray, and his eyes seemed not to see us.

Anticipating his second term, Nixon said he expected it to be "very interesting and provide great opportunities to many."

"What more could anyone ask?" he mused.

Devotion and loyalty were hallmarks of the Nixon "team," and no one was more dedicated than Manolo Sanchez. In an interview long before the Watergate trauma, Manolo told me simply: "I learned kindness from him [Nixon]. He likes everybody to be happy." Spanish-born Manolo and his wife Fina had worked for the Nixons for years. Fina told me, "I would prefer that something happen to Manolo rather than the President."

Considering the loyalty of the team, I could not understand why Nixon remained silent when Haldeman ousted Robert Taylor, the top-notch chief of the White House Secret Service detail. Haldeman had been gunning for Taylor even before Taylor, at the Providence, Rhode Island, airport one night during the 1972 campaign refused to let the crowds swarm around Nixon "spontaneously." Taylor thought it was a security risk and reportedly threatened to arrest Haldeman if he defied his edict to keep the fans behind the ropes.

Later, millions saw Taylor on TV during the inaugural parade take off his coat and put it around Nixon to protect him from the cold wintry day.

I heard of Taylor's dismissal while on a trip to California with Nixon. When I arrived at my office after midnight, I wrote the exclusive story. Ziegler tried to circumlocute the subject, but it was obvious that Taylor was fired. When I telephoned the Taylors Mrs. Taylor was upset and said: "I don't think Bob wants to talk to you." Her remarks were perturbing, but it was a story I could not ignore. Nixon did not publicly utter a farewell word of praise for a man who had daily put his life on the line for him. Their association dated back to Nixon's Vice Presidency when rioters in Caracas tried to overturn Nixon's limousine.

Several agents, as a protest against Taylor's dismissal, asked for transfers from the White House.

A Cabinet official had told me once sadly that "Nixon has a dark side." It was an oblique way of saying that at times Nixon was ruthless. Another top-ranking staffer said that Nixon would often order aides to carry out intolerable missions. They would frequently disregard these orders given in rage or as an example of the arrogance of Presidential power.

Whether Nixon was taken too literally by his staff in the Watergate affair is a question. He had plenty of opportunity to call a halt to any excesses. When my former colleague Norman Kempster of the *Washington Star* interviewed Charles Colson, one of Nixon's political operatives, Colson showed Kempster the famous memo he had sent around to the members of his staff during the 1972 campaign which stated that "I'd walk over my grandmother to elect Richard Nixon." He said he expected the staff to do the same.

In all the post-Watergate soul-searching, White House reporters have asked themselves why they did not uncover the facts, as had the *Washington Post*'s investigative team, Bob Woodward and Carl Bernstein. We were remiss, but we operated under many more wraps as regular White House reporters. We must take people at their word until it is proved otherwise, but once White House credibility is shattered, the road back is long. But hats off to those reporters who uncovered the Watergate scandal and other abuses by public officials and government agencies (such as the CIA).

During the Nixon administration, the press, under attack, lost ground in the eyes of the public and perhaps some prestige. There was no doubt in our minds, for example, that Vice President Spiro T. Agnew's attacks on the press, and particularly on the television media, were orchestrated by the White House. No Vice President, we were quite sure, was about to stick his neck out the way Agnew did unless he was programmed from higher up. Nixon aides confirmed it. But Watergate vindicated the press, I believe, and demonstrated the need for eternal vigilance by reporters who cover government officials.

On the evening of April 30, 1973, I was running down West Executive Avenue headed for the White House press center when out of a side door stepped President Richard M. Nixon. He was headed across the street to his hideaway office in the baroque Executive Office Building.

I came to a full stop, struck by the anguish and grayness of the President's face under heavy pancake makeup. He wore a heavy overcoat and his shoulders were hunched dejectedly. Steve Bull, an aide, was by his side, but he seemed very much alone.

In half an hour he was to deliver a televised address to the nation, the first of many statements proclaiming his innocence in the Watergate affair, the scandal that brought down his Presidency in shame and disgrace.

"Good evening, Mr. President," I said, "and good luck."

Nixon grabbed my hand warmly and appreciatively. "I know we

don't have the same religion but will you say a prayer for me?" he asked.

"I will, Mr. President," I said, deeply moved.

I did not fully comprehend the impact of his ordeal at that time, but I knew he was suffering. When I got to the press room, I said a silent prayer for the President and the country.

Earlier that day the White House had announced the forced resignations of Nixon's two most trusted aides, H. R. Haldeman, his formidable Chief of Staff, and John D. Ehrlichman, his domestic counselor, after news stories had linked them to Watergate.

After the broadcast in the Oval Office, during which he described his aides as "two of the finest public servants I have ever met," Nixon wiped tears from his eyes and told some of the TV cameramen and technicians: "It wasn't easy." Then, instead of heading back to the family quarters, he made a surprise appearance in the press room where he stepped onto the podium and told a cluster of reporters and cameramen: "When I'm wrong, keep giving me hell, I want to be worthy of your trust." Former Secretary of Defense Laird and political pro Bryce Harlow returned to the Nixon White House to pick up the pieces.

For a time former Treasury Secretary John T. Connally, who headed the 1972 "Democrats for Nixon" organization, acted as a consultant. He saw Nixon a few times and advised him to prune the pre-Watergate staff, and particularly to ax Ziegler. Laird had given Nixon the same advice. But Nixon did not listen. Connally announced that he was switching his party affiliation and came on board to help Nixon survive in office, but as Nixon did not call on him or anyone else for advice, Connally returned to Texas.

Ziegler's power grew as long as he was in the White House. He was made an assistant to the President and taken out of the line of fire of the daily questioning on Watergate by reporters. It was typical of Nixon to turn over the real Presidential domestic power to another Chief of Staff—Gen. Alexander M. Haig, whom he jumped over more than 240 higher-ranking Army officers to pin four stars on. Haig, amiable but tough, had been Henry Kissinger's deputy in the National Security Affairs office and one of the few aides Kissinger trusted. Soon Haig and Ziegler became Nixon's only companions, except for Rose Mary Woods, his personal secretary, who had suffered under the dominating Haldeman.

I had been in Florida covering Nixon in March 1973 when one of the convicted burglars in the Watergate break-in into Democratic headquarters, James McCord, chief of security of the Committee to Reelect the President, accused "higher ups" of perjury in the conspiracy trial. He said he doubted whether the FBI or the prosecutor's office could get at the truth of Watergate. His letter, read by Judge John J. Sirica in District Court, landed like a bombshell at the White House and marked the beginning of the end for Nixon. After this, White House counsel John Dean told Nixon there was "a cancer growing around the Presidency" and disclosed that money was paid to hush up the Watergate defendants.

From that point on Watergate consumed Richard Nixon. I flew with him in April 1973 to a dedication ceremony honoring Senator John Stennis, the Democrat who headed the Senate Armed Services Committee. Stennis, who was recovering from two gunshot wounds suffered when he was mugged in front of his Washington, D.C., home, gave a rousing introduction of Nixon, telling the President to "tough it out" in the Watergate crisis. And that is what he tried to do in every conceivable way.

With the start of the Senate Watergate hearings, Nixon's excellent health began to decline. He was in Bethesda Naval Hospital suffering from viral pneumonia when former White House assistant Alexander P. Butterfield broke the stunning news that Nixon had been taping all of his conversations in the Oval Office and in his hideaway office since 1971. Eventually the tapes became the weapon that destroyed him. While he was still in the hospital the taping system was shut off, but the damage had been done. All he could rely on now was to claim executive privilege and national security. Neither would prevail.

Even when it was disclosed that the Secret Service had wiretapped the telephone of Nixon's brother, Donald, at Newport Beach, California, the family rallied around him and later showed up at a White House State Dinner. To reporters who approached her, Mrs. Donald Nixon praised her brother-in-law as a "great President."

I rode back in the motorcade with Nixon when he left Bethesda Naval Hospital. A gathering of some 200 White House workers assembled in the Rose Garden to welcome the wan-looking and still ailing President. He thanked them and then told the audience that, in the language of his father, he wanted to say that "any suggestion that I am going to resign is just plain poppycock."

"Let others wallow in Watergate," he said. "We are going to do the job we were elected to do."

I ran to telephone a bulletin to my office. It was the first time that Nixon had taken public notice of the demands that he quit. Later there were many such statements in many different ways.

As the nation sat glued before TV sets, fascinated by testimony that drove one nail after another into the coffin, Nixon withdrew into his retreats in the White House. Press Secretary Ron Ziegler announced that Nixon would make no public reply to Watergate charges while the hearings were still going on. He held no news conferences. We went for days without seeing him physically. By this time, Ziegler had also retreated into the sanctum of his plush office, leaving his deputy, Gerald Warren, to fend off the reporters' more and more demanding questions. Warren took on the chore of counterattacking the damaging testimony piling up. He seemed to pride himself on being able to stonewall the questions in that desperate period—with answers supplied him by Ziegler.

We were again in California covering Nixon in the summer of 1973 when the news broke that the White House had kept an "enemies list" which included a number of outstanding journalists, actors, and other prominent persons. During a briefing Adam Clymer of the *Baltimore Sun* asked Warren why the name of Tom O'Neill, a deceased *Sun* political columnist, was on the list.

Before Warren could reply, I piped up: "How did he die?"

The reporters roared with laughter, and even Warren broke into a grin while chiding me for such irreverence. I was amused when Julie Eisenhower said she thought that keeping an "enemies list" was "silly." "After all," she told me, "we all know who our enemies are."

Watergate was inescapable. On August 1, 1973, I covered a State Dinner in honor of Japanese Premier Kakuei Tanaka. The beleaguered Nixon said in a toast: "Let others spend their time dealing

with the murky, small, unimportant vicious little things. We have spent our time and will spend our time building a better world."
Ironically, Tanaka fell from power only a few months after Nixon, following an exposé of his own involvement in a Watergate-style scandal.

Nixon's estrangement from the press and the public increased. Soon it seemed that he was talking to only two people: Gen. Alexander M. Haig, his Chief of Staff, and Ziegler.

One day, after we had not seen the President for some time, we went to the White House to take some photographs. I decided to wear a casual slack outfit to the White House: pants and a silk shirt, since pants outfits are most comfortable for the life-style of a White House reporter.

As we went into the Oval Office, Nixon teased me. "Helen, are you still wearing slacks?" he asked. "Do you prefer them actually? Every time I see a girl in slacks it reminds me of China."

Nixon continued to joke about women in pants. "This is not said in an uncomplimentary way," he said with a broad smile, "but slacks can do something for some people and some it can't."

Then he added: "I think you do very well—turn around."

I pirouetted, and the President said: "Do they cost less than a gown?"

"No," I replied.

"Then change," he said, but with a smile.

The slacks incident was widely carried in the newspapers and all hell broke loose with women's libbers, who sent irate letters to the President. All the women who were addicted to pants suits felt insulted. But the President got a bad rap on the incident. I believe he was trying to make a friendly approach to the press after the long estrangement, and I do not think he intended any rudeness. I do know that Nixon women never wore pants suits around the White House, although naturally they did at Camp David. Actually that afternoon I had to go to the mountaintop retreat to cover Nixon, so my attire was proper even from his perspective.

From the summer of 1973 on, Nixon's news conferences were all Watergate-oriented. At San Clemente in late August, aides reportedly had to push him toward the microphone because he so dreaded to face the press for the first time since the Watergate hearings.

The barrier between the President and the press grew more formidable. Questions became tougher and Nixon began to respond as though he truly was in an enemy camp. Hostility broke into the open on October 26, 1973, when, quivering with rage, the President said:

I have never heard or seen such outrageous, vicious, distorted reporting in twenty-seven years of public life. When people are pounded night after night with that kind of frantic, hysterical reporting, it naturally shakes their confidence.

I have a quality which is, I guess I must have inherited it from my Midwestern mother and father, which is that the tougher it gets, the cooler I get. . . . I suppose because I've been through so much, that maybe one of the reasons is when I have to face an international crisis, I have what it takes.

It was heartbreaking. I remember walking into the Oval Office one day for picture-taking and I read an appeal in his sad eyes as he looked up for one brief moment.

Millions of viewers saw a distraught President give Ziegler a rough push in New Orleans just before an appearance before the Veterans of Foreign Wars. He was furious because reporters were following him into the hall. I thought the White House permitted a rare moment of candor for those days when it was admitted after we flew from New Orleans to California that the President was understandably "under a strain." Never before had I ever heard a White House spokesman concede that a President was under emotional stress, even when I knew one was.

To me the most excruciating press conference of the Nixon years was held on October 26, 1973. A full-scale televised production, staged in the East Room, it came at the end of the three-week Arab-Israeli War, but more significant, it came on the heels of the "Saturday Night Massacre."

By October of 1973, the Watergate affair had heightened the President's hostility toward reporters, and I will concede that by this time many reporters were harboring resentment toward him.

We had gone too long without answers from the President about the Watergate muddle and Ron Ziegler had fed us nothing but a series of fairytales.

The President opened with a lengthy statement about U.S. peacemaking efforts in the Mideast and a brief, noncommittal statement about the "Saturday Night Massacre." But reporters refused to let him brush the matter aside. There was a barrage of questions. The President tried to take the offensive, boasting of his leadership in foreign affairs and his friendship with Soviet leader Leonid Brezhnev. Reporters went back to Watergate and the firing of Cox. The tension was almost palpable when Dan Rather of CBS News asked: "Mr. President, I wonder if you could share with us your thoughts, tell us what goes through your mind when you hear people who love this country and people who believe in you say reluctantly that perhaps you should resign or be impeached."

The President replied with a strained smile: "Well, I am glad we don't take the vote of this room, let me say." He charged that the TV networks had allowed commentators to call him a "tyrant" and "dictator."

In an answer to another question he digressed once more to deliver a lengthy harangue at the press, particularly the "electronic media," charging biased reporting.

I am not blaming anybody for that. Perhaps what happened is that what we did brought it about, and therefore the media decided that they would have to take that particular line.

But when people are pounded night after night with that kind of frantic, hysterical reporting, it naturally shakes their confidence. And yet, I should point out that even in this week, when many thought that the President was shell-shocked, unable to act, the President acted decisively in the interests of peace, in the interests of the country, and I can assure you that whatever shocks gentlemen of the press may have . . . these shocks will not affect me in my doing my job.

Robert Pierpont of CBS News was on his feet immediately seeking recognition from the President. He finally got it, several questions later, and the press conference culminated in this exchange:

Pierpont: Mr. President, you have lambasted the television networks pretty well. . . . What is it about the television coverage of you in these past weeks and months that has so aroused your anger?

The President: Don't get the impression that you arouse my anger.

Pierpont: I'm afraid, sir, that I have that impression.

The President: You see, one can only be angry with those he respects.

There was a long, low moan from the assembled reporters in the East Room. It was not a disrespectful gesture, for it was involuntary and it symbolized the nadir that the press conference had hit.

Those were trying days. Talk of impeachment filled the air. Nixon fired Special Prosecutor Archibald Cox, who took him to court to get the Watergate tapes, resulting in the domino resignations of Attorney General Elliot Richardson and Deputy Attorney General William Ruckelshaus and leading to a firestorm of public anger. Chief of Staff Alexander M. Haig admitted that the White House had vastly miscalculated public sentiment. October 1973 was catastrophic in other ways. Vice President Spiro T. Agnew was forced to resign. The Arab-Israeli October War flared, and Nixon declared a worldwide general military alert, which terrified Washington.

As early as August, Nixon apparently was aware that Agnew's days in the Vice Presidency were numbered. The United States Attorney in Baltimore had notified the White House that a scandal was unfolding, and it became necessary to convince Agnew to resign. His other choice was to stand trial. The President met with him several times. Little was revealed of those sessions but Agnew decided on resignation—on October 10, 1973—after pleading no contest to income tax evasion charges. I learned that, as the Vice President continued to protest his innocence in those sessions, the President would look out the window. The meetings in Nixon's hideaway office fostered a war of nerves in an administration that certainly didn't need another scandal.

What came afterward was tragic to anyone who cherishes his good name and reputation in this world. Spiro T. Agnew became a non-person. It was almost as if he had never existed, as far as the Nixon administration, and the country, were concerned. Certainly that seemed true when Nixon was host to a victory-style celebration at the White House to announce that Michigan Congressman

Gerald R. Ford was his choice as Vice President. In his television appearance Nixon did not mention the circumstances of Ford's appointment or the man he replaced.

The energy shortage gave Nixon a chance to shake the press by conserving Air Force One fuel. He arranged to fly secretly to California with his family during the 1973 Christmas holidays.

I learned of the trip as the Nixons were heading covertly for Dulles International Airport to take a commercial jetliner to Los Angeles. Deputy Press Secretary Warren indicated that it was true but declined to confirm the report until Nixon was airborne. That night I was on a "red-eye" special to California while other White House correspondents scrambled for reservations for the quickest flight to the West Coast. It took about thirty-six hours for everyone to catch up with the President and start covering him again. He had gone into hiding and I found it as heartrending as it was irritating.

Nixon had once jokingly referred to the White House as an "isolation booth," but as time wore on, it became a bunker.

I have often wondered when Mrs. Nixon first faced the tragedy that awaited her family.

During the 1972 campaign she passed off Watergate questions with a curt, defensive, "I only know what I read in the newspapers." She was with the President at the Camp David retreat, during the last weekend in April 1973 when her anguished husband told his two most trusted aides that they must resign as a result of Watergate revelations. The trauma of it all must have begun to hit her then. A week later, when Nixon wondered aloud whether he should resign, Pat joined her daughters in ardently persuading him that to quit would be an "admission of wrongdoing."

From that point on, Mrs. Nixon seemed to draw down a curtain on her public life. Her public appearances became fewer and she began ducking reporters for fear of being asked about Watergate. Perhaps she read the handwriting on the wall, yet she never stopped believing that her husband would prevail.

Her public statements were sincere; she kept the faith to the bitter end. She had fierce loyalty and was convinced that her husband was telling the truth. As the end neared, she confided to friends that she wished the President had burned the tapes, and justified this on the grounds that they were "like love letters." With tightened fists, she stressed his innocence even after he released the massive transcripts which sparked demands for his resignation. She read the transcripts over a period of about nine hours, and challenged reporters to do the same, strangely convinced they would prove that her husband had told the truth.

When Nixon, low in spirits and weak in health, suffered an attack of viral pneumonia in July 1973, Mrs. Nixon visited him at Bethesda Naval Medical Center. Uncharacteristically, she wore dark glasses. She obviously had been crying and pointedly turned the other way from reporters who were outside keeping the vigil.

I could not understand why Nixon did not summon her when chest pains awoke him in the middle of the night. She was not told until several hours later, after a medical diagnosis had been made.

I remember covering a brief ceremony involving Mrs. Nixon in which a young man brought her his hometown newspaper, and she held it up to show reporters. "See," she said, "no Watergate," and there was nothing about the scandal in the small weekly paper.

I pride myself on having the chutzpah needed to approach the high and the mighty, but I must say it took me quite a while, perhaps too long, to screw up nerve to ask Mrs. Nixon, "What are your feelings about the Watergate affair?"

The question upset her terribly. She replied tensely: "Like Julie, I have faith," and she fled from the Blue Room.

Later I heard that she had told some of her staffers, "How could Helen ask me such a question? I thought we were friends."

As a journalist I felt I would have been remiss not to seek her viewpoint, even when I knew it would hurt. At that moment I saw how much she was personally suffering and the toll it had taken of her self-confidence.

Following a trip to Latin America where she scored a triumph as an ambassador of goodwill in March 1974, Mrs. Nixon followed her habit of walking through the plane to talk to reporters, all of whom she knew on a first name basis. It was jovial at first, but then her temper flared when a newswoman mentioned the strain she had been under for the past year. "No, I really don't wish to speak of it," she said. "It is a personal thing and why bring that into the trip? You all who follow me day after day know how positive I feel about everything. And I really have faith in the judgment of the American people and the *press* people. I'm not going to rehash an innuendo and source story around in repetition."

The truth, she said, had sustained her. "I have great faith in my husband. He's an honorable, dedicated person. And when you know the truth you have nothing to fear. I have a very positive outlook."

Not to be deterred when another reporter piped up: "Did anybody in Latin America ask you about," Mrs. Nixon chopped her down. "No, this isn't covered there," she said. "It's only covered in the metropolitan newspapers—even out in the country in the U.S.A., it isn't."

The journey wound up in Nashville, Tennessee, on her sixty-second birthday. Nixon had flown in to meet her for a joint celebration at the Grand Ole Opry, but Mrs. Nixon's own staff was upset when they felt that the First Lady was being ignored by the President who claimed center stage all evening, bantering with the stars of the Opry and playing with Roy Acuff's yo-yo.

As the revelations compounded one another, Mrs. Nixon stopped reading newspapers. She told my friend Diane Beury they were going to "Fight, Fight, Fight."

A sense of persecution, of "They're trying to get us," pervaded the First Family. Julie began beating the bushes with an extra fervor to win support for her father and at the same time to lambast the press. She said she had taken up the battle cry on her own, but certainly Nixon wanted a defender of such winning charm and he was grateful. "It was as if they were one person, Nixon and Julie, and she was defending herself," said a friend.

AP's Fran Lewine and I interviewed Julie on her twenty-fifth birthday in San Clemente, California. We gathered at the San Clemente Inn for lunch, where a cake had been baked in her honor. As we talked, it was clear that Julie had not expected for us to probe so deeply on the main question of the day—Watergate—but this was no time for us to ask about the President's catsup-cottage cheese lunches. With Nixon himself in hiding, we had to probe the person closest to his thinking. I don't think I had ever grilled a

President so relentlessly, but she was candid and exposed the steel within her perky exterior. She gave us insights into Nixon's suffering.

When I asked her if it was true that her father had threatened to resign over Watergate, she related that a family powwow had been held at Camp David four days after Nixon forced Haldeman's and Ehrlichman's resignations.

He was playing the devil's advocate one evening, saying . . . you know, he would say, "Should I resign? Would it be better for the country? Would the wounds heal faster? Would it [the country] be able to move faster to other things?"

We said "No." We didn't think he should because resigning would be an admission of wrongdoing and we also felt that he was the man for the job and he had started things and needed to finish them. I think it was more than just a rhetorical question. I think he really thought, "Will this end everything?"

She also told us, "My father really just had complete faith in everyone around him. All I can say is that he was being assured that no one else [in the White House] was involved."

The next day, White House Deputy Press Secretary Gerald Warren denied that Nixon had contemplated resigning. Even though it was clear that Nixon at that time was simply seeking the reassurance from his loved ones, we believed the President's daughter.

What came through in the interview was Julie's misunderstanding of the public's concern and her belief in offense as the best defense. When wiretaps were brought up, she asserted that Attorney General Robert Kennedy had wiretapped more. As for government expenditures of some $1.3 million on Nixon's California and Florida homes, including a new furnace for his San Clemente Spanish-style villa, Julie charged, "President Kennedy had three homes and I'm sure that must have added up to more." Kennedy did own a summer home at Hyannis Port but he stayed at the family home or leased a villa at Palm Beach, Florida, during his winters in the White House.

When the subject of abuses of government agencies and invasion of privacy came up, Julie again cited alleged wrongdoing by previous administrations. Like Johnson, the Nixons were still fighting the Kennedy image.

She looked somewhat abashed when the interview was over. She confided later to her family that it was "rough." Fran and I knew that we were putting hard questions to Julie, but we felt that since she was speaking out on the major issues, we could not focus only on things stereotyped as "feminine."

Julie's reaction to Watergate continued to be righteous indignation. After a federal court jury in New York acquitted Mitchell and Stans in the Vesco case involving contributions to Nixon's 1972 campaign, Julie swung around to me on the South Lawn one day and snapped, "See, my father does pick men you can trust!"

She also revealed to AP's Ann Blackman that she, like her mother, had decided to "Fight, Fight, Fight."

Julie's interviews drew a portrait of her father as sitting at the piano late at night playing soft melodic favorite tunes and sometimes not wanting to get out of bed in the morning to face another day.

Sometimes Nixon would call her and other members of the family to tell them, "Don't read the newspapers today."

During this period, Julie was the only member of the family publicly standing her ground. Her mother and her sister, Tricia, remained in the background.

When the Watergate scandal swamped the White House, Tricia remained conspicuously silent, but not for lack of loyalty. In early 1974, she and her husband emerged from the White House one winter day and crossed the street to Lafayette Park to thank pro-Nixon demonstrators. Her eyes filled with tears when I asked her about rumors that she and Ed Cox were splitting up. "Ridiculous," she said. Then, looking at him, she added, "We love each other." He returned her loving look.

When I questioned Ed about Watergate, his defense of the President was passionate. He labeled Dean, who had implicated Nixon in the Watergate coverup, a "coward," charging that Dean was only seeking "immunity" in testifying against Nixon. He also struck out against the press for what he termed "persecution" of the President. When Nixon pulled a large team of lawyers into the White House to work on his defense, Ed offered to take leave from his Wall Street law firm to assist in the legal struggle for Nixon's survival in office, but the family decided against the idea.

David Eisenhower had first explained that he was not really privy enough to the President to speak on the matter; but in an interview I had with David which was published one day before Nixon forced out H. R. Haldeman and John D. Ehrlichman, David said, "I admire President Nixon for taking the action he did in starting his own investigation. I think everyone realizes he is doing the right thing. It would be a terrible irony if something like Watergate were to cloud his second administration." Among the entire Nixon family, he was the most detached and the most able to discuss the problem dispassionately.

I will always consider remarkable the joint news conference Julie and David held in the East Garden in May 1974. John F. Kennedy might have called it a "profile in courage," with both of them facing a barrage of penetrating questions on Watergate. I had pressed the First Lady's press secretary, Helen Smith, for an interview with Julie after the release of the massive White House tapes and subsequent calls for Nixon's resignation. Other reporters apparently did the same thing and a press conference was arranged to accommodate all of us.

I had the first question and asked, "Do either of you foresee any circumstances where the President would resign?"

"Absolutely not, no," said David. He added that his answer was "categorical."

Julie replied, "You know, Helen, I am not surprised by the question. In fact, Helen Smith called David and me yesterday and said so many members of the media have wanted to talk to us and that this was the number-one question. Then yesterday I got three calls from friends in different states saying, 'We have heard these rumors. Is it true they are drawing up papers of resignation?' That is one of the rumors floating around, and I don't know how those rumors get started, but there really is no truth to it at all. He is stronger now than he ever has been in his determination to see this through."

Julie and David had been primed for the question-and-answer session the night before during a cruise down the Potomac River with the President and Mrs. Nixon aboard the yacht *Sequoia.*

CBS correspondent Robert Pierpont shook Julie for a moment when he observed, "Mrs. Eisenhower, may I say first of all, that I feel I have to apologize for addressing these questions to you, since in our system we do not hold the sins of the fathers against the following generations, and we don't have a monarchy in which you are going to inherit the power. I am not quite sure why you are here to answer these questions."

"Mr. Pierpont," Julie responded, her voice quavering with emotion, "I am going to try to control myself in answering the question because it really does wound me. First of all, I am here to answer these questions because Helen Smith said that she received fifty-five phone calls from members of the media wanting to know the family's reaction and wanting to know if my father was going to resign.

"Now if the media has a hangup and an obsession about resignation and feels that they must be reassured from members of the family that my father is not going to resign, I feel that as a daughter it is my obligation to come out here and to say, 'No, he is not going to resign.' "

Julie continued, saying that her father "does not want me out here because he does not want anyone to construe that I am trying to answer questions for him. I am not trying to answer questions for him. I am just trying to pray for enough courage to meet his courage. Really."

Questioned on whether Nixon had discussed resigning with his family, she admitted he had and, "he has said—in fact last night, it was a very great quotation, very quotable—he said he would take this constitutionally down to the wire. He said he would go to the Senate, and he said if there was one Senator who believed in him, that is the way it would be. So if the Committee votes a bill of impeachment, if the House goes through with it, if it goes to the Senate, he has said if there is only one Senator that it is going to be a constitutional process."

Julie, in the same news conference, called the beginning of Watergate a "third- or fourth-rate burglary," reminiscent of Press Secretary Ronald Ziegler's first public comment on the subject in 1972. She commented that Nixon's enthusiastic aides simply tried to win "brownie points" with the President, but went too far.

No daughter ever had greater love for her father. Julie believed in her father and battled the growing forces seeking his resignation or impeachment. She insisted her father was not going to "bug out" and she and her mother were the last to be convinced he should relinquish his post.

In July 1974, as Nixon's days in office were fading, he and the family went to California. At a party in Beverly Hills given in his honor by longtime California supporters, I approached Tricia and asked her about Watergate. She let me have it in no uncertain terms. "My father is innocent, innocent. He is just being harmed by jealous politicians who want his job," she declared, and blamed the press as well for his troubles. She forecast that he would survive the ordeal and would not resign.

From the beginning of 1974, I knew Nixon would have to relinquish the Presidency. Nothing was working; there was no initiative and the government was severely crippled. Morale was worsening. White House secretaries were saying they worked at "1600 Pennsylvania Avenue" rather than at the White House.

In that period, Nixon's news conferences were few and far between. Each one became a confrontation between the President and the press. I know that on March 6, 1974, I felt pained by the way he looked when he strode into the East Room, defiant but forlorn. The President began that televised news conference by announcing that I had been named chief of the United Press International Bureau at the White House. Kind words and recognition. I responded with a polite, "Thank you, Mr. President." Then I began to sweat. I'll admit I was in a dilemma. I had come to the news conference with a tough question. I could see that my colleagues were waiting to see whether I would lay it on the line or soften the blow because the President, indeed, had been very nice to single me out. My hard question related to a tape of his March 21, 1973 meeting when he had learned that hush money already had been paid to the Watergate defendants. Nixon said that he had insisted "it is wrong for sure," but added "I know what I meant, and I know also what I did."

I know that many of the TV viewers, and perhaps even Nixon's staff, might have thought I was ungracious but I decided I could not pull any punches on a legitimate and fair question. When Nixon called on me for the second question, I did the only thing I could do. I asked what I intended to ask in the first place.

Mr. President, Mr. Haldeman, your former top aide in the White House, has been charged with perjury because he testified that you said it would be wrong to pay hush money to silence the Watergate defendents, and last August you said that was accurate. Can you, and will you, provide proof that you did indeed say it would be wrong?

The question was very painful and the transcript of that conference shows that the President uttered some 750 words in the course of a rambling and inconclusive reply. That evening I wrote a personal note to the President thanking him for his kind words.

From that day forward until Nixon quit, I wrote almost daily stories quoting the President as saying "Resignation is an easy cop-out," or Nixon says he is not going to "bug out of the job he was elected to do."

Nixon's last few news conferences were confrontations, and I am sure he felt that he was going into the lions' den. Each question put to him in those dying months revolved around his role in Watergate.

"If I were a liberal, Watergate would be a blip," Nixon told Rabbi Baruch Korff, his friend and supporter, in an interview for Korff's book, *The Personal Nixon: Staying on the Summit.* When Korff asked how he rated the performance of the White House Press Corps, Nixon replied:

I know, for example, my policies are generally disapproved of, and there are some, putting it in the vernacular, who hate my guts with a passion. But I don't hate them, none of them, individually I understand. Their philosophies are different, they don't agree with my positions and after all they want to write and take me on. An individual must not turn hatred for hatred. . . .

Nixon said that he was not consumed by "what consumed my friends in the press room. So I think you can put it this way—I can see, not all, but I can see in the eyes of them not only their hatred but their frustration, and as a matter of fact, I really feel sorry for them. . . ."

During his last months in office, Nixon took his family to Trader Vic's for dinner one evening after attending a birthday party for dowager Alice Roosevelt Longworth. After dinner, in front of the Statler Hilton hotel, Nixon paused to talk to reporters and in an emotional riposte told them that if Mrs. Longworth had been reading the Washington papers "she would be dead by now." Mrs. Longworth, however, was an inveterate newspaper reader.

Nixon afterwards began preparing for trips abroad to enhance his standing at home. Like Presidents before him, he knew the American people were generally very supportive of their Presidents when they go abroad in pursuit of peace. In foreign capitals, Nixon's plight had not hit home and it took a long time for leaders abroad to understand the true meaning of Watergate in our national life.

Nixon arranged summit trips to both Moscow and the Middle East early in the summer of 1974, hoping to demonstrate indispensable world leadership. Following the October 1973 Arab-Israeli War, Nixon had worked to bring the ceasefire into a permanent peace package. Although he had ordered a crash twenty-four-hour-a-day airlift of supplies to Israel (he told Rabbi Baruch Korff he believed Israel survived the war because of that assistance), the Arabs were also happy to let him take the lead in pushing for a final settlement of the perennial problem which had made the Middle East a tinderbox.

The Russians too had decided they could do business with Nixon and they were not anxious to have an unknown in the White House. Secretary of State Henry Kissinger also told reporters that Watergate had no strong impact on the conduct of foreign affairs. Kissinger later changed his tune.

From the moment we set foot in Moscow, I felt something was wrong. Nixon, the powerhouse, was not going to be able to cut a deal with the Soviets. It was clear that they had decided he was through. In his first toast at a Kremlin banquet Nixon stressed the importance of "personal diplomacy," meaning his special relationship with Soviet Premier Leonid I. Brezhnev, but Brezhnev, whose own power was limited by Politburo rivals, declined to rise to the bait. At a later banquet at the American Embassy which Nixon hosted Brezhnev rejected "personal diplomacy," a big snub to Nixon.

We flew to the Black Sea area with Nixon and Brezhnev where they continued their talks at a resort dacha in the idyllic surroundings of lily ponds, spring flowers, and a view of mountains against blue skies. I was in the "pool" that went to Brezhnev's dacha for picture-taking before the start of their talks. I took one look at Nixon in his casual maroon sports jacket, white shirt, and gray slacks and knew that something was seriously wrong. He walked slowly, pacing himself as if he were in a daze. All the life seemed to have drained out of him. He appeared to be only going through the motions. He probably knew then that he would fly home from the summit meeting empty-handed. The prize of a new strategic arms limitation treaty had eluded him.

Kissinger seemed to be staying in the background, walking ten paces behind Nixon and Brezhnev. In the past he had been right up there, always in the picture. I strolled up to Kissinger and asked him what was going on. "Nobody ever tells me anything," he said ruefully. His joking remark was interpreted as a sign that he was no longer in the power position he had once held and that Nixon was going to be more assertive as the foreign policy innovator. There had been several indications that that was so.

Reporters were always given a bad time in Moscow by the Secret Police. It was hand-to-hand combat all the way and sometimes I had to be rescued from the KGB by the Secret Service. White House aides also got pushed around, and if Nixon was aware of it, he did not show it or seem to care.

I went to the Kremlin in a "pool" with photographers and was the only American reporter on hand when the Soviet Police barred me from going into the room where the Brezhnev-Nixon meeting was to begin. A Secret Service agent kept me company outside the door as I angrily cooled my heels. Suddenly I looked up and coming down a long corridor was Nixon, looking haggard, surrounded by Russians and his aides. I appealed to him: "Mr. President," I said, hoping he would ask me what was wrong. Instead he glared at me and his expression, which needed no interpretation, was an inquiring "What is SHE doing here?" Later I was told he was most unhappy to see me there. I wondered whether other Presidents would have tolerated an American reporter being pushed around by a host government.

But perhaps understandably Nixon was weary of the press by this time and worried about himself. Nothing was going right. On the other hand, it seemed that when he visited a foreign country Nixon became plus royalist. I could not, for one, understand why there was not a bigger outcry when Nixon refused to permit any American interpreters to be in the room for his private talks with Brezhnev. Instead, they both used only a suave Russian diplomat, Viktor Sukhodrev, as the translator for both sides. But then he knew he had his tapes.

One observer who had seen the distraught Nixon before he had departed on his journey asked a communications official "What if he pushes the button?" "Don't worry," he replied, "there are too many safeguards, there are too many watching him."

On the Middle East journey, Nixon was lionized. Several million Egyptians danced in the streets all the way from Cairo to Alexandria to hail the American President. Banners strung across the boulevards along the Nile read "Nixon We Trust You" and other welcoming slogans that were uplifting to Americans. The Arab countries we toured, such as Syria and Jordan, were armed camps and we were escorted into Damascus and Amman in motorcades with jeeploads of machine-gun-carrying soldiers. What a way to go, I thought. In Israel, I went to the dinner at the Knesset honoring Nixon and heard Golda Meir jab him a bit on his problems at home.

Nixon had been observed limping, but not much was made of it at the time. When we got back to Washington CBS correspondent Dan Rather scooped us with the news that Nixon was suffering from phlebitis, a blood clot in his left leg. Gerald Warren, the Deputy Press Secretary, gave out a minimum of information but little by little reporters learned that Nixon's doctors had recommended that he go into a hospital in Salzburg, Austria, while he was en route to the Middle East. He had refused to do so and pledged his doctors to secrecy on the subject.

He had hoped that he would come back home heralded as a peacemaker. But when he returned to the White House he learned the bitter truth—the American people were more fascinated with the unfolding impeachment drama than ever before. The voluminous transcripts he had released on April 30, 1974, evoked widespread calls for his resignation in many of the nation's leading newspapers and on Capitol Hill. The dialogue showed Nixon to be a man who used profanity as much as his predecessors. But Americans across the land just had not thought of Nixon in terms of "expletives deleted." In fact, few reporters had ever seen him in those relaxed moments when he used earthy expressions but we knew he cussed when he was angry, as all Presidents do. In the case of Lyndon B. Johnson, we all took his barnyard irreverence in our stride, and it could be explicit and colorful. John F. Kennedy also apparently often relied on a stream of profanity to get the message across to his cronies in privacy. Reporters remembered that during the 1960 Presidential race Nixon had attacked Harry Truman's use of profanity and called for a clean-cut President like Dwight D. Eisenhower in the White House.

When we flew to California with Nixon in July 1974, I was convinced it was all over for Nixon and I told my boss, Grant Dillman, so on several occasions. It was just a question of time and there was little of that left for Nixon.

There were so many indications that spelled his doom in the Presidency. When we arrived at our favorite motel, the Surf and Sand, at Laguna Beach, the former owner and manager, Merrill Johnson, a great friend of the press, greeted me and said: "This is your last trip, isn't it?"

"Yes," I said. It was all intuition, but it was so clear. There is a word in Arabic that seemed to sum it up: *Maktoub*. It means "It is written"; "Destiny."

The equipment in the Surf and Sand press room was all on rollers indicating that we were temporary, indeed. Soon after our arrival for a summer stay, we were told by the San Clemente Inn where we had another press room closer to the Western White House, that we could no longer use the Inn. We moved to a nearby schoolhouse. The Secret Service agents and White House aides also got the word that there was "no room at the inn" for them.

We saw little of Nixon in those days, but we sensed the emptiness. It became a charade, with most of the White House statements responding to Watergate or impeachment charges. White House counselor Dean Burch likened the Judiciary Committee counsels to "hired guns." Ziegler called the impeachment proceedings a "kangaroo court." Vice President Gerald R. Ford dropped by and during a news conference on the lawn at the Nixon compound, declared that the President had not committed an impeachable offense.

James D. St. Clair, Nixon's chief lawyer who had argued Nixon's case for retaining possession of his Watergate tapes in the Supreme Court, arrived a day before the Court ruled and refused to say unequivocally whether Nixon would obey the Court. St. Clair hedged when I asked at his news conference if he would quit as Nixon's lawyer if the President refused to abide by a Supreme Court decision.

Reporters who interviewed St. Clair when he took the job in January 1974 had tried to find out if he would have complete access to Nixon and the Watergate tapes. But he made it clear his relationship with Nixon was confidential. He must have known that a lawyer should have the full facts, but apparently he believed that he should operate within the perimeters set by the President, even if he was his client. St. Clair told reporters he had not listened to the tapes.

On July 24, 1974, the momentous tape decision was handed down. The Supreme Court, including the four members Nixon had appointed to give it a conservative, "strict constructionist" cast, decided eight to zero that he must turn over the Watergate tapes to Special Prosecutor Leon Jaworski as evidence in the coverup trial of former Nixon aides. The White House had not realized that the ruling would come that soon or be so devastating.

That day began early for me with a call from my Washington office informing me that the decision was imminent. The rumor around the nation's capital was that the decision would be unanimous against Nixon. Reporters began converging on the press room to take up the vigil. When the first bulletin came through I tried to reach Warren for comment. But that comment did not come for eight hours. I never thought for a moment that Nixon would defy the law, although his lawyers and spokesmen refused to say flatly that he would obey. Nixon, after all, had capitulated to a court order for the first batch of his tapes after the "Saturday Night Massacre."

We were told that Haig did not inform Nixon of the decision until forty minutes after it was handed down. Incredibly, all the world knew, except Nixon. It was explained that Haig wanted to be thoroughly prepared to explain the decision before discussing it with Nixon. There were also indications that it was going to be difficult to break the bad news to the already tormented President.

Among the tapes sought was the June 23, 1972 conversation between Nixon and Haldeman, which came to be called the "smoking gun" by Nixon defenders on the House Judiciary Committee who argued there was no proof that the President had taken part in the coverup. During the conversation, Nixon authorized the use of the CIA to block the Watergate break-in investigation. Haldeman told Nixon that Mitchell and Dean had suggested that the CIA tell the FBI to "stay the hell" out of the investigation because it would expose cloak and dagger CIA operations.

In Watergate terms, Nixon apparently knew the "jig was up," since investigators were going to hear that incriminating chat. According to Nixon's close friend, Rabbi Baruch Korff, both Haig and St. Clair had heard the June 23 tape in May 1974 and were aware of its possible impact. Nixon had also listened to it and had lived with the knowledge that it could destroy him as President.

After many hours St. Clair went before TV cameras in our press room to say "this President of course would abide by the Supreme Court ruling." St. Clair had spent the day with Nixon. He saw for himself the President's personal anguish. The Boston lawyer also attempted to put the best face possible on the cataclysmic defeat. Earlier that day, Nixon had telephoned Fred J. Buzhardt, a member of his Watergate legal team at the White House, to listen to the June 23 tape again, probably hoping against hope that it would not be as damaging as it appeared and that he could survive in office.

St. Clair flew back to Washington that evening. When a White House aide called him to confirm that he would appear on the ABC-TV network show "Issues and Answers" Sunday, July 28, St.

Clair brushed him off, saying "No Way." He could no longer publicly defend Nixon's proclaimed innocence.

On July 27, the House Judiciary Committee voted its first article of impeachment—obstruction of justice. Nixon was walking along Red Beach at nearby Camp Pendleton when the final vote came. Ziegler did not inform him until almost an hour afterwards and then it was in a telephone call to the shoreline where the Secret Service had set up special communications for him. We were banned from the area.

The next day the Nixons flew home with their daughter and son-in-law, Tricia and Edward Cox, and, as I had observed so many times in the past, the President stood at the ramp with his wife and they smiled and waved their arms, just like old times.

The flight back to Washington was melancholy. We had been told by Ziegler that Nixon had the strength and would go down to the wire in the impeachment process. But when we were aboard Air Force One, Haig seemed to sing a different tune. He was not his old confident self, and when pressed he said that Nixon would resign if he decided it was in the "national interest."

Haig had become acting President in the months before. At first he resisted the power thrust upon him but, according to other White House aides, "he grew to like it." He also became supersensitive about his own role and would make late night telephone calls to try to track down news leaks. Military man that he was, he often used the expression "Your Commander-in-Chief has ordered you" in order to stress his instructions. He obviously made some day-to-day decisions that belonged to the President; but on the other hand, a distracted Nixon had handed him the power.

When I covered Nixon on his last trip to California as President, death was in the air. We could smell it.

When we returned to Andrews Air Force Base in Washington, I followed Nixon to the fence where he shook hands with well-wishers. When I tried to ask a question, his Press Secretary Ron Ziegler typically chastised me, and it was Mrs. Nixon who saved me from another useless confrontation with Ziegler. She came over and said,

"I want you to see someone." With her arm around my back, she led me to the fence where my husband, Doug, was standing. "I know how you feel," she observed of our reunion. "I love Dick very much, too."

I gave Doug a quick kiss and walked toward the Army One helicopter with Mrs. Nixon. She had kept the President waiting because of me but it did not disturb her.

In the days that followed, we saw nothing of Nixon. He had holed up in the Lincoln sitting room listening to the deadly tapes. It was his favorite retreat and even on the hottest day of summer, he would have a fire in the fireplace and turn on the air conditioning.

The sights and sounds of those days remain vivid. Rumors were rampant in the capital that Nixon would resign, but none of the top echelon of Nixon staffers would confirm it. On the contrary, Warren said repeatedly at the news briefings that Nixon would go through the "constitutional process." He conceded at one point that the House might vote impeachment. Even when he knew it was almost certain that Nixon was going to resign, he continued to say the opposite from the press room podium.

Nixon's Communications Director Ken W. Clawson tried desperately to hold back the tide, but even he seemed to have lost a sense of reality. The loyal band had dwindled, and gradually it was every man for himself. Some devoted defenders remained until the bitter end and beyond. Among them was Clawson, who had produced one administration spokesman after another to defend Nixon publicly at the so-called "Cocktails with Clawson." Also staying in line were Father John J. McLaughlin, the silver-tongued Jesuit who was on the speech-writing staff, and Bruce Herschenson, who kept in touch with Nixon supporters in the losing battle to save him in the Presidency.

By July 31, Haig, with the help of St. Clair, apparently made a command decision that Nixon was through. How best to ease him out of the White House? From then on it was brilliant orchestration by Haig, who touched all the bases, giving Nixon only one option—to resign. But he had to convince the man himself. In some ways I have likened it to a silent coup d'etat, but Haig was determined to have Nixon depart with dignity. It was human, too, I suppose, that Haig and others began to think of their own reputations and their own futures, which were in jeopardy.

Later, Nixon's closest intimates spoke of Haig as "That SOB, and the President jumped him from colonel to general." In their masterful execution of Nixon's demise, Haig and his coterie lined up Kissinger and speech writer Pat Buchanan, both of whom were influential with Nixon.

Nixon's family fought against the resignation. On August 2, they went to Camp David for the weekend. Nixon isolated himself at Aspen Lodge, while St. Clair, Haig, Ziegler, Buchanan, and chief speech writer Ray Price labored at a nearby cabin on the draft of a statement disclosing the contents of the June 23 tape. They were depressed, knowing from past experience what the impact would be when Nixon would reveal that all his prior statements were "at variance" with the facts. Throughout the ordeal, Haig and St. Clair kept in touch with important figures on Capitol Hill who learned before the public did the contents of the devastating tape. Many were outraged.

Only Haig and Ziegler shuttled back and forth to see Nixon, who was withdrawn but determined. When they passed on the suggestion that he resign, Nixon reportedly told them "I wish you hadn't said that."

I was at home celebrating my birthday that Sunday, August 4, but I gave up plans to go to dinner with my husband and friends and stayed by the telephone. I was certain something big was happening because the speech writers were clustered at Camp David. None of them would talk, but I knew from the super-secrecy involved that the resignation was probably in motion. Frustrated, I finally put in a transatlantic call to Helen Smith, the First Lady's press secretary who was vacationing in London, and asked her if she could find out what was happening at Camp David. Helen called Julie Eisenhower who reassured her that all was well, unless, as Julie told Helen, "you know something I don't know."

Actually, Julie had known since Friday that her father was seriously considering resigning. The family returned to the White House Sunday evening. She prayed he wouldn't.

Monday, taking the family and Rose Mary Woods on their last sail on the Presidential yacht *Sequoia*, Nixon kept in contact with Haig, who informed him that the Southern Senators, his last stronghold, were lining up for his impeachment. "Soft bastards," responded the emotionally wrought Nixon.

Reporters waited on the front lawn for a Tuesday Cabinet meeting to break up. When they emerged Treasury Secretary William E. Simon told reporters Nixon had said he was not going to resign and that he had the will to fight. But we extracted from him and others that no member of the Cabinet had applauded Nixon when he finished his fifteen minute monologue on his determination to remain in office.

Vice President Ford, who had been told the week before that he should be prepared to take over as President, nevertheless went ahead with a speaking tour the weekend of August 3, stating that Nixon had not committed an impeachable offense.

Meanwhile Kissinger, at Haig's insistence, had been privately urging Nixon to resign on grounds that uncertainty in United States leadership in the world could lead to a miscalculation by the enemy. Kissinger said Nixon was very "agitated" in those last days, and they talked intermittently by telephone. The trusted Kissinger was in a handholding position, simultaneously trying to comfort and coax the President to resign. "It was a very human problem," Kissinger told me later.

Nixon ordered his speech writers to go to work on a Resignation Address, but still had not definitely decided.

Rabbi Korff had been summoned to the White House by Julie Eisenhower and members of the family who needed support to urge Nixon to stay the course. Before Rabbi Korff went in to see Nixon in his hideaway office on Tuesday afternoon, Haig and Ziegler begged him not to persuade Nixon to stay on and suffer through an impeachment trial. Korff said later he felt that he was "used" by Haig. That night Korff passed the word to Douglas Wilson of the *Providence Journal* that Nixon was going to resign and that his decision was painful but irrevocable.

The next day I found Nixon's physician, Dr. Walter Tkach, and said, "It's over, isn't it?" He gently ignored the question, but a few days later admitted that my remark had surprised him. He told me that Nixon had appeared concerned, but never distraught, although the doctor said he would have considered a breakdown a natural reaction.

Wednesday, August 7, was the clincher. Key Republican leaders Senator Hugh Scott, Representative John J. Rhodes, and Senator Barry Goldwater came to the White House and brought the bad tidings that Nixon could count on only about fifteen Senators to stand by him through an impeachment trial.

Nixon once told an interviewer: "What helped keep us close together were my defeats and the great crises. All three women in my family never admitted my defeats in 1960 and 1962 the way I did. It's sort of the opposite of what some psychologists say about children." Now, even the tight family circle was not enough to sustain Nixon in office. That evening he gathered his family in the "California Room," the solarium on the third floor that had been Caroline Kennedy's nursery school and the room in which Luci and Lynda Bird Johnson's husbands had proposed, and told them he was quitting. Julie sobbed and her mother and sister broke into heartbreaking tears.

General Haig had dispatched Chief Photographer Ollie Atkins to take historic pictures of that heartbreaking family meeting. When Julie ran sobbing into her father's arms, Atkins caught a memorable picture that was distributed when Nixon went on the air to announce his resignation on Thursday, August 8. Most of the White House aides had sensed for days that it was coming. Some said he was martyred. Many who had stood by Nixon felt "betrayed." Others uttered profanities when mentioning his name. Julie herself thought her father was being made a "moral example," and that the same "ethical slide rule" had not been applied to his predecessors.

I practically moved into the White House, eating meals "catered" by press room candy and Coke machines. My one hot meal arrived when Helen Smith and her young secretary Terry Ivey brought me soup and sandwiches. Leaving the White House on Wednesday evening, I was still unable to confirm that Nixon would resign. On the walk I ran into his valet, Manolo Sanchez, who had tears in his eyes and anger in his voice. He felt his boss had been done in by enemies from within his own trusted circle and without.

Afterwards I picked up the tip that Nixon's speech writers were working on a resignation statement to be delivered the next evening. The UPI scoop hit the wires about 11:00 P.M. There was no denial, and we knew it was solid.

Thursday morning, August 8, I got to work early and waited. At the news briefing Ron Ziegler, his voice choking as he tried to hold back the tears, told reporters the President would deliver a speech on nationwide television at 9:00 P.M. that evening. Reporters in the press room fell over each other in the hurry to get to their telephones.

Later I walked into Gerry Warren's office. He was crying but wanted me to know that the farewell speech was being written by Nixon, not by his aides, as I had reported. "This will be HIS speech."

"I know, Gerry," I said, putting my arm around him in sympathy. "I know." Ironically, in a CBS interview on "Face the Nation" in August 1975, Warren said, when asked if Nixon had committed a crime, that he believed he had—obstruction of justice.

I found out that Nixon had been in the Oval Office since early morning. He requested that Marine Lt. Col. Jack Brennan be allowed to accompany him back to California. Brennan, who was his loyal aide, knew that trip would hurt and end his military career. He was right, and he left the service afterwards to become Nixon's chief aide in San Clemente.

Staffers recall that Nixon wondered if he would be able to get a set of the Camp David mugs he liked so much to take with him into retirement. Camp David mugs in the midst of debacle!

Even though the Vice President had held several sessions with Haig, and had his own staff preparing to take over, Ford told me months later that only when he walked into the Oval Office at 11:02 A.M. that morning and Nixon greeted him with "You will do a good job, Jerry," did he know for certain he would become President of the United States. The two men remained together for a strained off-the-record seventy minutes.

Shortly before six o'clock, as we readied ourselves for the address, we found ourselves locked in the press room. A policeman stood guard at our door. Every door of the White House and Executive Office Building was locked. No one could leave or enter.

During those forty minutes we were greatly concerned that something may have happened to Nixon. Warren tried to quell our protests by telling us "It's all a mistake," but even at that point the White House saw no need to be credible. Nixon had told the Secret Service he wanted to cross from his hideaway office to the White House without seeing the press or anyone else. Grasping his arm to comfort him, Ziegler walked with the sobbing President.

Nixon did not permit any reporters or photographers in the Oval Office when he delivered his address. Only TV technicians were present. He did not want Secret Service agents in the room either, but they stayed anyway.

Before going on the air he had met with two separate groups of Senators and Congressmen and expressed the hope that he had not let his friends down. Nixon said he had lost his "political base" and so had decided to resign. "I would have preferred to carry through to the finish whatever the personal agony it would have involved, and my family unanimously urged me to do so. But the interest of the nation must always come before any personal considerations."

A couple of hours after, Ziegler came into the press room and delivered his own astonishing valedictory:

I have been proud to be President Nixon's Press Secretary over the past five and a half years. I have tried to be professional, as all of you are professional, and I hope I have never underestimated the difficulty of your jobs or the energy and intelligence you bring to them. We have been through many difficult times together, and we have been through many historic times together. I know that I will remember the good ones and I hope you will, too.

There was dead silence when he finished. Not even a "So long, Ron."

Ziegler had told Nick Thimmesch in an interview in *Potomac* magazine on February 24, 1974,

Do you know where I will be January 20, 1977? I will be standing on the inaugural stand with the President of the United States, as the new President takes his oath of office. I will look over those stands and see all of the people. And I will know that I have seen a man under vicious attack show the courage and strength to last it out. . . . He will go out with dignity.

On their last night in the White House, Nixon and his wife strolled through the corridors for one last look. Again the White House was bolted and guarded to permit him to have the run of the mansion for one last time. Reporters were told to leave the press room.

Throughout the resignation ordeal Haig was in charge of the exit scenario. Days before, the Pentagon had been alerted that all commands from the White House must go through the Secretary of Defense, James Schlesinger. Nixon was in a grave emotional state, according to many aides around him, and Schlesinger moved to retain control of the armed forces.

During those agonized last days, Haldeman and Ehrlichman asked for pardons through intermediaries, but Nixon turned them down. There was talk of pardons, according to Haig. It was even rumored that Nixon was being urged to pardon himself.

On Friday morning, the household staff asked to say good-bye to him. Nixon came out in his pajamas and robe on the family floor for the tearful farewell and was joined by Mrs. Nixon. The maids and butlers, who were very fond of the Nixons, were overwhelmed with the sadness of the occasion. Holding hands, Tricia and her husband stole down to the Rose Garden where they had been married for a nostalgic stroll.

Shortly before ten o'clock on the morning of August 9, 1974, the President and his entire family, staring straight ahead, marched into the East Room where live cameras had been set up for Nixon's farewell remarks to his Cabinet and staff. I stood on the sidelines. It was impossible not to feel the pain. I wondered how he and his loved ones had the courage to stand there, emotionally exposed before the world.

But Nixon wanted to say again one final time that he was not a quitter. No one in that room will ever forget his personal anguish, nor the tragic faces of his wife and daughters. In his melancholy farewell, he evoked Teddy Roosevelt, his mother, and his father. He identified with Roosevelt saying, "He not only became President, but as an ex-President, he served his country always in the arena, tempestuous, strong, sometimes wrong, sometimes right, but he was a man."

He also warned that one should never permit oneself to be

destroyed by hatred. Dr. Tkach said that Nixon at that moment was more emotional than he had ever seen him.

I was struck by the fact that Nixon, in his swan song, delivered lines from Teddy Roosevelt which JFK often quoted:

The credit belongs to the man who is actually in the arena—whose face is marred by dust and sweat and blood . . . a leader who knows the great enthusiasms, the great devotions and spends himself in a worthy cause—who at best if he wins knows the thrills of high achievement—and if he fails fails while daring greatly—so that his place shall never be with those cold and timid souls who know neither victory nor defeat.

Pat Nixon stood on a platform in the East Room looking like a martyred Madonna, her face convulsed, holding back sobs. I kept remembering her words in an interview I had had with her a year after she entered the White House, "I just want to go down in history as the wife of the President." She had been the last holdout against resignation.

Typically, Nixon wanted his family beside him during his hour of torment, but the First Lady did not know that his poignant, yet defiant farewell would be on live television. It was a staged public ceremony to the end.

Head high, Nixon walked out of the White House as the President of the United States. He went down the elevator with his family to the first floor where he met Vice President Gerald Ford and his wife, Betty. The Nixons and the Fords embraced, and with Julie and David joining them they walked down a long red carpet leading from the diplomatic reception room to a waiting helicopter on the South Lawn. Many people sympathized with Julie, especially, on the grounds that she too may have been deceived by her father. But while she admits to mistakes made, she never ever lost faith in him. I marveled later when she held her head high and attended, with her husband, the first address the new President, Gerald R. Ford, made to a Joint Session of Congress. She was determined not to let crushing hurt defeat her. One sensed that the country was going to hear a lot more from Julie as time goes by.

The press was roped off, and Ziegler, running behind the Nixon party, shouted to the White House police with a sweeping angry gesture. "Hold them back. Hold them back." As the door of the helicopter closed, two Marines began rolling back the red carpet. Nixon looked out the window at the White House and his daughter Julie gave him the "thumbs up" sign and then sobbing bent her head on David's chest.

Airborne aboard Air Force One, Nixon passed down the aisle chatting, but no one brought up the resignation. He observed to a Secret Service agent, "I guess I won't be having your protection any more." Then he was told that, as a former President, agents would remain with him. "What if I do it to myself?" he asked.

On the ground, Secret Service agent Richard Keiser, chief of the White House detail, choked up as he watched "The Boss" leave without him. "I thought how I had always been at Nixon's side to protect him and now I couldn't do anything to save him."

Chapter 9

Right On, Martha!

Martha Mitchell was one of the first victims, and perhaps the only heroine of the Watergate tidal wave that engulfed the White House.

Manhandled and tranquilized in California to prevent her from speaking out on the Watergate burglary, she refused to suffer in silence. Instead, she dramatically alerted the country to the bizarre happenings in Washington.

"Why did Martha Mitchell call you?" I was asked after I first flashed the story of her outrage a few days after the break-in at the Watergate. She simply knew that as a wire-service reporter I could quickly reach millions of readers across the nation, and she also knew I liked and trusted her. She once told a *New York Post* interviewer, "Helen Thomas knows me well enough to know I'm not going to give her a line of bull. We just kind of fell into each others' arms." She would often explain that: "Several other reporters had been recommended to me, but when I talked to them they were cold fish. They were calculating, and, I thought, unwilling to stick their necks out. Helen Thomas, I knew, would print the truth no matter what it cost her personally, and I wanted the truth to be known."

I was not the only reporter she called, but I think I was special to her because I consistently took her seriously. Indeed, I found at times that her credibility has stacked up higher than that of Presidents.

Martha Elizabeth Beall Mitchell had not wanted to leave her home and the social life she enjoyed in Rye, New York, to come to

Washington and the unknown. But she had been instrumental in persuading her husband, John N. Mitchell, then a Democrat, to become a political supporter of Richard M. Nixon, and Mitchell became Nixon's campaign manager in 1968. After that triumphant election victory he was tapped to become Attorney General. Like many other Nixon appointees—and the Democratic National Committee—the Mitchells moved into the plush Watergate Apartments.

I met Martha along with other Nixon Cabinet wives at the White House early in 1969. I was struck by her warmth, her dimpled vivacious smile, and her quick intelligence. My contacts with Mitchell himself were at those White House social occasions and I could never quite understand why he felt that he must engage reporters by telling us dirty jokes.

Nixon wanted the administration wives to be active, and Martha lost no time in involving herself in several worthy projects. She enlisted Justice Department wives in a national narcotics education program for parents and teenagers and took them on a tour of the riot-damaged ghettos of Washington. When Nixon wanted the wives of his Cabinet members to help promote the administration, at the behest of Herbert Klein, then White House Director of Communications, she gave an interview to CBS's Marya McLaughlin. "As my husband has said many times," she declared, "some of the liberals in this country, he'd like to take them and change them for Russian communists. I don't think average Americans realize how desperate it is when a group of demonstrators, not peaceful demonstrators but the very liberal communists, move into Washington. This place could become a complete fortress." She made headlines with those quotes.

After that the press besieged her for interviews. She became an instant celebrity. In a society where Cabinet wives were seen and not heard, her comments caused an uproar.

In my own interviews with her, I found that she had a spontaneous sense of humor and a sense of humanity even though her observations were frequently illogical. She called the shots as she saw them and that was refreshing in a lackluster administration where everyone, even the President, was programmed like a robot. Martha, of course, kept wandering off the reservation, but Nixon was excited about the bright star in his galaxy. He liked her spirit.

As her popularity grew, the irrepressible Martha was swamped with speaking invitations. She charged ahead, even telephoning her home state newspaper, the *Arkansas Gazette*, with the declaration that "[Senator J. William] Fulbright should be crucified." Nixon was tickled and phoned her to say "Give 'em hell, Martha." Later on he probably wished he had not egged her on but at the time he was enjoying her meteoric rise into the national limelight.

She soon became more sought after as a personality than Nixon himself. "She's a phenomenon," Mitchell told me proudly. He marveled at her popularity and once when confronted with a way-out remark by his wife, he shrugged and said: "I love her, that's all I can say." Later he jokingly told reporters that he would permit her to be interviewed, but only in "Swahili."

A genteel Southern woman, born in Pine Bluff, Arkansas, Martha Mitchell sometimes came across as a Tennessee Williams heroine, very feminine and striving for understanding. She said of herself, "I think most people realize that I am politically naive and what I am saying represents my own viewpoint. When I talk to anyone, I talk from the heart instead of the head. I have always been open and frank and honest."

As she became an outspoken superstar, many women in the nation identified with her, and applauded her freewheeling tell 'em off attitude.

Martha liked public attention and applause, as do most celebrities. She became "hot property" for the Republican Party, which sent her on the road to promote the cause. In a sense she was exploited but she tried to play the game. But lonely hotel rooms, a fear of flying, and the strain of public appearances caused her great anxiety at times, and beneath the surface of sometimes outrageous remarks and a flamboyant style was a sensitive, seeking person who kept her integrity intact, which is more than can be said for many in the White House coterie of those ill-fated days.

Martha Mitchell has said it was only later that she realized that she was ill-prepared for the personal consequences. She had naively believed that a Cabinet wife had a right to speak out. She had taken her cue literally from President Nixon, when he asked Cabinet wives to attend some of the Cabinet meetings and to speak up on national issues. Of course, he meant "speak up" only in agreement with administration policy. Martha had no problem following that course in the early days. She did agree with Nixon's philosophy and became a vocal defender of his nominations of Southern G. Harrold Carswell and Clement Haynesworth as Justices of the United States Supreme Court. Both nominations were rejected, much to the outrage of Nixon and Attorney General John Mitchell.

Her flamboyance did, however, send shudders through the East Wing of the White House, the First Lady's domain, where Pat Nixon and her daughters, Julie and Tricia, schooled in the protocol of the political wife and aghast at her behavior, gave her a cold shoulder. Martha has said she will always remember a telling bit of advice she was given by Pat Nixon early on. "Just remember, Martha, your best friends will become your worst enemies," Pat Nixon had said. She was well aware that Mrs. Nixon was snubbing her and it was painful, but she did not lack for friends.

To the Cabinet wives also, her candor was too much, although several, like Lenore Romney, wife of the Secretary of Housing and Urban Development, had a genuine affection for her. She was too recherché for their taste, with her blond bouffant upswept hairdos and her unfashionable sling pumps, though she had elegant taste all the same, beautifully reflected in her Watergate apartment and in her gracious hospitality.

She soon became fair game for comedians. When she would appear at a head table, an outsized telephone would be placed in front of her, a comic symbol of her notorious phone calls to reporters. But she was a drawing card and the autograph hunters had a field day when she was around. Martha began to evoke as much curiosity as Jackie Kennedy. Journalists flocked after her because she had something to say and we suspected that she often reflected the views of her husband, and of Nixon as well. Martha was not a gossip. When she called you knew darned well it was for a reason. She was on top of the news, and as time went on she found out that people were interested in her views, stunning as some of them were.

When Nixon began to rely heavily on Mitchell as his mentor, Martha was well aware of his late-night telephone calls to her husband. Mitchell was heavily involved in national security as well as in Justice Department matters. To reporters Mitchell said, "When the President wants to say something important, he calls her up and says, 'Now, just how would you put it, Martha?' " FBI Director J. Edgar Hoover, who had a high regard for her, called her "the most lovable girl."

Martha Mitchell first strained Nixon's affection with her comments to the press aboard Air Force One in September 1970. Nixon, Mitchell, Secretary of State William P. Rogers, and their wives were returning to Washington. I was in the pool of reporters traveling with them and we were assigned, as usual, to the tail of the plane, away from the VIPs. Occasionally a VIP would wander back to use the lavatory, also as usual. Martha strode back deliberately, looking for action among the press. "I did my knitting years ago," she declared, declaring her difference from the other official wives. She said she wanted to see what we, "her favorite people," were up to. My colleagues were playing gin rummy, so I saw her first. For openers, I asked her what she thought of calf-skimming midi-skirts and broached other trivialities. "Oh, Helen, why don't you ask me something important?" she said. I accepted her invitation. "Okay, what do you think of the Vietnam War?"

"It stinks, and if it weren't for Senator Fulbright we'd be out of it," she said, her eyes flashing.

With that salvo, reporters dropped their flushes, picked up their notepads, and I lost my exclusive as we began quizzing her.

"If this country would stick together . . . if everyone felt a common cause in Vietnam, we would have been out sixteen months ago and it makes me so mad I can't see straight," she exploded. She careened onto touchier ground, declaring, "We shouldn't have gotten into the war in the first place. The Nixon administration inherited it and they're trying their best to get out of it."

At this point, other VIPs started our way. Secretary of State Rogers tried to squelch her with "Martha, why don't you stick to the Justice Department and I'll take care of foreign affairs?" Mitchell then stepped to the rear of the plane, puffing a pipe with studied nonchalance. "Would you like to hear what your wife said?" I asked mischievously.

"Heavens, no," he said, casting his eyes upward. "I'd jump straight out of the window." On landing, we ran for phones and called in the story of the Cabinet wife's denunciation of the war on Air Force One. After that, Martha was grounded from Presidential trips. She was never told of the ban officially, but she heard that the order came from the White House Chief of Staff H. R. Haldeman and, perhaps, from Nixon himself.

Her prominence did not come without other costs. She was swamped with mail, including a dead mouse and threats that made her fear for her life. While her husband was Attorney General she had FBI protection. Later when he became Nixon's campaign manager security agents were hired.

Martha sensed doom as the first Nixon administration drew to a close. Her calls to me became more frequent and she expressed foreboding that her husband would leave the Cabinet to become Nixon's campaign manager for his 1972 election drive. "Nixon can get someone else for the campaign," she telephoned to say on the day Nixon announced Mitchell's resignation from the Cabinet. "The country needs him at the Justice Department."

Martha had an instinct for danger. She would, for example, tune in quickly to perils that Jay Jennings, her son by a previous marriage, encountered as an army lieutenant in Vietnam. As weeks passed and she did not hear from him, she grew agitated. She would call in tears, wailing, "They won't tell me anything." On two occasions when I was in Laguna Beach, California, the press center for White House correspondents covering Nixon at San Clemente, she called me from the Newporter Inn to ask me to find out what was happening to her son. She insisted he was in danger and would not be comforted until she had definite word as to where he was and his condition. I was sure she had more direct channels than I did. "But Martha, you can find out in a minute. Why don't you call Laird at the Pentagon?" I suggested. Melvin Laird was Secretary of Defense in the first Nixon Cabinet. She insisted she was unable to get any information from the Defense Department despite her husband's official position. So each time she asked I cabled the UPI Saigon Bureau and each time I received word that, although

Jennings was safe, he was indeed in heavy fighting in a fire zone in South Vietnam. Her intuition was right. I always felt that her intuition, plus her keen sense of right and wrong, were her outstanding attributes.

Once her son was safely home, her fears focused on Mitchell. She was given a desk and was tapped to speak at rallies and such for the Committee to Reelect the President from its inception. She and Jeb Stuart Magruder, who was Deputy Campaign Director, were among the first two people there. Also there was James McCord, Security Director for CREEP from September 1971 on. More would be heard of him later.

When the Nixons vacationed in Key Biscayne, Florida, the Mitchells also wound up at the sunny resort. They leased a house on an island owned by Nixon's best friend, "Bebe" Rebozo. In this villa Martha later said that she overheard planning for covert campaign operations of which the Watergate break-in was one. She also recalls that back in the spring of 1972 she sat in the living room of their Watergate apartment and her husband sat in his favorite armchair and read a "campaign strategy" book, exclaiming as he read: "This is foolproof." She believes that the book was destroyed after the break-in, as were other documents at CREEP.

In mid-June, she planned to go to New York for her regular dental and physical checkups. But Fred LaRue, a close Mitchell associate, begged her to fly to California for the weekend with Mitchell and the LaRues instead. She did not want to go but LaRue insisted that his wife could go only if she did. In retrospect, Martha feels she was set up, that they wanted her a continent away from Washington when the Watergate burglary was underway.

After arriving in California, the Mitchells and their daughter Marty, then eleven years old, moved into one of the villas set aside for governmental personages at the Newporter Inn in Newport Beach, accompanied by an entourage which included Mitchell's secretary, Lea Jablonsky, and Steve King, the bodyguard provided by CREEP.

There was much partying going on there that weekend; meanwhile, back in Washington, mischief was afoot. The Democratic National Committee headquarters was broken into by five men, including James McCord, bent on bugging Nixon's opponents.

Martha was not aware of the telephone calls between Mitchell and other CREEP and White House officials, but she felt that something was amiss. On the Sunday afternoon before he returned to Washington, she urged her husband to quit the campaign. He promised he would do so in two-and-one-half months. He urged his wife to stay on in California to relax for a few days and flew back to Washington leaving her behind, apparently with instructions to keep Martha incommunicado. Marty, Miss Jablonsky, and King also stayed behind.

Martha did not actually find out about the break-in until Monday, two days after it occurred. Then she read a newspaper account carrying large photographs of McCord and the others who had been arrested. She knew immediately that CREEP was involved. She telephoned her husband and he assured her that there was no big problem.

When I answered the phone after finishing dinner with my husband, Doug, in our Washington apartment, I heard Martha's voice, uncharacteristically subdued. She was calling from California and it was nine o'clock at night our time. We chatted awhile, then I asked her what she thought of the break-in at the Watergate. My question ignited the conversation, and her voice rose in answer: "That's it, I've given John an ultimatum. I'm going to leave him unless he gets out of the campaign. I'm sick and tired of politics. Politics is a dirty business."

Suddenly, Martha sounded more agitated. She was protesting to someone. I later learned it was King, the bodyguard CREEP had assigned to her. "You just get away. Get away," she said.

I shouted to Doug to get on the bedroom extension. I was not sure of what I was hearing and wanted him to verify the struggle. By the time he picked up the telephone, Martha's line had gone dead.

I later learned that King had ripped the phone from the wall in her bedroom.

Martha told reporters a hair-raising story of her personal humiliation that night at the hands of the bodyguard, a doctor, and others. She told me more about the incident recently: "They threw me down on the bed—five persons did it—a doctor, a nurse, Lea Jablonsky, and her daughter Marty—pulled my pants down, and stuck a needle in my behind, the longest needle you ever saw. I've never been treated like this before."

I tried several times to phone her again at the Newporter Inn that night but the switchboard blocked me. I attempted to reach Mitchell through the White House, assuming they would alert him quickly, but the operator was not responsive to my insistence that this was an emergency. Finally I did get through to him at his Watergate apartment and poured out my fears that Martha was in jeopardy. Far from being surprised, he tried to soothe me. "She's great. That little sweetheart. I love her so much. She gets a little upset about politics, but she loves me and I love her and that's what counts. I'll tell you a secret. I've promised Martha I will give up politics after this campaign."

I found Mitchell's calm reaction strange, but with his assurance that Martha was not in any danger, I phoned my office and dictated an "urgent" story to Bob Taylor, our desk man. He accepted the bizarre account as creditable and I will always be grateful for that.

It was played up big across the country, but mostly on women's pages of the newspapers. Editors apparently thought it was just another Martha Mitchell story, tantalizing only because it revealed a spectacular marital rift in the Cabinet. Administration spokesmen intimated Martha was hallucinating, that she was deranged or drunk, but later revelations have shown that Martha Mitchell was right.

The following day, a Friday, I called Mitchell again and he again dismissed Martha's possible plight.

"She's sitting around the swimming pool," he said in a calm voice. "She's fine."

I was at Key Biscayne covering Nixon the weekend of Watergate. White House Press Secretary Ron Ziegler dismissed the break-in to us as a "third-rate burglary." But Nixon was furious. We were told that he hit the ceiling.

The following weekend I was covering Nixon at Camp David. My colleagues and I registered at the Thurmont Motel, six miles from the mountaintop retreat. On Sunday morning I called my office and discovered that Martha had been trying to reach me. I reached her at the Westchester Country Club in Rye, New York.

She had lived across the street from the club when her husband was a bond attorney, a member of Caldwell, Mitchell, and Trimble; his firm merged with Nixon's law firm in New York in January 1967. Martha told me she had persuaded her husband to go with Nixon. When I got her on the line, she was still distraught and furious. She complained that she had become a "political prisoner," a strong indictment. "It's horrible. I don't like it. Martha isn't going to stand for it," she told me. I was used to her referring to herself in the third person, but she sounded desperate and I was upset for her.

We barreled out her story in fuller detail on the wires. This time, instead of winding up with the cooking columns and garden club schedules, it was on the Monday front pages. Reporters and cameramen converged on Rye, and I tried to put through several telephone calls to her, but the operator would only take messages. Martha has told me that she never received the messages from any of the dozens of reporters and friends who tried to contact her.

That weekend, her husband drove to Rye to see her. She said he cried as they talked and promised he would quit the campaign. He even showed her a list of possible successors to run the reelection drive. Nixon also phoned her to express concern. The Mitchells hid out and after a few days he smuggled her back to the capital. Martha dropped from view. I telephoned her and sent telegrams, but she did not respond. The campaign committee began to hint that Martha was guzzling. When the smear hit the newspapers, the committee issued a formal denial.

Martha was particularly bitter over a remark Pat Nixon made about her at a news conference. In response to a question about Martha in the summer of 1972, Mrs. Nixon replied: "I understand she is ill."

Martha was so infuriated by that remark that she called me up to say, "If she thinks I'm ill, why doesn't she send flowers?"

She was also incensed at reports that the First Lady had expressed sympathy for the families of White House aides Haldeman and Ehrlichman after they were deposed.

"What about others who are suffering?" asked Martha.

Martha had her troubles with the White House switchboard, particularly if she wanted a call put through to the President or other administration officials. After all, the President had telephoned her home many times, and had called her personally. She often told me that Nixon had "telephonitis" because of his "loneliness." Once when she tried to use the White House switchboard, she was told by a sarcastic operator: "Why don't you call Helen Thomas?"

She telephoned me in California to protest that kind of treatment. She was always a few jumps ahead of the headlines. Not only were her vibes on the beam, she also had sources who told her what was going on in the White House.

Doug got used to the early evening and late night calls I got from Martha. He sympathized with her plight. He was also a good newspaperman and understood that news does not always break at a convenient hour. I always tell my office to call me at any time. I want to be in on a breaking story and major news events do not wait for proper business hours.

Oftentimes when she would call she would be very upset, but I believe her sense of righteousness and moral outrage helped her survive her own personal fears. "Martha doesn't like it," she used to say.

She protected her husband for a long time and tried to pin the blame solely on Nixon. She seemed not to want to face the fact that her husband was deeply involved. "President Nixon always knew what was going on about the Watergate affair," she told me. "I'll be damned if I'll let my husband take the rap for Mr. President. Between you and me and the gatepost, Mr. President always knew what was going on."

In late June 1972, Nixon granted one of his infrequent press conferences and denied any White House involvement in Watergate. I wanted to ask him about Martha Mitchell, but resisted. I had received so much personal publicity as a result of her early pronouncements that I thought that bringing up her name might seem self-serving. She chided me later for not asking the President "about Martha" and I think she was right.

In early July, Mitchell issued a formal statement that he was quitting the Nixon campaign to spend more time with his wife and daughter. Martha was blissful. She loved him all the more for having such compassion for her. In truth, Mitchell saw he'd have to slip away from a situation that was about to involve him.

Washington Post reporters Bob Woodward and Carl Bernstein were looping Mitchell's noose by interviewing his cohorts. Presidential tapes later revealed that he and Nixon had figured that Mitchell could use his wife as a cover to evade the public eye, and Mitchell could burrow into CREEP. His law office was in the same building and telephone wires became puppet strings. Nixon felt he still needed his former Attorney General. He relied on Mitchell, who showed no weakness and seemed to have an answer for everything, qualities which Nixon prized.

Martha soon realized that her husband remained enmeshed in the campaign and was a frequent guest of Nixon aboard the Presidential yacht *Sequoia*. She says, incidentally, that the break-in was planned on the *Sequoia*. But she loved her husband and refrained from any further blasts during the campaign. In fact, she went underground and was not seen publicly for weeks. She later explained to me that she was afraid.

"Free Martha" was a coveted button young women in blue jeans wore at the Democratic National Convention in Miami. She became a folk heroine and a rallying point for people she had once called "radical demonstrators." They believed in her truthfulness.

Martha Mitchell remained silent until after Nixon's landslide victory. Then she phoned often with more urgent appeals regarding her personal safety.

"If you don't hear from me, call the police," she told me. She was disturbed and I knew Mitchell was also. Nixon wore his new mandate like a crown and tossed the accusations of dirty campaign tricks in Mitchell's direction. CREEP and White House officials linked arms to protect themselves as the Watergate coverup began to unravel.

Except for Martha, women in the Nixon administration's inner circle stayed clear of political trouble. Those who worked at CREEP had believed in Nixon, but now they suspected wrongdoing and expressed shock and surprise at the furtiveness of the national campaign. They had been kept ignorant.

In the spring, Martha threw herself into decorating the opulent New York apartment Mitchell later dubbed "The Taj Mahal," but in blue moments she still dialed the press saying, "Mr. Nixon knew all about the whole goddamned thing." In mid-March, as the tapes later showed, Mitchell was summoned to a White House conference which clearly was intended to urge the "Big Enchilada" to take the rap for Watergate. But he declined, and returned to Martha in New York. She telephoned me: "John Dean wasn't big enough. They want John to take the rap."

In May 1973, Martha tracked me down at a small hotel in Madison, Wisconsin, where I was to make a speech the following day and she minced no words. "Nixon should resign," she declared. "He has lost his credibility in the country and in the Republican Party. I think he's let the country down."

She said it more in sorrow than in anger and when I called the UPI bureau in Washington, there was no question that Martha Mitchell's call for a Presidential resignation would be a bombshell. She was the first to call for Nixon's resignation, a battle cry picked up nearly a year later by the most eminent officials in the land from Capitol Hill to the editorial rooms of the nation's leading newspapers.

President Nixon was sunning himself that weekend at Key Biscayne, and his aides obviously burned up the wires with calls to Mitchell, bitterly protesting his wife's interference. Mitchell issued a formal statement, saying it would be "ridiculous" for anybody to take seriously his wife's suggestion that the President resign because of the Watergate scandal. His disclaimer, issued through Nixon's campaign office, which still had not disbanded, claimed UPI should not have reported her comments.

"Martha's late-night telephone calls have been good fun and games in the past," said Mitchell. "However, this is a serious issue. I'm surprised and disappointed that 'a news organization' would take advantage of a personal phone call made under the stress of the current situation and treat it as a sensational public statement." He said he thought, under the circumstances, that his wife was entitled to more consideration and courtesy, "particularly from a reporter whom she considered a personal friend." He ended: "Any thought of the President resigning is ridiculous."

After ordering his aide to suppress his wife and despite her loving, if emotional, attempts to save him, he was still discrediting her. I was not perturbed by his comments because I had not violated a personal relationship. Whenever Martha phoned, it was to make her views public, and pronto.

Martha never once said whether her husband was guilty or innocent. I later learned that, throughout the Watergate crisis, even when a schism between Mitchell and Nixon seemed imminent, the two men were in almost daily contact. Mitchell publicly supported Nixon's claim of noninvolvement in Watergate. If Nixon had known anything about it, Mitchell said, he would have "blown the lid off." Even after Mitchell was convicted in the coverup conspiracy trial, he visited Nixon at San Clemente.

There was nothing Martha could do to convince Mitchell that he should "tell all" and especially about the President. She could never break her husband's will to remain loyal to the President. It probably was actually a mutual protection society. Martha told me that her husband came home one night and said: "The President is going to keep me from going to jail." Once Martha said, "Nixon used to call us every night and used to say that Mitchell was the 'real' President and he was the Secretary of State."

Early one morning when Martha called to predict Nixon would resign or be impeached, she repeated that the White House was trying to make her husband "a fall guy." Mitchell was apparently listening in on an extension and interrupted. He wanted her to hang up, but I sensed he did feel cornered and was prickly enough to be coaxed into talking. I was right.

"Are you willing to take the blame?" I asked.

"Any attempt to make me do it isn't going to work. I've never stolen any money. The only thing I did was to try to get the President reelected. I never did anything mentally or morally wrong," he insisted.

When this went out over the UPI wires, the White House read it with horror. They were trying to defend themselves against the outside world and now it appeared that Mitchell might blow the whistle on them. But Mitchell had no such intent. He remained faithful to the Nixon cause.

Martha often said she wanted her husband to reveal what he knew and stop "protecting King Richard." She believed Mitchell was aware of her plight, including the rough handling at Newport

Beach, but I guess she couldn't face that bitter truth. She blamed Nixon, not Mitchell. "Nixon bleeds people. He takes every ounce out of everybody and then throws them out," she said in a telephone call.

Another thing she said of her husband, "I love him very much. He loves me because I've stood up for him. But he is defending the President who planned the whole goddamned thing. I'm under surveillance day and night. I'm no fool."

Each time Martha called during the uncovering of Watergate she insisted her phone was tapped. Among other signs, this seemed possible. She grew wary. When she called in the early evening, she would say, "Now don't go writing that I called you at three A.M." When I phoned her, she cautioned, "Now remember. You called me."

One of Nixon's close associates taunted me, "Why don't you get some class, Helen, and hang up on Martha Mitchell?" He was in the White House inner council and knew the truth.

Martha Mitchell was fear-ridden, especially about the future. In our tête-à-têtes, she seemed to be trying to understand what was happening. I sensed her fatalism. She often wailed in wonder, "When I was in school, I was never sent to the principal's office."

Mitchell was depressed by the headlines, and his law firm wanted to disassociate itself from the tainted partner. "He never moves," Martha called to say. "He won't see our friends. He's broken up. He has been taken." She loved her husband, and wanted to save him, but he was disconsolate, became a recluse, and would not talk to her. Their family life suffered under the strain. Marty, their daughter, had been close to her mother, but when Watergate broke and her mother broadcast the troubles, the child sided with her father. Once when Martha called, I heard Marty screaming in the background, "Don't talk to her, she's no friend."

In September 1973, Mitchell moved out and took their daughter with him. Many sympathized with Martha's agony and believed her to be a lone woman fighting the most powerful government in the world to keep her home intact. Romantics saw it as a tragedy and asked me if I thought they'd reconcile. I felt the break was inevitable in view of the tremendous tensions. Television talk-show hosts and others constantly asked me to assess her mental state and drinking habits. I always said that I could not speculate, that all that mattered was that she told the truth and that her credibility held up while that of others in high places crumbled.

Only weeks before he deserted her, Mitchell told Martha: "You are the most wonderful woman I have ever met." But after he was convicted in the Watergate coverup trial, Mitchell said: "It's better than spending a lifetime with Martha Mitchell." This remark did not win him any votes and in fact probably lost him some supporters. It was at the very least ungentlemanly.

Martha's charges seemed incredible until the President of the United States faltered under challengers in the courts and Congress. Martha used to call the Watergate episode a "cops and robbers" administration. It went against her grain and her sense of patriotism, not to mention the personal hurt and the shattering of lives.

To be vindicated in your own time is a good feeling, and she had that as the Nixon Presidency came to a close. She had been ridiculed, vilified, admired, and loved for her outspokenness, bucking the most powerful people in the country even though she was afraid.

Martha sensed that if she could reach the people, and she knew she could do that only through the press, they would rise up to save her and the nation. One woman sent a letter to me to pass along to her. It said: "You are a brave heroine who stood alone against terrifying odds. They are doing their damnedest to make you appear a 'kook' just as they vilified Billy Mitchell when he advocated airplanes for defense. It takes guts to stand alone and my hat is off to you."

Unlike most other political wives, Martha never learned the rules—smile and speak only when spoken to. It's ironical to remember that Nixon himself used to say in the early pre-Watergate years, "Right on, Martha."

Chapter 10

Kissinger:
Survival of the Fittest

Henry A. Kissinger dominated American foreign policy through the Nixon years and Ford's early Presidency, a charismatic personality who viewed the world as a chessboard. His foreign policy was based on one principle ingredient—military power. He used to joke that power was the "ultimate aphrodisiac."

The Nixon foreign policy was loaded with threats of force. After the Vietnam setback, Kissinger said that the United States would have to become more abrasive so that there would be no miscalculation on the part of potential enemies. His concepts were based on power politics and were short on the FDR ideals that brought about the truth of the United Nations and the Good Neighbor policy. It appeared that he believed that the best the United States could achieve was a Churchill-like "balance of power" with the Soviet Union to head off a technological explosion of nuclear know-how around the world. It remains to be seen how history will treat him, whether he will stand with the greats and whether his initiatives will be a lasting stimulus for peace. His is a world of super powers and pragmatic statesmen.

White House reporters used to see Kissinger often since he met many times a day with President Nixon and he always sat in on meetings with visiting heads of state. Seated on a sofa with a portfolio or a yellow legal pad on his lap, Kissinger would look up with a quizzical smile when reporters and photographers would pour into the Oval Office for picture-taking. I would see him in his office, our old press room, peering over his papers when I walked past the window on my way into the White House in the mornings.

Kissinger was very much a part of the Nixon White House, officially and socially. He and Nixon seemed to decide all foreign policy matters between them. Kissinger was a guest at every State Dinner. On those occasions especially, we found it great fun to buttonhole him for comments and he was usually forthcoming to reporters, though he would often turn aside my serious questions with an easy quip.

He was famous for his "step-by-step" diplomacy, and for trying, as he put it to us, to "start a process of peace" between the Arabs and the Israelis, to get them to substitute negotiation for confrontation. Sometimes it seemed he was just buying time.

"I have a first-rate intellect and third-rate instinct about people," he has said. His own sense of survival was keen and he knew that he was accountable to and needed the support of only one man, the President. There was awe and yet, it seemed, some envy of Kissinger's exalted position in both the Nixon and Ford administrations. He was a celebrity and even with the President in the room, reporters would gravitate to Kissinger. He had a sharp wit but was never rude to reporters as far as I could observe.

I became acquainted with Kissinger on Air Force One, the President's plane, when we would jet off to summits and high-level talks for days on end. The "pool" of reporters was allocated several seats near the rear of the plane. When Kissinger and other officials would walk through from time to time, heading for the lavatory, we nabbed them for what were tagged "men's room press conferences." My own greatest fears while on board were that I would doze off or have to go to the lavatory myself and miss a chance to collar a spokesman. I don't know how many Presidential guests restrained themselves rather than storm the flank of the inquiring press, but Kissinger didn't.

Instead, it became tradition that, right after takeoff, Kissinger would stroll back to chat, usually to brief us on the American position at the upcoming meetings. He would be wearing the special slate blue flight jacket embossed with the Presidential seal which Nixon had made for staffers who came aboard. More often, he would drift back to our section in shirt sleeves.

Our seats on Air Force One were arranged like booths and on our table would be a dish of chocolates and hard candy. Before airborne briefings ended, we would find that Kissinger had emptied the bowl and plowed into a basket of pretzels besides. He complained he always gained weight during tense negotiations, and no wonder. After a China trip, and there were several, he would find himself at least ten pounds heavier. He crash-dieted after such trips. Sometimes when Kissinger talked to us, he would be summoned by a harried aide: "The President wants you." He would take his time about returning.

Kissinger would not let us attribute the information he gave us to him, but he fooled no one, certainly not those in foreign chancelleries. We would write our stories "on background," crediting a "senior American official" or one from the White House. I often threatened to write "A high-ranking White House official with a thick German accent said today," but never did. We played by the rules, incongruous and ridiculous as they sometimes seemed.

Kissinger used the so-called "backgrounder" more than any other government official I have ever known. He believed it gave him more latitude to make his points. It did; it also made him less accountable. Kissinger was obsessed with the idea of leaks and most of his criticism of the press related to stories he could not control. His saving grace was his sense of humor and irony about himself, even when he seemed, as he always did, to be on the defensive.

Kissinger and I got along, even when I ribbed him about his Metternich machinations and his girl friends. He took it very well.

When one-time newsman John A. Scali was named United States representative to the United Nations, Kissinger teased the pool—"See, there is hope for you yet."

"That's more than we can say for you," I said, but with a big smile. Kissinger was taken aback.

Kissinger revelled in his secret swinger image. As *Chicago Daily News* correspondent Peter Lisagor put it: "As a reputed ladies' man he undoubtedly has given aid and comfort to every squat, owl-eyed, overweight, and middle-aged bachelor in the world."

Once I wrote that Kissinger was seen "walking along the beach at San Clemente, California, hand in hand with a beautiful dark-haired girl."

The next day, he sidled up and said: "Auburn-haired."

I later found out it was actress Marlo Thomas. Marlo shared billing with her father, comedian Danny Thomas, at the White House Association dinner where I was inducted as President, and I had forewarned Marlo that Kissinger would be there. So, after I introduced Marlo, who wore a black gown with dramatic decolletage, she called out, "Hello, Henry, I haven't seen you since you got married." It brought the house down. He loved it and followed her around later in the evening.

On another occasion I twitted Kissinger about Madame Katerina Furtseva, the Russian Minister of Culture, who flirted outrageously with him.

"Do you blame her?" queried Kissinger, cocking an eyebrow.

Kissinger and TV star and author Barbara Howar were friends when he first came to Washington. At the height of the Vietnam crisis, Barbara called Kissinger a "warmonger."

"But I like Barbara," he protested, not one to bear a grudge. He belonged to the celebrity school of "write anything you want about me as long as you spell my name right."

In his swinging days, before he married Nancy Maginnis, a New York socialite and Rockefeller aide, Kissinger dined nearly every night with a striking blonde. And when he was in California, he made many friends among the stars. He seemed to be fascinated with their life-style. He told us, kiddingly, that one day he was going to become head of a movie company.

After we covered the Moscow summit in 1972, the American party returned by way of Iran. Nixon remained at the palace in Tehran while Kissinger went nightclubbing. Nadia, a belly dancer, plumped herself in his lap as his Iranian hosts and reporters sat convulsed with laughter over his startled expression.

The next day on the Presidential flight back to Washington, I asked him about "Nadia."

"I want to make the world safe for belly dancers," he joked.

Kissinger's sardonic wit ran away with him sometimes. After the bizarre report of attempts by an anti-Vietnam War group to kidnap

Kissinger, he referred to "sex-starved nuns" and had to apologize to the Vatican.

Often, in his briefings, Kissinger gave us incisive insights into the personalities of world leaders, revealing himself and what he admired about people in the process. His greatest respect was reserved for Chinese Premier Chou En-lai, whom he saw as his peer. Their friendship transcended the tough diplomatic maneuvering, and when Chou was hospitalized for several months with a heart ailment, Kissinger spoke of his illness with tears in his eyes.

Kissinger considered Soviet Communist Party leader Leonid I. Brezhnev as a rough-hewn Russian peasant—tough, unsubtle, and unsophisticated. He sized up Le Duc Tho as extremely shrewd and delighted in telling the story of how the North Vietnamese negotiator once leaned over a table and said, "Dr. Kissinger, I want to tell you frankly and candidly—you are a liar."

Tho had lost intellectual ground with Kissinger when the two met in Hanoi. Kissinger had heard that the city's anthropological museum was one of the world's best. Tho, who had never been there before, was interested only in his own experiences in the cities from which exhibits had been taken—"I spent two years in jail there, six years here, I had to flee from that town," he would say. He ignored the cultural landmarks that Kissinger found so absorbing. On Air Force One I heard Kissinger say that, at the peace talks Tho, instead of negotiating, pored over communist newspapers, noting broad popular support for North Vietnam. "So we had a little bombing," Kissinger said. "And Tho got down to business. In a while we bogged down again, and again we bombed. Then Tho became so friendly, you would have thought he was homosexual."

The superstar fame of Kissinger did not sit too well with other members of the Nixon administration whom he eclipsed. Diplomats used to say they would rather have ten minutes with Kissinger, than Assistant to the President for National Security Affairs, than an hour with Secretary of State William P. Rogers, who took second place and was not in on some of the highest foreign policy planning between Nixon and Kissinger. Kissinger coveted the Cabinet job and eventually got it. But he had already been the true Secretary of State in the minds of world leaders.

Attorney General John N. Mitchell described Kissinger as an "egomaniac," and Kissinger responded to this and similar assessments with self-deprecating humor. "I have been accused of megalomania," he said in a toast at a dinner party at the West German Embassy. "Actually I suffer from paranoia and the good thing about working in the government instead of the academic world is that—I can have real enemies."

Kissinger came to Washington with Nixon in 1969, on sabbatical leave from Harvard University. When I wrote later that it was doubtful that he would be welcomed back at Harvard because of his stand on Vietnam, Kissinger was distressed. While he had no intention of returning to Cambridge at the time ("Why should I be running Harvard when I can be running the world?"), he certainly did not want to feel that the choice was not his to make, or at least that he would be unheralded.

The "incursion" into Cambodia outraged Kissinger's former faculty colleagues, including Richard Neustadt, and a dozen of them came down from Boston to make a personal protest. Kissinger listened, tried to persuade them that the operation was limited—to help speed withdrawal of American troops from South Vietnam—but they were not appeased. I ran into the group as they were leaving the White House grounds, still fuming. They virtually disowned Kissinger as a member of the academic community. They had had a painful confrontation. The professors had served notice that they would no longer serve as consultants to the administration—actually their views were seldom solicited in the Nixon era anyway. Kissinger retorted "I can always teach at Arizona State."

Most Washington observers had enough evidence to support their conviction that Kissinger was a "hawk," but Kissinger had many elite friends on what was known as the "Georgetown liberal circuit" who felt he went along with the Vietnam bombings and the Cambodian "incursion" reluctantly. Nixon's aides said otherwise and disclosed that he strongly supported Nixon's controversial decisions.

Kissinger has been called a "Modern-Day Metternich," a "Dr.

Strangelove," "Rasputin," and "Svengali" by detractors. But his admirers were placed where it counted. Kissinger had a strong following on Capitol Hill, and he kept a close relationship with Senator J. W. Fulbright, then chairman of the Foreign Relations Committee, though he crossed swords often with Senator Henry M. Jackson of Washington on concessions to the Soviet Union on behalf of détente.

But Kissinger knew that his primary power lay in his proximity to the Oval Office, and he later insisted on keeping his National Security Affairs position as well as his Cabinet post because it entitled him to a White House office near the center of power. Nevertheless, Haldeman tried to keep tabs on whom he saw in his office. Other Presidential aides tried to undercut him, but Kissinger managed to maintain his one-man constituency where it counted most—right in the President's office.

Kissinger's sun was dimmed for a time, however, after his sensational interview with the Italian correspondent Oriana Falacci rocked the White House. Kissinger was distressed by the revealing interview and claimed that his quotes may have been garbled in the translation. But he was stuck with it. He had told Falacci, "The main point comes from the fact that I have acted alone. The Americans love this immensely. The Americans love the cowboy who leads the convoy, alone on his horse, the cowboy who comes into town all alone on his horse, and nothing else. Perhaps not even with a gun, because he does not shoot. He acts, and this is enough, being in the right place at the right time. In sum, a Western."

Kissinger pointed out that although he had opposed Nixon in three electoral campaigns, Nixon "showed a great vigor, a great ability, even in picking me. . . ."

The Palace Guard was livid. I observed that Kissinger began to stress more often in his briefings that he was acting on behalf of the President. That he had regained the lost ground with the White House was apparent when I asked Ford in an interview in December 1974, whether Kissinger was "indispensable to his administration." His reply took me by surprise. "He is indispensable to the country," he answered. I had never heard even Presidents described in such terms before.

He was protected as no other Secretary of State in American

history, with round-the-clock Secret Service agents moving with him and guarding his home. He had a Presidential jet at his command ready for short-notice takeoffs, and often two limousines would be flown abroad, one for the Arab countries, the other for stops in Israel during his days of Middle East shuttle diplomacy.

He did not seem to object to imperial trappings, but created what author Tad Szulc termed "the impression that he and American foreign policy are indivisible."

The announcement of a Kissinger briefing at the White House brought reporters rushing over to the press center. It was the best show in town, and Kissinger would put on a virtuoso performance, a professor lecturing to freshmen students. His briefings were so detailed he sometimes seemed to explain: "There is something called the Middle East. It is divided into Israel and the Arab world." Once he opened his remarks by saying, "I hardly know where to begin." I suggested: "Begin at the end." And even he chuckled.

Kissinger held a briefing following the Cambodian invasion on May 9, 1970, and as usual it began with Press Secretary Ronald Ziegler cautioning reporters: "You can attribute what Dr. Kissinger says to White House officials, no direct quotations." He began with banter, even when the subject matter was war and peace. I would have preferred my jokes elsewhere, but on that occasion, Kissinger was asked, "Did you watch the sun come up?"

"No," he replied. "I was in the situation room plotting the war."

Then Ziegler interjected: "Put that off-the-record."

"It sounds better in German," Kissinger quipped.

Another common opener for Kissinger was: "Does anyone have a question for my answers?"

Ziegler referred to Secretary Kissinger as "Henry," during the briefings and reporters also used his first name freely.

At another White House briefing, a reporter said: "Henry, I think it would be of value to some of us if you could describe how the administration views Greece, Italy, and Spain as Mediterranean powers? Why are they important to the Mediterranean? What do they do?"

Dr. Kissinger: "For one thing, they are located in the Mediterranean."

Kissinger sometimes had a credibility problem. One day he told us at the White House that the United States was taking a neutral position in the India-Pakistan War over Bangladesh. Yet soon afterwards columnist Jack Anderson made public National Security Affairs secret papers in which Kissinger was quoted as saying, "The boss [Nixon] is giving me hell every half hour to tilt toward Pakistan." The Indians already understood this, and only the American people had been kept uninformed. This was also true of the secret bombings of Cambodia and North Vietnam. The bombed countries were aware of the air strikes, obviously, so why not the American people?

I am sure that both Nixon and Kissinger felt that secret diplomacy was necessary to bring about the diplomatic breakthrough with China after a twenty-year Cold War gap. Kissinger, using the pretext of having a stomachache to stay out of the public eye in Pakistan, stole away on a Pakistani government plane for the China capital. Even his Secret Service agents were kept mystified, and as Kissinger put it, they "dropped their teeth" when they spotted Chinese navigators as they boarded the plane.

Once aboard the Middle East shuttle, Kissinger gave reporters a piece of information that turned out to be untrue. When the reporters confronted him with this, he simply grinned and said, "You are now part of foreign policy."

When I asked Kissinger whether the President hears any voices that dissent from his views, "Of course," he said in all seriousness, "and I am with him ninety percent of the time when he does."

My colleague Richard Growald, who has traveled extensively with Kissinger, calls him the "mirthful paranoid." He often says he plants rumors that he is going to resign "to lift the morale of my staff."

Despite his protestations that he was going to shape up the State Department, Kissinger did little in that direction. Assistant Secretary of State Dixy Lee Ray resigned when she could establish no contact with him. She did not see him once after she was sworn in. But when asked to comment about her departure, Kissinger didn't even know her name. He said, "I like Dixy Ray Lee."

A demanding perfectionist, Kissinger drove his aides as he drove himself. He was always in his office in the West Wing at 7:30 or

8:00 o'clock in the morning, and often would leave a State Dinner or embassy in the evening and return to work.

With underlings Kissinger could be tyrannical. He plainly terrorized members of the foreign service. He often belittled them and expressed his contempt for them. I was at a news conference at San Clemente after he became Secretary of State when Kissinger said he would "institutionalize" foreign policy in the State Department. This gratified the foreign service after his long policy of "benign neglect"—or worse. But, of course, a one-man foreign policy-maker was not about to share his policy-making power with other diplomats.

He preferred his own staff to cherish a passion for anonymity. Sharing honors was not Kissinger's habit, nor did he want anyone but himself and the President to make foreign policy pronouncements for the administration. After the Cambodian incursion, five top staffers quit in protest over the move.

I experienced first-hand his compassion in minor things. Flying home from China, a reporter taunted me for having a private interview with Pat Nixon aboard the plane. I was exhausted from working eight straight days with only a few hours sleep. Upset, I struggled to hide my tear-filled eyes. Kissinger saw this and held back giving substantive information until I had composed myself and could put on dark glasses. Soon he had us laughing and I forgot my tears.

Kissinger had a private constituency among the State Department correspondents who traveled with him, particularly on the flying shuttle between Tel Aviv and Cairo. He used to speak of "my fourteen" reporters in a possessive way, and their colleagues sometimes referred to them as the "groupies." But they did not feel they were in any sense committed to Kissinger and, as reporters, they called them as they saw them.

There has been much machismo in Kissinger's foreign policy. He believes ardently that without the threat of force he cannot negotiate. Eight months after peace accords were signed in Vietnam, the North Vietnamese seemed to be on the move again, but by this time Kissinger no longer had any interest in trying to shore up the peace or to condemn the North. He said it was up to the Vietnamese to determine their own fate.

In January 1972, Nixon, in a nationally televised address, disclosed that Kissinger had been flying back and forth across the Atlantic for a year-and-a-half for secret meetings with North Vietnam's peace negotiator, Le Duc Tho, in an effort to reach a permanent peace settlement. Nixon made his dramatic announcement at a time when the talks were stalemated and he was heading into an election year with the nation restive for a peace settlement.

On October 26, 1972, Kissinger told reporters "peace is at hand" in Vietnam. But only the Presidential election was "at hand," it appeared later. For weeks sardonic "Peace is at Hand" buttons cropped up on lapels. Nixon, with Kissinger's apparent approval, resumed three weeks of round-the-clock bombing of Hanoi and other parts of North Vietnam during the Christmas period in December 1972 and early 1973.

As a matter of protocol, Secretary of State William P. Rogers was dispatched to Paris to sign the Vietnam peace accords in late January 1973. I asked at a briefing exactly where Kissinger was at 6:00 A.M. Washington time when the agreement was signed. "Making love, not war," was the reply he relayed to reporters.

Kissinger's preoccupation with foreign affairs may have made him slow to realize the impact of Watergate. Even though he and the President had always worked closely together Kissinger later admitted, "I never know what's really on his mind."

Kissinger was on a mission in Moscow during the week of the "Saturday Night Massacre" when Nixon fired Special Prosecutor Archibald Cox in a showdown over releasing his taped Watergate conversations. With Attorney General Elliot Richardson and Deputy Attorney General William Ruckelshaus quitting the government in the aftermath of the Cox firing, a "firestorm" of public outrage engulfed the White House, but Kissinger was far from the scene and not clued in on the temper of the times.

That incredible October also saw Vice President Spiro T. Agnew resign and a new Arab-Israeli War.

When Kissinger and Defense Secretary James Schlesinger held crisis meetings at the White House after receiving what was described as a "brutal" note from Russian Ambassador Anatoli

Dobrynin implying the dispatch of Russian troops to the Mediterranean if the temporary cease-fire did not hold, Nixon did not attend, apparently because he was too disturbed over the public uproar after the White House firing of Archibald Cox in the Watergate affair.

As Kissinger related the chronology to a few of us later, he and Schlesinger, in a midnight telephone call to the President, recommended a military alert to warn the Russians to stay out of the Middle East. The President agreed. About three o'clock in the morning the Pentagon alerted U.S. forces around the world and Kissinger went to sleep. When he awoke at seven o'clock, he turned on the *Today* show and to his surprise found that the worldwide military alert was a sensational news story.

I was astonished to learn later from Kissinger that he believed that such an alert, intended as a silent signal to the Russians, could fail to reach the American people. In Washington, already alarmed by Watergate, the news stimulated wild rumors of a possible military-political coup. Kissinger was stunned by the response.

That same month I was assigned to join Kissinger on his twelve-day trip to the Middle East, Pakistan, and China (the second trip to China for me), a journalistic plum, but I was reluctant to go. I felt certain that Nixon was going to resign.

As it turned out, my bets with a few press colleagues were about nine months short of the mark. I asked Kissinger a number of times if Nixon was going to resign. His denials were adamant: "He will never resign."

Kissinger was caught up in the eager welcome of the Arab world. The news of his "peace plan" for a stronger cease-fire between Arabs and Israelis broke on that trip. But when we reached mainland China, Kissinger finally began to respond to the consequences of Watergate. In a toast at a lavish banquet at the Great Hall of the People, he assured the Chinese hierarchy that United States foreign policy was constant no matter what administration was in power. It was an oblique reference to the scandal.

When we checked with Ambassador Robert McCloskey, Kissinger's press officer, he tried to steer us away from such an interpretation. I asked Kissinger the same question and McCloskey, almost apoplectic, shouted he would not answer any more questions from me.

We hailed our Chinese driver and I filed a bulletin story ignoring McCloskey's efforts at dissuasion, saying that Kissinger had reassured the Chinese that détente would continue despite the threat to Nixon's leadership. As late as the following June, however, when the White House tapes had been revealed, Kissinger was still telling us that Watergate had no impact on foreign policy and that Nixon would go to Moscow for the third summit and to the Middle East.

With the Russians aware of the growing crisis of confidence over Nixon in the United States, the Moscow summit failed. On the way to the Middle East summit in Salzburg, Austria, Kissinger held an impassioned news conference in which he denied that he had initiated wiretaps against members of his staff and newsmen, and, almost in tears, threatened to resign unless he received a vote of confidence from the Senate Foreign Relations Committee. It was an astounding performance. Nixon, we learned, was furious that Kissinger had diverted attention from the upcoming Middle East summit to vent personal difficulties.

The Senate Foreign Relations Committee gave Kissinger a clean bill of health, though Kissinger had admitted to acquiescing in the surveillance from 1969 to 1971. I thought it bizarre that some of his staff who had been victims of the wiretapping would accept his rationale that he had done it to prove their innocence, but they stayed with him.

It is ironic that Kissinger was also bugged by the President's taping system in the Oval Office and elsewhere. He recalls once mentioning the fact that there was no stenographer in the room for Nixon's long secret talks with Brezhnev. "Don't worry," he remembers Nixon saying, "we have a perfect record." Kissinger had not known about the taping system.

On one occasion, Kissinger exploded to his deputy, Gen. Alexander M. Haig, Jr., about a "leak" in the newspapers on national security matters. He wondered aloud if his office was "bugged" and was assured by Haig that the Secret Service had made a sweep of the office for hidden microphones and electronic gadgets. Laughing about it now, Kissinger shakes his head and says, "and it was the Secret Service doing the bugging."

During our last stay in California in July 1974, the White House staff gave a fiesta-style party for the press at the San Clemente compound. None of the Nixon family showed up. All the Watergate shoes were falling and Nixon understandably was in no mood to see reporters. Kissinger and other senior advisors showed up and mingled with the press and munched on tacos.

During the day the Cyprus situation was becoming more tense and all the White House would say was: "We're watching it closely." Kissinger was sipping a margarita and holding forth when I approached him. We chatted about Cyprus briefly and he said, "I think they're coming in," meaning the Turks.

I was astounded. There was about to be a major invasion of a Mediterranean island which would bring two NATO countries— Greece and Turkey—into conflict, and the United States seemed about to permit it to happen without any effort to prevent it. Kissinger, this time, seemed to be withholding the power to act.

By this time, other reporters had gathered around him and I did not want to pursue Cyprus for fear of tipping them off. I was in a dilemma. It was a social occasion. Would he have said so, unless he wanted the world to know? But on the other hand, would I be fueling the fires of international conflict if I wrote it? I called my Washington office and quoted a "high-ranking official" as saying that the Turks might invade Cyprus.

A short time later, the Turks did land on Cyprus. I felt the United States did not exert its good offices to the full extent to try to persuade the Turks not to invade. Perhaps it would have been to no avail. In any case, war did break out and at a tragic human cost. While we were still in California, at a dinner party given at the Beverly Hills home of Budget Director Roy Ash, Nixon announced that he had achieved a cease-fire.

When General Haig, who had assumed the position of Assistant to the President, or Chief of Staff, as we called him, in the aftermath of the Haldeman-Ehrlichman departures, and chief Watergate counsel St. Clair decided that the President must resign or be impeached, Haig went to Kissinger's office in the State Department and enumerated the facts. At Haig's urging, Kissinger joined trusted advisors in private talks urging him to quit. He told Nixon that it would be in the national interest.

On Tuesday, August 7, two days before he left office, Nixon had several private chats with Kissinger. In the evening, he called the Secretary five times, deeply distressed, still groping, trying to make up his mind. Then Kissinger was summoned to the White House at midnight Wednesday, on the eve of the resignation. He wanted Kissinger's reassurance that he was doing the right thing and he wanted the solace of knowing he had earned a place in history for his foreign policy initiatives.

I was remembering the earlier days of triumph.

"Am I on your man of the year cover?" Henry A. Kissinger had asked a *Time* magazine correspondent on Air Force One in December 1972. The reporter said it was top secret but that Kissinger and Nixon might have equal billing. Kissinger's face fell. But he ended up alone on that coveted January 1973 cover.

My thesis may not be shared by my colleagues or by Kissinger, but I credit the dramatic diplomatic achievements of the Nixon years—the breakthrough to China and détente with the Soviet Union—to the President himself. The two practiced summitry together as if they'd invented it, but while Nixon gave Kissinger wide leeway, the grand design was Nixon's. He made the extremely tough decisions and Kissinger was his brilliant implementer who translated theory into policy, gathering significant laurels and status.

I had been in the White House in October 1973, when the bulletin from Oslo came over the wires announcing that the Nobel Peace Prize would go jointly to Henry Kissinger and Le Duc Tho for hammering out the Paris peace accord which "ended" the war in Vietnam, though their pact later proved to be meaningless. After the fall of Indochina two years later, as Kissinger told me in 1975, he had considered returning the Nobel Prize. Hanoi's Tho, perhaps wisely knowing of things to come, never did formally accept the award.

Kissinger had recently been named Secretary of State, retaining the post of National Security Affairs Advisor to Nixon, and he was in his White House office that day when the news of the award broke, but it was at least three hours later before we were all summoned for a picture-taking ceremony with Nixon congratulating Kissinger.

Reporters and cameramen who were ushered into the Oval Office observed an awkward scene: Nixon trying to smile and Kissinger sheepishly happy. They shook hands and Nixon asked "How much money will you get?" He was making conversation, but it hurt. I knew Nixon had cherished the goal of winning the Nobel Prize and the title of "Peacemaker" in the world. A campaign to get it for him had been waged by his supporters. When he spoke, as he did often, of his desire to help create a "generation of peace," I had asked "Why just a generation?" but perhaps the failure of the dream of the war to end all wars had made predictions of a longer peace unbelievable.

Later that afternoon, Nixon and members of his family flew to Camp David on an unscheduled trip. A sympathetic White House aide said that the entire family was upset, that they believed the peace prize rightfully belonged to Nixon. They had wept for him, then. And they would again.

Kissinger kept in touch with Nixon about once a month after Nixon left office and remains convinced that Nixon will be "rehabilitated" and that history will remember only a few elements of the scandal and some of the "tawdry" financial arrangements of his Presidency. He contended that people would not understand the meaning of Watergate in the esoteric terms of ethical conduct by a government servant.

Kissinger was one of the few key figures of the Nixon administration to survive the debacle virtually unscathed. He is a master of survival. In 1975, despite a fading of the Kissinger legend as a miracle worker, and what appeared to be a well-organized behind-the-scenes campaign against him, Kissinger, determined not to leave under a cloud, won assurances from President Ford that he could stay on until the end of his term—and even longer if Ford won the 1976 election.

Chapter 11

Ford: Instant President

When Gerald Ford was sworn in as thirty-eighth President, he rested his hand on a family Bible, which was open to his favorite passage, in Ecclesiastes, "a time to keep, and a time to cast away . . . a time of war, and a time of peace."

In his inaugural address in the East Room, Gerald R. Ford told the American people that "our long national nightmare" is over and "truth is the glue that holds government together." He promised "straight talk" and told Congress with emotion that he would seek "conciliation, compromise, and cooperation."

Right after the inaugural, in a demonstration that straight talk would have concrete application, he popped into the White House press center and jauntily introduced to us his new press secretary, Jerry terHorst of the *Detroit News*. Ford announced that he would run an "open . . . candid administration." Where had we heard those words before?

It seemed for one brief, shining month we did have that reporters' Camelot. TerHorst was the reporter's ideal of a Press Secretary. He understood the ambivalence of the role of Presidential spokesman and dispenser of legitimate information. He believed the public was entitled to the facts from the White House.

The idyllic situation ended the day Ford gave Nixon a full pardon, some ten days after he had announced that such a pardon, if it came, would come only after judicial proceedings were completed. Jerry terHorst, convinced that he had been seriously misled by the White House, and in turn had misled his colleagues in the press, decided he had no choice but to resign. He had set a standard of integrity for the job and established the principle that you can say "No" to a President and walk away from a White House job.

Ford searched before he found a replacement. Ron Nessen was handed the job. Ron had been with UPI and was an NBC-TV broadcaster before going to the White House. Now he wanted to test the water on the other side, to be a participant in policy-making, he said. He told reporters, "I'm a Ron, but not a Ziegler" and "I will never knowingly lie." But reporters, evaluating his early days in the job, began to say, critically, "Two Rons don't make a right."

On the flight back from the Vladivostok summit meeting with Brezhnev, Nessen told reporters (the summer of 1975) that in three months Ford had achieved more on nuclear arms limitation than Nixon had achieved in five years. A howl went up from the other Ron in San Clemente, and Nessen softened his appraisal.

Nessen was intent on clearing away the hostility that remained between the press and the Presidency in the aftermath of Watergate. But he soon found himself accusing the press of being "blind" and "mistrustful." He began to tell reporters that there are no "blacks" and "whites" in terms of truth, only "grays."

However, Nessen did initiate many long-needed innovations. He established as a reporter's privilege the right to ask the President a follow-up question when an answer required amplification. And he dispensed with what we called "tricky track" White House announcements by passing out memos on such routine matters before his briefings. He took criticism well, and most of all he had the backing of the one man he most wanted to please, the President. Ford told reporters, after Nessen had served as his press spokesman for nearly a year, that he was "doing a darn fine job."

Like other Presidents, Ford, too, had his "honeymoon" with the press. For reporters, the press room seemed a bit brighter when Ford took over in the White House. He promised to hold regular news conferences and did during his first year, about one or two every month. He maintained an easy rapport with reporters and frequently would greet us with a cheery "Good morning" when we bounced into his office for a picture-taking session.

I had seen Ford in action many times as a Congressional spokesman on the White House podium for the Nixon legislative program, side by side with GOP Senate Leader Hugh Scott. Under the watchful eye of Ziegler, the two would emerge from their legislative breakfast meetings with Nixon and report to the press. Scott was the more glib and articulate, but Ford was a steady team player and a loyalist, strongly defending the administration on all issues, though he also made friends among Democrats.

As President, to our astonishment, he actually seemed to thrive on press conferences. I was able to get an exclusive interview with him at Christmas time at Vail, Colorado, within six months after he took office. He was to give many such interviews.

By tradition the UPI and AP wire services get the first two questions at a Presidential news conference, and rotate each time. I am sometimes teased, even by strangers who come up to me and repeat the President's words, "Miss Thomas, I believe you have the first question."

Ford was approachable and accessible. He usually suppressed any anger, and sometimes a little laugh would give away his nervousness.

The atmosphere was often merry at news conferences. Once when Ford had his news conference on the wet muddy South Lawn, he asked me how I liked the setting. "Slogging through the mud," I said with a laugh. "Next time, in the swimming pool."

"How deep?" Ford shot back with a grin.

And about the time the new White House pool was to open there were stories that JFK used to go skinny-dipping in the old indoor pool. When I asked Ford if he was going to "skinny-dip," he responded, "Is that an invitation?"

I often thought that LBJ would have been apoplectic if he was asked whether he thought he was smart enough to hack it in the Presidency, but when NBC-TV correspondent Tom Brokaw asked Ford a question along that line, he took it in stride. "I was in the upper third of my class at Yale Law School," he said. Ford assured Brokaw that he had no sense of inferiority about his ability to handle the job. Brokaw received many letters protesting his question. But that is par for the course. The public often takes umbrage at reporters' questions even when a reporter feels that a question must be asked, touchy as it may be.

Ford, like his predecessors, has insisted on some secrecy and protested leaks to his staff, but nowhere nearly as obsessively as Johnson and Nixon. Ford's own tendency is to play his cards close to his chest. Sometimes he leaves his own staff guessing, a good way to conceal his moves from the press.

Although he never aspired to the Presidency and his greatest ambition was to be Speaker of the House, Ford gave us the impression that he felt perfectly competent to cope with what his predecessors had termed the "splendid misery" and the "awesome burden."

Many of his colleagues on Capitol Hill, though they dubbed him "Mr. Nice Guy" and a "Decent Man," shook their heads and maintained that he would remain the Congressman from Grand Rapids, provincial in his outlook, stubbornly showing no growth or depth in the job. But Ford, who had an inner poise and security that both Nixon and Johnson apparently lacked, took the job in stride, shaping the Presidency to his own style—more casual, more down-to-earth, more Middle American. He stressed the values of the pre-New Deal days. His peer models were Lincoln and Truman, and he placed busts of them in the Oval Office, but his perspective of the Presidency at times appeared to be a draw between Hoover and Coolidge.

Ford projected the image of a man at ease with himself. In the early days of his Presidency he toasted his own English muffin for breakfast, put his feet up on the desk in the Oval Office, puffed on a comforting pipe, and worked with his sleeves rolled up. He downed martinis in front of reporters who were more accustomed to a pretence of abstinence from Presidents, in public at least. He shunned the imperial trappings that had become a part of the Presidency. He said he "enjoyed" being President and that his number-one goal was the restoration of confidence and trust in government. By the end of his first year in office, he thought he had achieved that goal.

In a matter of days after he took office, Ford passed the word that he would probably run for election for a full four-year term on his own. Determined not to be considered a lame duck President, he wanted to turn the "accidental President" label into a full-fledged mandate.

The President's deep conservatism and lack of vision for the future quickly came into focus. He was retrospective, not forward-looking. His economic advisors at times seemed to be tearing a page out of Adam Smith's laissez-faire philosophy. His own philosophy added up to "maximum individual freedom for businessmen" and less government regulation and red tape and interference in the lives of American citizens, as he stated in several speeches. In Congress he had voted against Medicare, the poverty program, federal aid to education, and the 1965 civil rights legislation.

No prominent pieces of legislation bear his name as a legacy of his twenty-five years in Congress. In private sessions with reporters, President Johnson often laced into Ford's voting record. When someone pointed out that Johnson himself had not built an unblemished "liberal" record in Congress, Johnson would say, "I'm President now." Ford, as President, has shown no similar inclination to move away from his conservatism on domestic affairs. He saw the Presidency rather as an opportunity to begin reshaping the nation in conformity with his own philosophy of fiscal responsibility and frugality—except in defense spending.

He slipped into the Presidential shoes with ease, and he told the world he loved the job. After the collapse of Indochina early in his administration, he urged the nation not to indulge in recriminations over the follies of the past, and not to search for answers on why the sacrifice of American lives and fortune had been in vain. When I asked Ford what were the "lessons of Vietnam," he only spoke of the need for a strong defense.

Often accused of a lack of compassion for the poor and the disadvantaged, Ford insisted that he knew the problems of the elderly and poverty-stricken. "For a good part of my career in politics I saw firsthand by visits to areas such as that, so I don't have to go through the process again of seeing tenements, of seeing people on welfare or the like," he said. "I know from firsthand experience."

In retrospect I should have been forewarned about his pardon of Nixon. Ten days after he became President, Ford flew to Chicago and stunned the Veterans of Foreign Wars by announcing a limited amnesty for Vietnam War evaders. He inserted the announcement into his prepared speech as we scrambled for telephones. Louis Foy, a sophisticated Agence France Presse correspondent, said to me then, "He's talking about amnesty for Nixon."

I was remembering Nixon's words on amnesty for draft dodgers during his 1972 campaign swing through Ohio. "Never, never, never." Ford could never have pardoned Nixon without offering some form of amnesty to the Vietnam War evaders. Ironically, while Nixon was pardoned, the amnesty, criticized as inadequate, was accepted by relatively few.

I remember that on the flight back from Chicago, Ford came to the back of Air Force One in his shirt sleeves to chat with us. This President was going to be more casual, more informal. I still kick myself for not asking the President then whether there was any connection between amnesty and the possibility of a pardon for his predecessor. I do remember he seemed delighted that he had succeeded in taking everyone by surprise. All Presidents I have covered love to confound the press, perhaps because it keeps everyone guessing or at least off balance.

We did not have to wait long for another surprise. On Sunday, September 8, 1974, less than a month after Ford assumed the Presidency, I went to St. John's Church across Lafayette Park from the White House. Ford was attending Holy Communion mass at eight o'clock in the morning. When he emerged, I asked rather routinely, "Mr. President, what are you doing for the rest of the day?" He paused a moment and then told me rather tersely, "There will be an announcement shortly."

AP's Gaylord Shaw and I looked at each other and made a mad dash across the park to the White House where we found reporters already gathering on summons from the President's press office.

A couple of hours later, I was in a small pool of reporters ushered into the Oval Office to watch the President read his statement announcing that he had granted Nixon a "full, free, and absolute pardon." We had been given a text of the announcement moments before he entered the room and so we knew what he was going to say. We stood behind a red velvet rope and listened. His expression was grim. He had banned any picture-taking or television—that, in itself, was extraordinary for a statement of such momentous news value. It was plain that Ford wanted the episode to be as low key as possible. But the timing was electrifying. Only ten days before, in answer to my question at a news conference, Ford had said he would not act on a pardon until the judicial process had been followed, meaning until there had been an indictment or conviction.

There were no formal charges against Nixon, although he had been named as a co-conspirator in the Watergate coverup. It was a period when reports about Nixon's mental and physical condition were spreading through Congress. Phone calls had been received from the man in exile in San Clemente, and from members of his family. Ford himself had told his aides that he realized that Watergate could hang over his head until 1976, the Presidential election year. The scandal would remain a national issue and injure the Republican Party unless he could exorcise it.

Ford told the American people he acted out of conscience, but he lost a lot of ground in public confidence, temporarily at least. He dropped sixteen points in the popularity polls.

In tandem with the pardon, Ford negotiated an agreement with Nixon to give back his tapes and official papers. Nixon would be free to dispose of his tapes within five years. The agreement fired a protest in Congress and legislation blocked the move. Nixon then challenged the decision in the courts, claiming that other Presidents had received their papers.

With the pardon Ford had effectively barred for all time disclosure of the full facts of Nixon's involvement in Watergate.

At the news conference of September 26, 1974, I had the second question, and asked, "Throughout your Vice Presidency you said that you didn't believe that President Nixon had committed an impeachable offense. Is that still your belief or do you believe that his acceptance of a pardon implies his guilt or is an admission of guilt?"

The President answered, "The fact that thirty-eight members of the House Committee on the Judiciary, Democrats and Republicans, have unanimously agreed on the report that was filed that the former President was guilty of an impeachable offense, I think is very persuasive evidence."

Ford had forgotten the last half of the question and I repeated "Was the acceptance of the pardon by the former President an admission of guilt?"

"Acceptance of a pardon I think can be construed by many if not all as an admission of guilt," he said.

At another point in the interview he said Nixon had resigned in "shame and disgrace."

Ford remained in contact with Nixon on holidays and when Nixon was ill. Nixon said he would return the pardon if it was causing Ford too much trouble. Ford refused.

Nixon himself displayed no strong sense of guilt and continued to explain in the early days of his retirement that he had placed too much trust in his aides. He called the pardon "the most humiliating day of my life."

Some of the reporters who covered Ford during his Vice Presidential days were to some extent skeptical about Ford's candor. Ford was told by Haig on August 1, 1974, that he should prepare to become President and that the "evidence is overwhelming" against Nixon. Yet on August 3 and 4 during a Southern swing, Ford had said that Nixon was "innocent" of any impeachable offense. The President has justified these remarks by stating that he did not want to undercut his predecessor. Throughout the many months of Watergate disclosures, Ford had maintained that Nixon was not involved in Watergate. He told interviewers even later that he still had trouble understanding the scandal.

Ford brought some new men into the Cabinet but kept Nixon holdovers, including Kissinger, Secretary of the Treasury William Simon, and Housing Secretary James T. Lynn, who became his Budget Director. Donald "Rummy" Rumsfeld, former NATO ambassador, who had been in the Nixon White House, became his Chief of Staff, and Robert T. Hartmann his chief speech writer and political mentor.

President Ford showed Vice President Nelson A. Rockefeller more open respect than his predecessors, who traditionally behaved as though Vice Presidents should be seen and not heard. Ford, in the beginning at least, gave Rockefeller a voice. Rockefeller had weekly appointments with Ford, unlike Agnew, who rarely saw Nixon. Two of Rockefeller's aides became members of the Domestic Council, giving Rockefeller some influence on the direction of Ford's home-front policies. But the Council itself had little power and Ford's own conservatism weighed heavily there.

But then Rockefeller, as the election season rolled around, got the same treatment his predecessors got. Ford began to make equivocal statements about his admiration and respect for Rockefeller, while warning in the same breath that "Rocky" would have to line up his own Republican delegates to win the GOP Vice Presidential nomination in 1976. Conservatives in the party remained suspicious of Rockefeller's political views. They remembered the old days when Rockefeller had a reputation as a "liberal" or at least as a "moderate." Ford's apparent fickleness may have been a Ford maneuver to keep the Reagan forces off balance but, in any event, it put the Vice President in an awkward position.

Rockefeller played the game like a pro. In every public utterance he praised Ford unstintingly, sometimes embarrassingly, perhaps to demonstrate his unfailing loyalty. He also took up Ford's advice to seek more support in the party ranks and began traveling to woo conservatives to his side or at least to soften their opposition to his candidacy.

Ford displayed a decisive, if one-dimensional personality, early in his Presidency. Like Truman, once he made up his mind he did not belabor the point or agonize over the ramifications of his decisions.

In foreign affairs, the new President deferred wholly at first to Kissinger. His public statements about his Secretary of State verged on the worshipful. Ford found himself rising to Kissinger's defense every time the Secretary of State was criticized. In the beginning of the Ford administration, Kissinger told reporters that he did most of the negotiating in talks with Soviet leader Leonid I. Brezhnev at the Vladivostok summit while Ford looked on quietly. But Ford's aides gradually let it be known that the President was calling the shots in foreign policy. Although behind-the-scenes maneuvering against Kissinger surfaced, Kissinger triumphed in his strong insistence that he be allowed to remain in the dual role of Secretary of State and National Security Affairs advisor.

Ford got into the foreign travel swing promptly and, like his predecessors, enjoyed the trappings of summits and state visits. In the tradition of Senator Arthur Vandenberg, a fellow Republican from Grand Rapids, he became an internationalist in foreign affairs. His journeys abroad were viewed as successful in establishing his own position as the new American President. He had followed the Nixon foreign policy, including a hawkish approach to the Vietnam War, with little deviation.

In the aftermath of the Indochina debacle, Ford acted swiftly when the Cambodians seized the merchant ship *Mayaguez*. With a naval task force steaming to the scene, he managed to rescue the thirty-nine men of the crew and the ship. The death toll was forty-one Marines. Ford's stock rose in the nation as a man who could act decisively in times of crisis. In the aftermath of the humiliating defeat in the Indochina War many in the nation rejoiced in the show of strength. Others viewed it as a risky and dangerous gamble and Kissinger told reporters Ford and his advisors lucked out.

When the Fords moved in, the White House came to life. The Fords used the Mansion as their home, more so than earlier occupants. Their parties were fun, and State Dinners lost their austerity when the Fords danced with their guests long after midnight. Ford and his wife liked to entertain and obviously enjoyed each other's company at White House social events and at dinner in chic Washington restaurants.

Ford kept his cronies, political friends, and wealthy Washington lobbyists, and played golf with them every week he was in town at the exclusive all-male Burning Tree Country Club. Neither women nor working reporters are admitted.

President and Mrs. Ford made sure that some White House correspondents and media representatives were invited as guests to each of his State Dinners. I was invited to the first of their State Dinners. This particular one was in honor of King Hussein and Queen Aliyah of Jordan. After dinner the Fords escorted their royal guests to the East Room where small tables were placed around the dance floor cabaret-style. His Majesty stayed late and the dancing went on past midnight. Ford, twirling his wife on the dance floor, told reporters: "We love to dance." Whenever Ford saw reporters clustering around the guest of honor, he would come to the rescue, not that a head of state cannot take care of himself. The Shah of Iran was happily conversing with some women reporters when Ford came up and chided them with, "Now, girls, this is not a press conference." After one young cub reporter approached Ford after another State Dinner, the President fumed about it.

According to the usual party scenario, the President's guests of honor arrive at the White House at 8:00 P.M. and are escorted to the family quarters for a drink in the yellow Oval Room. This is always the relaxed moment of a state visit, no matter what First Family is in the White House. This is the time for building friendships and trust. I've never seen a state visitor at a White House dinner who did not respond to the cordial atmosphere, and this is where we may get an interesting story.

The President and First Lady and the visiting head of state and his wife leave the family quarters about 8:30 P.M. and go to the East Room where the other guests have gathered. A military color guard goes before them. A Marine Band combo plays "Hail to the Chief" as they make their grand entrance into the great hall. Reporters watch from a reasonably inconspicuous vantage point. Our American hosts have always appeared unnaturally stiff at this moment; they are not trained in the regality of it all—not in Stonewall, Texas, or Whittier, California, or in Hyannis Port, Massachusetts, or in Palm Beach, Florida, or in Grand Rapids, Michigan. Jack Kennedy would sometimes give us reporters a low wave of the hand at such a time as if to say, "This is not really my bag."

When the guests file in to dinner, we wire service and other pool reporters go into the library or the theatre on the first floor and listen to the toasts which are piped in from the State Dining Room. Then we call in a story from one of several telephones in these rooms. Usually we already have a list of guests and a description of the gifts exchanged by the President and the visiting chief of state. We even find out what china is being used. Inconsequential? Not if a guest breaks one of the gold-plated dinner plates purchased during the Harry Truman administration.

It always pays to cover the toasts whether the President is entertaining at the White House or elsewhere. When President

Ford met with French President Valery Giscard d'Estaing in Martinique in December of 1974, a highlight of their meeting was the poolside dinner party President Ford gave for President Giscard d'Estaing on the patio of the Meridian Hotel. Presidential Press Secretary Ron Nessen had assured reporters that there would be nothing "substantive" in the toasts. "Baloney!" I told my colleague Richard Growald, who was covering the story with me. There's no way you can assure me that two world leaders are not going to say something newsworthy at an important dinner party. Under the influence of good food, good wine, and good companionship, human beings—Presidents included—are quite likely to depart from a prepared text and ad lib something significant. Other reporters, who relied on Nessen's statement, left for a press party in an adjoining hotel. But I asked my UPI colleagues Growald and Ray Herndon to stay behind and help me cover the Ford-Giscard d'Estaing dinner. I was one of the "pool" reporters assigned to cover the picture-taking session and I needed a backup reporter to catch the toasts piped into the press room.

Ford, as it turned out, said nothing of consequence. But when d'Estaing toasted Ford, he heralded a breakthrough in Franco-American relations. "I now know that it is quite clear that we will be able to work together," d'Estaing told Ford. "It has occurred to me during these two days of talks that we were in fact going to take initiatives and perform actions which would lead to solutions which could well have a lasting effect, not only on our own relations, but also, perhaps, on world affairs." Clearly this signaled a thaw of the rivalry and bitterness that had plagued U.S.-French relations since the time of President Charles de Gaulle. Growald had the story on the wire ten to fifteen minutes before other newsmen got wind of what had happened.

After a State Dinner, the guests usually return to the East Room where gilt chairs have been set up for entertainment, then the Marine Corps Dance Band strikes up for dancing in the Cross Hall. Champagne is served on trays. Pool reporters have now returned from the library or press room and mingle with the guests. We never know when and from whom we will get a story, and we cannot risk missing out on whatever story there is.

At first Ford banned reporters from covering his afternoon and early evening receptions, as they had traditionally done. He passed the word that he thought reporters eavesdropped on his conversations. Other Presidents had managed to take reporters more in their stride, although they, too, no doubt did not particularly enjoy having them around. Ford's edict banning reporters from many social affairs and discouraging their conversations with guests at others, therefore, distressed many of us. It seemed to us inconsistent with an open administration. Formally arranged interviews with the chief of state and his advisors are no substitute for spot news. We need access to both.

Other Presidents and First Ladies had tried to ban reporters from certain social events, but they bowed to the press when we reporters wrote about the restrictions. With Ford, it took longer. For nearly a year, he closed us off from such coverage. I decided that we had to make one last ditch fight and enlisted the White House Correspondents Association, the Washington Press Club, the National Press Club, and the National Society of Journalists to write a joint letter of protest to President Ford in July 1975.

The President yielded in August, permitting a small pool of reporters to cover such events "on a trial basis" provided we did not carry notebooks or taperecorders! This was unacceptable if we were not to misquote. So AP's Fran Lewine and I went to see Ron Nessen and he assured us that we would be allowed to take notes on the spot, but inconspicuously, and provided we did not interview the President. Not a total victory but a victory all the same.

THE WHITE HOUSE
WASHINGTON
August 7, 1975

Dear Helen

Thank you for your thoughtful and persuasive letter concerning press coverage of social receptions here at the White House. As you know, I consider it useful to be able to chat privately on occasion with guests at the White House to hear their views and suggestions and to discuss their problems without the inhibiting presence of notebooks or microphones. I consider these conversations at receptions to be an important part of my effort to keep in touch with the views of my fellow Americans.

At the same time I recognize your legitimate news interest in White House social events. As your letter states, we have made considerable strides in improving access by reporters at the White House and your observations persuade me that we should now turn our attention to resolving the problem of covering the social events.

I have asked Ron Nessen to work out arrangements to enable a small pool of reporters to circulate at these social events on a trial basis, with the understanding that the pool reporters will respect the privacy of personal conversations between myself or Mrs. Ford and our guests.

It seems to me that the presence of taperecorders or notebooks would not be appropriate at social functions.

I believe this arrangement may meet your needs for coverage and also mine for some privacy in conversations with guests. At least, let's give it a try.

I appreciate the spirit of your letter, and I hope this arrangement will work out well for all of us.

Sincerely,

Jerry Ford

Ms. Helen Thomas
President
The White House Correspondents Association
1029 National Press Building
Washington, D.C.

After Betty Ford held the family Bible at the swearing in, she had said, "I really felt like I was taking the oath, too." No one hit White House family quarters with more candor or more determination to be herself than the red-haired, green-eyed First Lady, who told interviewers, "I know I can't lie."

Considering the subjects she has tackled since then, Mrs. Ford seems fearless. She enchanted reporters from the outset with her frankness and strong stands on controversial issues. She expressed support for legalized abortion in certain cases. She speculated out loud that her children had tried marijuana. She said she wouldn't be shocked if her eighteen-year-old daughter had an affair; indeed, she thought premarital experimentation might even be a protection against divorce. Evangelist Billy Graham expressed his dismay and said he and his wife would have wept if told by any of their children that they were similarly involved. The hubbub that resulted from these candid remarks in a televised interview echoed from coast to coast, but her daughter said she appreciated her mother's frankness. Betty Ford swept aside other taboos as well. She took a drink in public, picked up a cigaret, admitted to having taken tranquilizers for years, and to being a divorcée. She freely discussed her visits to a psychiatrist for more than a year-and-a-half when she found her four growing children difficult to cope with during a time when her husband was on the political circuit 200 days a year. She had suffered a pinched nerve in her neck for nearly a decade before. Diagnosed as osteoarthritis, it kicked up often when she was under tension and it caused her much suffering.

There was no shyness when the Fords moved into the White House. Reporters were told that the Fords had slept in "one bed" for twenty-five years and there was no reason to change now, a fact that made news. (The Trumans, incidentally, also shared one bed.) About a year later Mrs. Ford made headlines when she said to Myra McPherson in a *McCall's* interview if she was asked how often she slept with her husband she would say "as often as possible." The comment was criticized by some members of the clergy, and by others who expressed shock. The other recent Presidential couples had separate bedrooms, though this fact may reveal nothing whatever about their intimate lives.

At Mrs. Ford's first news conference a month after she became

First Lady, she spoke to 120 reporters, including many curious males. Sitting at a table in the State Dining Room, she fielded questions like a veteran.

I asked, "Your son Jack says that you were very disturbed when you heard that your husband would probably run for the Presidency. Are you disturbed?"

"No," she said, hedging. "I was very surprised at my son's statement."

"You want him to run again or how do you feel about that?"

"Well," she said, "I feel at this point two years is quite a long ways away and I wouldn't want to commit myself one way or another." When Ford was named Vice President after Agnew's forced resignation, his wife had made it quite clear that she did not want her husband to run for Vice President, or President, in 1976. Her husband had promised that after twenty-five years in the House as a Republican Congressman and then as GOP leader, he would quit politics. But it was a promise he could not keep.

No marriage is perfect and Ford, who is always prompt, was caught glaring at his wife on several occasions when she showed up late for a receiving line. Promptness was not one of her virtues, but a politician's wife is expected to arrive on time. But Betty Ford always managed to tease her husband out of his obvious pique. She later said she has broken the habit and gets everywhere ahead of him.

The White House gave Mrs. Ford a new perspective. Her sons, Michael (the oldest), Jack, and Steven, had left home. Susan was around to keep her company, but Susan was in college in Washington and had her own life. While she was protective of her husband, she felt no qualms about differing with him on public issues. Mrs. Ford became a patron of the women's movement in her vigorous crusade in support of the Equal Rights Amendment, calling on members of state legislatures and Senators on Capitol Hill fearlessly. She was criticized and picketed as a result, but her husband defended her right to speak her own mind. In fact, his admiration grew as she took her stand, heedless of the flack. No other First Lady had lobbied so openly for a woman's cause.

Betty Ford had invited Lady Bird Johnson and her two daughters, Lynda Bird Robb and Luci Nugent, to come to tea one afternoon after dedication of the Lyndon B. Johnson Memorial Grove on the Potomac. I never guessed, watching her at that dedication that she was facing a personal ordeal. She entertained the Johnson women in the afternoon, accompanying them graciously around the house that had been their home for five years. There were still nostalgic touches for the Johnsons—a strip over a drawer still read "Lynda's hope chest."

But as soon as the Johnsons left, Mrs. Ford, bag already packed, departed in a waiting car for the hospital. Her former personal secretary and companion, Nancy Howe, had earlier urged her to get to Bethesda Naval Medical Center for a check-up and after two examinations, one with a leading Washington specialist, Mrs. Ford had agreed to undergo a biopsy. But before she left for the hospital she asked that Lady Bird be informed. She didn't want them to "read it in the newspapers," Luci told me.

In telling her own story of those trying hours and days, Mrs. Ford said, "I believe in living day to day—or hour to hour—and my only concern at the time was entertaining the Johnsons."

I was in the press room around 7:00 P.M. on Friday, September 27, when reporters were summoned for a briefing. White House Press Secretary Ron Nessen announced that Mrs. Ford had entered the hospital to undergo surgery the following morning. It was bulletin news and I had no sooner called the story in than I was on my way to the hospital in a motorcade with President Ford. Reporters scrambled for telephones and tried to piece the news together.

The next morning I was there at six to buttonhole nurses and orderlies. The two-line medical bulletin told everything: "The results of the biopsy performed on Mrs. Ford were unfavorable. An operation to remove her right breast is now under way." Ford, on a vigil at the White House, learned from his personal physician, Dr. William Lukash, that cancer tissue had been discovered and that his wife's right breast had been removed. When Ford left the hospital after his wife's surgery, he had been crying and he appeared stricken and could hardly speak.

Afterwards, her doctors in a news conference made it clear that she would not carry on the normal demanding life of a First Lady for some time.

Ironically, within a few months, Happy Rockefeller, wife of the new Vice President, Nelson Rockefeller, also underwent two breast cancer operations, also with great courage. I admired Betty Ford and Happy Rockefeller tremendously for the way they carried off their roles, so naturally and with great warmth. "We're proud of you," Happy told me. "Just keep on doing what you're doing." Though she had not had a career herself, she admired women who had. She got to know women reporters well and called us by our first names. Unlike many other wives at the top, she was not afraid of us. At one of the first parties the Fords gave for the Cabinet, Happy hugged me and laughed with me over the two-step her husband resorted to for every dance number that the Marine Band played. Politics obviously was not her bag, but it was his and she wanted him to be happy.

The waves of telegrams and letters that came to Betty Ford were a great comfort to her in her convalescence. Thousands of women, identifying with her, flocked to cancer clinics for examinations. She told her husband she believed she had saved lives.

Betty Ford was a woman with a heart. She sympathized with Pat Nixon and, particularly, with her daughter Julie Eisenhower. A close confidante of the Nixon family told me that, after seeing Julie several times in August 1974 after the Nixons moved out of the White House in disgrace, Mrs. Ford had urged her husband to pardon Nixon. She was one of several persons who did, of course, but I was told that the First Lady's opinion was a crucial factor in the President's final decision.

The Ford children were taught at an early age to be themselves. The three boys, Michael, Jack, and Steve, touched base at the White House, but had no real desire to live there. Mike was twenty-four in 1974, married, and a graduate student at Gordon Conwell Theological Seminary when his dad became President. Steve, at eighteen, liked ranching and the life of a cowhand and he headed West.

Jack Ford was graduated at twenty-two from Utah State University with a major in forestry during his father's first year in office. The only member of the family who showed an interest in politics, he spent the summer of 1975 around the White House, learning the ropes to help his father in the 1976 campaign. He flew to the Helsinki summit conference with his parents that summer. When the "pool" of reporters talked to him aboard Air Force One, we were astounded by his conservatism.

He said that "overall I agree very much so" with his father's philosophy, "but I admit that, if anything, I may be more conservative." He was convinced that "people are really getting tired of throwing money around for twenty years. It hasn't solved all the problems."

Jack had no sense of reverence about the White House. He did not "like the way people are so awed by the White House," he told us. "I don't like living in an institution. I see the need for it, but it doesn't sit well with me. If I had my way I'd like to see more of the house opened up."

But it is Susan who made herself most at home in the White House. She is independent, and instead of taking one of the bedroom suites on the second floor where the family resides, she chose a bedroom for herself on the third floor where overnight guests usually stay. She had often been in the White House before, having gotten herself a job at the White House the summer her father was Vice President and sold White House guidebooks. She said that every time a bell would ring, the salesgirls would have to hide behind a screen so that any member of the Nixon family who happened to be passing could do so in privacy. During the few months she worked she never saw any of the Nixons. Susan was seventeen at the time of her father's inauguration. At first she treated reporters warily, but gradually loosened up and she would pop into the press room to chat. In fact, the tall teenager joined our own ranks, in a way. She was an amateur news photographer and soon she was running in and out of the Oval Office with the herd. We would see the President's eyes light up when his daughter walked into the room. She has been tutored in photography by David Hume Kennerly, Ford's chief photographer, who was treated like a member of the family. Kennerly loaned Susan White House cameras and encouraged her and so did her parents. In the summer of 1975 after her graduation from Holton Arms, an exclusive girls school, she worked as an intern photographer with the Topeka *Journal*.

After her mother's surgery, Susan lost her hoydenish quality. She became much more serious. She says her brother Mike, with whom she is very close, helped her through that sad time.

I was used to seeing Susan in blue jeans and T-shirts. One day I saw a tall, shapely blonde in a clinging jersey dress talking to the secretaries in the press office. "Helen, don't you recognize me?" asked Susan. I was startled. She had lost a lot of weight; the White House does that to you. She was following a diet laid down by Dr. William Lukash, the President's physician, of 1,200 calories a day. She had lost her baby fat and she was a knockout.

"I'm not interested in politics," she used to say. She had been quite turned off by the political demands that kept her father on the road during her early growing years. Her brothers felt the same way. Ford had some recouping to do with his family after he moved into the White House and got reacquainted with them.

Susan found the White House limelight too dazzling for some boyfriends. Gardner Britt, who was her beau when she moved into the mansion, fell by the wayside. Britt, incidentally, won the label of being a "male chauvinist" from White House circles after comments in a magazine that a woman's place was in the home. He had said that a wife should seek a career only after she has raised her children. When I asked him about his views, he said: "I knew you press ladies wouldn't like it." Susan defended him but soon afterwards she chopped Britt as a steady boyfriend, and began dating other young men.

It was easy to see that Susan was sometimes lonely in the White House. But White House secretaries became her friends and her Secret Service agents gave her room to spread her wings. From her mother, who had studied modern dance with the Martha Graham company, she inherited a love of dancing. From her father she inherited a love of sports, and she would ski and swim avidly, and jump energetically on the Camp David trampoline. Susan made no pretense about being a good student. Books did not interest her.

The Ford children seemed much more independent in their views from their parents than had the Johnson or Nixon girls. During the early days of his Presidency, Ford found his children speaking out on Vietnam, amnesty, and whether he should seek a full term in the White House, often with views contrary to his own. In response, he said:

"All my children have spoken for themselves since they first learned to speak, and not always with my advance approval, and I expect that to continue in the future."

After a year in the White House, Betty Ford told me and other reporters, "It's been very happy. We've traveled a lot of miles, covered a lot of ground. I don't feel any differently than I did as wife of the Vice President and Minority Leader.

"I feel at home in the White House as much as anyone could," she said. "I say that advisedly because it belongs to the American people. We're only a page in history. I have a great love and appreciation for the White House. It's really a great place."

Did she want him to run for the Presidency? "Of course I want him to run; he wouldn't be running unless I wanted him to."

Here was a man who was preparing to bow out of public life. Now he had a chance to become President in his own right and during the nation's 200th anniversary year. The question was would he be able to win the support of the people and to reaffirm the ideals of the Republic?

Epilogue

"The Right to Know"

On September 18, 1974, in the first days of his own administration, President Ford attended an inaugural at the Washington Press Club. He joined in the humorous banter during the mock swearing in of Ronald Sarro of the *Washington Star-News* as president. Some of the banter was directed at me.

Anybody in public life is well aware of how important the judgments of the press are. I'm firmly convinced that if the good Lord had made the world today, he would have spent six days creating the heavens and earth and all the living creatures upon it. But on the seventh day, he would not have rested. He would have had to justify it to Helen Thomas.

Nothing he could have said would have pleased me more. On my epitaph, I want only one word: WHY? In the press, that question is central to our search for truth.

An Associated Press managing editor's report several years ago, on the role of the White House press, expressed my own views: "A constant spotlight on governmental officials lessens the possibility of corruption."

John Kennedy once said: "We are not afraid to entrust the American people with unpleasant facts, foreign ideas, alien philosophies, and competitive values. For a nation that is afraid to let its people judge the truth and falsehood in an open market is a nation that is afraid of its people."

But many Presidents have chafed under press criticism from George Washington on. FDR handed one reporter the Nazi Iron

Cross when he was provoked by a question. I used to hear that Roosevelt would tell offending reporters to "put on a dunce cap" or "go stand in a corner." Truman called columnist Drew Pearson an SOB and fired off a hot letter to *Washington Post* music critic Paul Hume objecting to a critical review of his daughter's concert. Kennedy cancelled his subscription to the *New York Herald Tribune*, annoyed with its reporting. The press doesn't ask to be loved. It prefers to be respected.

No President likes to be quizzed, to be the target of hostile or even penetrating questions, but most accept it most of the time as a requirement of his job.

"When the press stops abusing me, I'll know I'm in the wrong pew," Truman said.

FDR autographed a picture that hangs in the White House press room: "From their victim."

Nixon ultimately convinced his aides that when reporters grilled him for information they were attacking his programs. Aides were told not to talk to us. We were labeled "the enemy" by his staff and "the leeches" by Constance Stuart, Mrs. Nixon's chief of staff. He once had been able to field tough questions with relative ease. I think he even respected some reporters for their sense of fairness even after Watergate.

I believe in the people's right to know what is going on in the White House where the President has life and death power over millions of lives. After the Bay of Pigs fiasco in the spring of 1961, Kennedy confided that he wished *The New York Times* had not gone along with his request for a suppression of news of American military operations leading up to the planned invasion of Cuba. In retrospect, he believed that if the news had been published he might have seen the folly of the plan in time to stop it.

Ironically, former White House Press Secretary Ronald Ziegler also once expressed the view that President Nixon might have become more aware of the dangers of the Watergate scandals to his Presidency if we had asked more questions about it at his news conferences. Presidents and reporters can learn from each other, and the American people benefit if they do.

Columnist Walter Lippmann once said that the Presidential

press conference, no matter how imperfect, was not a privilege but an organic necessity in a democracy. I agree.

Woodrow Wilson was the first occupant of the White House to hold regular press conferences, an exercise in democracy that was not practiced in other parts of the world at the time. After he became ill, his news conferences were abandoned. Warren G. Harding, a newspaperman himself, revived the practice. His successors, Coolidge and Hoover, would answer reporters' questions only in writing—and then reluctantly.

The press conference hit its heyday in the Franklin Delano Roosevelt era when FDR held news conferences twice a week. He enjoyed sparring with reporters. He also understood it was a two-way street and told the White House Correspondents Association in 1941: "For eight years, you and I have been helping each other. I have been trying to keep you informed of the news from the point of view of the Presidency. You, more than you realize, have been giving me a great deal about what the people of this country are thinking."

Truman used to fence with reporters. In 1952, as his White House days were ending, he said that press conferences were a good way to put over his ideas, and in addition, they were "fun."

Eisenhower held the first televised news conferences, not live, however, but taped for later viewing. Kennedy mastered the art of television. His televised debates with Nixon had helped win him the election and he was the first to hold "live" televised news conferences, although he complained that it was like cramming for an exam. News conferences put the President "in the bull's-eye," Kennedy said.

FDR holds the record for news conferences, 998 of them in 12 years in office. He averaged 83 a year. Truman averaged 40 a year. Their successors have been less accessible to the press forum. Eisenhower averaged 24 a year, Kennedy, 21, and Lyndon Johnson, 25.

Johnson was never comfortable with television or with any large, formal press conference. "I don't see why y'all want to sit out there and keep popping up and down like ducks," he once told some of us reporters who were flying with him on Air Force One. He preferred the small, informal press session like those he had held in his Senate days. So, he improvised. In addition to his "walkie-talkie" specials, he held outdoor conferences on the ranch. Often he announced them in the middle of a party. We would be biting into a sparerib when Johnson would begin to talk. We had to drop the sparerib and grab our notebooks. LBJ held one such a conference beside a bale of hay; another at the New York World's Fair, another on the South Lawn where he invited reporters to bring their wives and children. The Marine Band played and aides served lemonade and cookies. It was unbelievable. Johnson was, essentially, playing games with us. George Reedy once said that LBJ thought that "press relations consist of supplying the press with material quite unrelated to his functions as President; and that the function of the press really is to entertain the public." He often behaved accordingly. Nixon favored the full-dress televised press conference during his first two years, but he pulled away from the cameras as he began to withdraw to the bastion of the White House, and began to meet reporters more often in the Oval Office or the press briefing room, where cameras were permitted only for taping.

We fought for more press conferences during the Nixon administration and I believe, as Ziegler said he did, that the President might have saved himself the agony of losing the public trust if he had subjected himself to more questioning. As the Watergate affair became more convoluted, Nixon, who had been controlled and cool, became agonizingly tense, diffident, and defensive, particularly in his last three press conferences. Reporters grilled him about the labyrinthic web of stories spun by the protagonists in the Watergate affair; it became more of an ordeal for him to face us. In some ways he must have felt we were the Inquisitors. But the press is the only institution in our society that can question a President and make him accountable for his policies and actions.

Ford is more at ease with reporters than any chief executive since JFK. He seems actually to enjoy the Presidential press conference and he does his homework well. Before each meeting he is thoroughly briefed by aides who try to anticipate reporters' questions and draft suggested answers. He approaches reporters before television cameras with much less fear, trepidation, hostility, and perspiration than his two immediate predecessors.

The Presidential news conference, of course, is not the end-all in Presidential press relations. Reporters have other means of getting news out of the White House. They interview the President, the First Lady, the President's children, the White House staff. They query the President's Press Secretary and they cultivate sources in the time-honored way. They listen and they watch. White House reporters follow Presidents everywhere. To the press, almost everything a President does is official business.

During the campaign, the candidate and family will have to submit to blanket coverage of their lives. They will have become public figures and must endure prying and intrusion into their private lives. The candidate who wins the election must face the loss of privacy during his term in office. Although he has drummed up massive press coverage to help him win, once in the White House, a President and his family will often try to regain their privacy and to control press coverage. But it is too late to call a halt. The Presidency does not give the man—or woman in the future—who holds it the right to determine the limits of reporting in a democracy.

Protective reporting, that is, following the President everywhere in public, seems to annoy Presidents the most. They believe it invades their privacy and that they can have a private life in public. But that is not possible and it is the price of public life. Personally I don't believe there is any such thing as overexposure. Many times Presidents have escaped our watchful eyes, and probably will again; they can easily slip out of the White House for secret meetings if they choose.

Not that the press writes and publishes everything it knows. It doesn't. But rather that it is the press and not the President in a free society who must determine what is news and what is not. It is the people's right to know that must take precedence. And the press is the guardian of that right to know.

In March 1975, President Ford congratulated me at a Presidential press conference for becoming the first woman member of Washington's Gridiron Club, a century-old journalistic fraternity. I had just asked the President a question and after he digressed to refer to my breakthrough, I came back to the question. No reporter can put aside any question. We are not there to curry Presidential favor, nor can we respond to efforts at Presidential intimidation. Our priority is the peoples' right to know—without fear or favor. We are the people's servants. As for Presidents, my own feeling about what they should be is summed up in the John Adams' prayer inscribed on the side of the marble fireplace in the State Dining Room below the brooding portrait of Lincoln: Blessings on this house. May only honest and wise men live here.

Index